C000247013

BREAKTHROUGH

Memoir of a British-Trained Bangladeshi

BREAKTHROUGH

Memoir of a
British-Trained
Bangladeshi

SUHAIL AZIZ

The Book Guild Ltd

First published in Great Britain in 2020 by
The Book Guild Ltd
9 Priory Business Park
Wistow Road, Kibworth
Leicestershire, LE8 0RX
Freephone: 0800 999 2982
www.bookguild.co.uk
Email: info@bookguild.co.uk
Twitter: @bookguild

Copyright © 2020 Suhail Aziz

The right of Suhail Aziz to be identified as the author of this
work has been asserted by him in accordance with the
Copyright, Design and Patents Act 1988.

All rights reserved. No part of this publication may be
reproduced, transmitted, or stored in a retrieval system, in any form or by any means,
without permission in writing from the publisher, nor be otherwise circulated in
any form of binding or cover other than that in which it is published and without
a similar condition being imposed on the subsequent purchaser.

Cover design by Jack Wedgbury of the Book Guild
Front cover – Suhail Aziz as a midshipman with backdrop of the Britannia Royal Naval College Dartmouth
Back cover – Ann and Suhail on a P&O Mediterranean cruise 2010

Typeset in Garamond Premier Pro

Printed and bound in the UK by TJ International, Padstow, Cornwall

ISBN 978 1913208 653

British Library Cataloguing in Publication Data.
A catalogue record for this book is available from the British Library.

FSC
www.fsc.org
MIX
Paper from
responsible sources
FSC® C013056

To Anna –
in memory of our life together

Contents

Acknowledgements

I am indebted to all those who helped me in writing this book with ideas, stories, comments, advice and suggestions. However, this is my memoir: things remembered from digging into my past. The views and opinions expressed are mine. If I have erred and offended anyone, I beg their forgiveness – it is unintentional.

So many people have helped me with ideas in writing this memoir. My wife passed away in June 2014. The loneliness and sadness struck me. The late Rukhsana Samad, a cousin's wife, had called me from Dhaka: 'Rana Bhai, start a project – maybe start writing.' Others have similarly asked me to get busy, to move on. This book has been my "work in progress" for the past four years or so, off and on from 2015. The people who have encouraged me to write are too many to list. But they know how much I am indebted to them for their help.

I got to know about Arvon from the people we bought our house from in Sydenham. Probably inadvertently, they had left a copy of an 'Arvon inspires' information booklet in one of the desk drawers! So, by chance I got to know about their creative writing courses in the UK. They ran courses in various parts of the country, and I registered for one in Exeter on prose writing. Due to upcoming surgery I could not attend the course. But reading the initial course material whetted my appetite. In getting me motivated I acknowledge the important role played by Arvon. I felt inspired to write.

Jon Magidson, a freelance coach and tutor, ran a six-week long intensive course – "Magpie Writing Introduction to Memoir Writing Workshop" – from his base in Peckham, South London. I enrolled. There were about six others registered for his workshop. Jon would set us tasks followed by presentations and discussions. His unique style in questioning taught me a lot – 'How did you feel? Show us the "why" behind the "what". Show us what these amazing events meant to you then, and mean to you now.' I am grateful to Jon for his help, and also to my fellow students on the course for their insightful comment and suggestions.

Most importantly, I must express my utmost gratitude and sincere thanks to Gordon Thynne, editor of the *Croydon U3A Magazine* (University of the Third Age – www.u3a.org.uk), who read through my typescript, correcting and suggesting, until it became acceptable to the publishers. Without his help, this book would not have been possible. I am also grateful to his daughter, Catharine, for guidance on using my computer.

Finally my publishers, The Book Guild. I have been fortunate to have a team of people mobilised to help with the publication of my memoir: Lauren Bailey, my initial point of contact who got me started in a business-like manner; Rosie Lowe, in charge of the production processes, for her suggestions and advice along the way, in a very helpful manner; Philippa Iliffe, with advice on the book's title and marketing strategy; and Jack Wedgbury, for his ideas and suggestion about the cover design. I am greatly obliged to the Book Guild team for working with me in a spirit of partnership and co-operation.

Suhail Aziz
Selsdon
28 August 2020

Introduction

This book has some interesting origins. It came about from informal chats with friends and family members, who listened to me relating my life's experiences and encouraged me to write.

Delbert Sandiford, a West Indian friend with whom I studied Economics at the Central London Polytechnic (now University of Westminster) and Birkbeck College, University of London, once invited me to lunch at the Royal Society of Arts and Manufacture (RSA). In the quiet ambience of the historic RSA restaurant near Charing Cross, we talked about his experiences and mine. He said, incidentally, that he wrote, about anything that came into his mind. I asked, 'Are you writing a book?' and, 'Who would be your audience or readers?' He said that was not his intention – he just wrote. Then he said to me, thinking about my emotional state (Anna, my wife, had just passed away), 'Suhail, you should write.' I asked, 'Who would read my book?' He said, 'Don't worry about that, Suhail. Just write. You have a story to tell.' Delbert's encouragement is infectious. He is a great, charming motivator. I respect him very deeply. He has been a true friend for many years.

Tol Bedford, a learned senior civil servant, now retired, was a psychologist of high repute, renowned for recruitment and assessment of people for the top grades in the Civil Service. I had made quite an effort to find Tol at the Recruitment and Assessment Service (RAS) of the Civil Service Commission (CSC). At my first meeting with him, at the RAS offices in Basingstoke, he listened to me attentively. At the mention of World Bank projects that my company, Brettonwood Partnership, was engaged in, Tol asked me, 'How do you know about these things?' I explained. I succeeded in persuading him to be Brettonwood's team leader on the World Bank-funded long-term project: '*Institutional Improvement of the Bangladesh Public Service Commission*'. Tol and I have kept in touch since the late 1990s. Once I invited Tol to lunch at my club, the Royal Air Force Club, in Mayfair, London. We talked about a multitude of things. I narrated my life's experience – my career in the navy, how it ended early, Anna in my life, life for us in England, how Anna and I coped. After hearing me, suddenly Tol said, 'Suhail, you have a story to tell, you should write a book!'

I knew Judge Daphne Wickham and John Harding from my days as chairman of the London Probation Board. Daphne was the chair of the pre-merger Inner London Probation Committee, where John was the chief officer. Following due competitive process, I was appointed by the Home Secretary chair of the newly formed London Probation Board. In that capacity I got to know Daphne and John well. We would meet at our respective clubs: Royal Overseas League (ROSL), John hosting; the Reform Club, Pall Mall, Daphne hosting; and the Royal Air Force Club, Mayfair – me, Suhail, hosting. In December 2015, John and Daphne invited me to one of the lunches at the ROSL. It was a poignant occasion, as it was soon after Anna's passing away. They expressed deep sympathy for me. John and Daphne listened to some of the stories of my life. They asked about my background, my family back home, what my father did, how I came to England, my time in the Pakistan Navy following training at the Britannia Royal Naval College, Dartmouth and being commissioned by the British Admiralty, my marriage to Anna, and what I had achieved in England from very small beginnings. Some interrogation! Then both Daphne and John said, 'Suhail, you should write a book, you have so much to tell.' I said that I had thought about doing so but had wondered who would read it. John said, 'Don't worry about that. Your grandchildren will read your book. They will like to know who their grandfather was, what he did in England, where he came from and where he got to. They would be your audience.'

And of course my friends from school days in Sylhet, Bangladesh, who now live in England – Rafi, the late Putul and others – several of them have encouraged me to write about my experience in England 'in the mainstream'. Rafi had told me, 'Rana, you must write your memoir. You have done so much in Bangladesh and England. Very few people from Bangladesh have your background and experience. So, write a book.' Rafi has a special affection for Sylhet. He knows I am also proud to be a Sylheti. So Rafi asked me to write particularly about why Sylhet is so important.

After Anna passed away at the St Christopher's Hospice, in Sydenham, London, some of the recently bereaved relatives formed a group called the 'New Horizons'. One of the group members, Mrs Pauline Donovan, after hearing a bit about my life's story, wrote, 'I look forward to reading more and I encourage you to keep writing because real stories are the ones people want to read.' As a member of the Croydon Branch of the University of the Third Age (U3A), I belonged, amongst others, to the Creative Writing Group. The group leader was a learned Danish lady. I wrote a few pieces of prose as set tasks for the sessions where each member of the group read out what they had written. After hearing some of my writing, Mrs Tove Lamb once told me, 'You can write!'

So, with all this encouragement, I decided to have a go at writing, because I believed I had 'a story to tell'. After Anna's death I listed some of my unfinished jobs. First among them was to write this book. So here it is, I hope it will be of interest to readers.

My book is my love story, which started while I was training at the Britannia Royal Naval College, Dartmouth, England. It proceeds to my dismissal from the Pakistan Navy on account of disobeying government orders concerning marriage with foreign nationals. Then the martial law government invited me to go back to the navy if I wished. I declined! My love story is interwoven with my career, my experience, impressions and insights. On coming back to England, I started at the bottom as a ticketing clerk at a tiny British Rail Station (Motspur Park, Surrey) and eventually rose to the top, as chairman of two UK National Health Service (NHS) trusts and chairman of the Greater London Probation Board. Overcoming prejudices, discrimination and obstacles, I made it in the UK.

Although my book is written principally for family, friends and acquaintances, I hope it will find a more general readership. It should be of interest to policymakers in UK government departments and to the governments of Pakistan and Bangladesh. It should interest the hundreds of Bangladeshis in the restaurant and catering industry who have made the UK their home. I hope it will engage the interest of the British and foreign media, including TV and radio. Libraries and institutions will no doubt add it to their catalogues. Whoever opens its pages, I hope they will find encouragement in a story about the overcoming of obstacles.

Chapter One

Early years – Sylhet

'Join the navy to see the world'

Early years

I was born in Sylhet, the north-eastern district of Bangladesh. Previously Sylhet was part of Assam Province of the then British India. Sylhet joined East Pakistan (now Bangladesh) through a referendum at the time of the partition of India in 1947. My nationality went through some changes. My birth was as an Indian; I became Pakistani for a while (1947–71), then with the break-up of Pakistan I became a Bangladeshi (1971). Now I am a British citizen – a British-Bangladeshi. I can speak Hindi, Urdu, Bengali and my mother tongue, Sylheti. That just about sums up my historical background!

Our large family was well educated and middle class. I was one of nine children: six boys and three girls. Using family nicknames, the eldest was my sister Ruby, then myself, Rana, followed by a sister, Mina, then brothers Raja, Molik, Nripa, Lama and Koysor; and the youngest was our third sister, Nargis. My father chose all the brothers' names following the names and titles of kings and rulers of Indian history. My sister Ruby was very bright; she was to gain a Master's Degree in Political Science and teach Politics and Philosophy at the Government Women's College in Sylhet. My brothers and Nargis all went on to higher education and followed different careers.

My first school was the Lama bazar Pathshala, a primary school about ten minutes' walk from home. It had been established by the Lal Brothers of the famous Hindu family in Sylhet, whose substantial property was spread around the area. The Lal Brothers were well known, friendly, diplomatic and philanthropic. They were much loved and respected by the Hindu, Muslim and other communities of Sylhet. They owned the two cinema halls of Sylhet town: the Lal Kuthi (the Red Cottage) and the Rong Mohol (the Colourful Mansion).

About that time, 1950, my father decided to farm at nearby Goalgaon, about four miles out of Sylhet town to the north along the road to Shillong, India. Built by the British, the road leads to the land border between Bangladesh and India, and on to Shillong, Meghalaya State (formerly Assam) of India. From Goalgaon the nearest secondary school was the Model High School, where I studied up to class V. The school was about four miles from our farmhouse. Sometimes I walked to school but mostly I would accompany my father in a rickshaw to work. He would drop me off and carry on to the Mukhtar Library – his law practice office for *mukhtars* (civil lawyers). Our day was fairly long – from 8am to 7pm most days. My father and I would bring some food in tiffin carriers from home or eat in cafés, risking stomach upsets from poor hygiene.

We moved back to Sylhet town to our own house, which was still in relatively good condition even though we had been away at the Goalgaon farm for the intervening few years. I was admitted to the Government-Aided High School and continued there till class VIII. I was fond of that school. The proportion of Hindu and Muslim students was about half and half; there were also a few Monipuri and Khasi students. We all mixed and mingled together. The teaching staff, too, was Hindu and Muslim, happily working together. However, I began to feel some peer-group pressure, as most of my friends from my neighbourhood were studying at the Government High English School. Also the school had a reputation for achieving better results at the important matriculation examination at the end of secondary schooling years. My own uncle, Uncle Bozlu, the youngest brother of my mother, was there. I persuaded my parents that I should move across Sylhet town, telling them the school got more students passing matriculation with a distinction. I told them I could get a 'first division' pass too. It was a tough job persuading my father, who said, 'Rana's results are poor, he gets 2 or 6 out of 100 in maths at half-yearly exams, how can he possibly do well at the

Government High?' Anyway, I got my chance. I moved to the government school at class IX, and did well in the annual exams, getting promotion to class X. I got ready for my matriculation exams, consisting of eight papers. These took place in 1952. As the results were due to come out, a telegram arrived from an uncle (my Aunt Dudu's husband) in Dhaka, the seat of the secondary education board, with the following words: 'Rana First, Bozlu Third, passed. I had passed the matriculation examination in first division with a distinction (i.e. over 80%) in mathematics. So I beat my maternal uncle, Bozlu, whom I had followed to the Government High School. My parents, brothers and sisters and close relatives and friends were delighted with my unexpected results, as indeed was I.

I did well in my final school exams and went on to study sciences at Murari Chand College, obtaining a first class pass. This 'standing out from the rest' was to play an important part in my later life. But it has to be said that in the educational performance of my elder sister, Ruby (Razia Khatun), and myself, our father's deep interest in our education, which included some caning, played a not insignificant role! The youngest brother of the family, Koysar (a variation of 'Kaiser'), achieved a distinction in exams and studied civil engineering at the Bangladesh University of Engineering Technology (BUET). During his early formative education, Koysar lived with us in Chittagong when I was working as the personnel manager of Lever Brothers Pakistan Ltd (Unilever). I got him admitted to the best secondary school in Chittagong. Anna, my wife, and I were very pleased to see his seriousness in studies. Anna was fond of Koysar; she looked after him dearly when he lived with us. I think Koysar, too, was very fond of his sister-in-law, 'Bhabi', as he used to affectionately and respectfully address her. Koysar recently retired as an additional chief engineer, Roads and Highways Division, of the Ministry of Communication, Government of Bangladesh.

I continued my studies at Murari Chand (MC) College, Sylhet, and was admitted into the first year of Intermediate in Science (I.Sc.), under the University of Dhaka. Because of my matriculation first division pass I was awarded a stipend which lasted all my two years of I. Sc. education. So my father did not have to find the monthly fees .

M C College was a philanthropic gift by a Hindu gentleman of Sylhet, Mr Murari Chand. The college still retains that name, even though its administration has moved to the Ministry of Education. Sylhet has always received much by way of bequests and philanthropic gifts from the famous Hindu sons of Sylhet. The college occupies a huge area of hilly land, with the principal's bungalow situated on a hill top in the college compound. Nearby are students' accommodation, sports and recreation grounds, and staff quarters.

My activities at schools and colleges were nothing outstanding really – mediocre. But I played most games – football, volleyball, badminton, cricket, hockey – and was included in competitive matches on occasion. I participated in school dramas and variety shows. I was an active member of the MC College University Officers Training Corps (UOTC). My compatriots in UOTC included Rafi Choudhury, Obaid Jaigirdar, Enayet Ullah and Mushtaq Qureshi. We went for a week-long camping trip near the famous Shrine of Baiyazid Bostami, in Chittagong.

Sylhet

Sylhet was my birthplace. Sylheti people all over the world regard this name with affection. Why is Sylhet so acclaimed? In Britain, Sylhet is famous for two obvious reasons: first, almost all of the so-called 'Indian tandoori' restaurants and takeaways one sees throughout the UK are Sylheti-owned. This process started from the early 1950s. You will find Sylheti-owned tandoori restaurants not just in the UK, but also in many European cities – proof positive of this adventurous community's love for 'life across the seven seas'. Today the foreign exchange earnings of 'non-resident Bangladeshis' – mainly Sylhetis – add to the GDP of Bangladesh in no small way, running into billions of pounds and dollars, second only to the export earnings from Bangladesh's garment trade. Also contributing to Bangladesh's income is the involvement of young Bangladeshis in the peace-keeping operations of the UN, for example during the Bosnia and Kosovo wars, and engagements in the Democratic Republic of Congo (DRC) and elsewhere in Africa. Participation in UN peace-keeping forces is important not just for GDP growth, but also politically by demonstrating Bangladesh's positive contribution to international affairs.

Second, Sylhet is famous for tea. In quality, Sylhet's tea is next to Darjeeling tea from Assam. Tea has been grown in Sylhet by Scottish tea houses, – e.g James Finlay, James Warren, etc. – for a very long time, going back to the East India Company time. Following independence in 1947, the management of tea gardens has slowly moved over from British to indigenous managers. Now it is Bangladeshi managers who manage the gardens, although in some cases the ultimate ownership remains in the hands of the original Scottish tea houses. One can argue whether the standards of production and distribution of tea under Bengali management are as effective and efficient as previously. But the fact remains that income from tea exports is an important foreign exchange earner.

Despite these achievements by the Sylhetis, recognition by non-Sylheti Bangladeshis is given grudgingly: our Bengali friends refer to Sylheti people in a belittling way – 'Syletian'. News about positive aspects of Sylhetis is suppressed in the national media. The part played by Sylhetis in the Bangladesh fight for independence is not given due acknowledgement in Bangladesh's history and educational books or in Bangladesh literature or media. We hear of discrimination between 'Bengalis' and 'Sylhetis'! It is well known that the difference between the Bengali and Sylheti languages is such that you need an interpreter. In social circles Sylheti-speaking people are seen as 'inferior'. The failure to declare the old Sylhet District (created under the British rule) as a 'Division' of Bangladesh at the time of the creation of the other three divisions (Dhaka, Chittagong and Khulna), led to a campaign organised by the Greater Sylhet Development and Welfare Council, not only in Bangladesh but in the UK and other places, until Sylhet was declared a Division. Finally, the number of Sylhetis in the public services – civil service, foreign service, defence services – is disproportionately low. It is to be hoped that this imbalance will be addressed by the Government of Bangladesh. There is no justification for any unfavourable treatment.

Sylhet has a distinctive history and culture. It was an ancient commercial centre, populated by Indo-Aryan Brahmins and Assamese. Old feuds and wars between chieftains have been traced to the tenth century or before. Sylhet was known in the rest of India and was mentioned in ancient Hindu texts and literature. The fourteenth century saw the beginning of the spread of Islam. Many battles took place. Later, King Gour Govinda of Sylhet was defeated by Shah Jalal and his accompanying 360 disciples, who arrived from Mecca. Shrines dedicated to Hazrat Shah Jalal, and his nephew Shah

Paran, today attract many thousands from Bangladesh and beyond to pay annual homage.

The seventeenth century saw Sylhet coming within the sights of the British East India Company. They saw its strategic importance in their fight against Burma (now Myanmar). The company appointed Robert Lindsay to govern Sylhet and the region. They appointed 'Lashkars' as their agents for tax collection. Lindsay made a fortune from his appointments. His role as Deputy Commissioner and Collector of Sylhet is told in a chapter of his own memoir, *My Twelve Years in Sylhet*. (This narrative has been translated into Bengali, and published by the Kandryo Muslim Shahitya Shongshod (KMSS – the Central Muslim Literary Institution). It gives an insight into the colonial exploitation at the time but also shows the affection and esteem in which Sylhet was held.)

My own familiarity with the word 'Lashkar' (or 'Laskar') goes back to my childhood days when I used to hear my father and his peers mention the name of a distinguished Sylheti. His name was Omor Ali Boro ('the Big') Lashkar; everyone knew who he was! Those days a British-appointed Lashkar was something of a status symbol. It was always a man, and seen as someone in authority.

In 1781 a devastating flood struck Sylhet. The people blamed the British rulers for not taking flood control measures. Following an uprising, Lindsay's army was defeated by the local fighters – the 'Pirzadas'. But the adventurous Sylhetis saw opportunities in serving on British ships as cooks and coalmen. They would cook curries for the ships' crews. An increasing number of Lashkars served in the British Army during the Second World War. They joined British merchant ships as lower-level crew members. Later some of the Lashkars were to jump ship at the docks of Liverpool and London. They set up the first cafés and restaurants in England selling rice and curry, thus stimulating the great British love of curries. The late Robin Cook's mention of 'chicken tikka masala' reflected a widespread recognition of the successful multi-billion-pound Bangladeshi catering trade in the UK. Today chicken tikka masala is sold as a packaged dish on the shelves of supermarkets.

My ancestors came from the Middle East. They were Muslims. Muslims in India thrived during the Mughal period. Although Muslim and Hindu cultures differed, in Sylhet both communities lived harmoniously without apparent religious discord. The Hindus had their temples for gatherings and prayers; the Muslims had their mosques and madrassas around which their community's activities took place. I personally had as many Hindu friends at school and college as I had Muslim friends. That is until partition when the major population movement took place, with Hindus moving to India and Muslims moving to Pakistan (Sir Richard Attenborough's film *Gandhi* gave a glimpse of what happened). Some still viewed Pakistan as an anomaly – proof of the pressure Mountbatten was facing both from the Attlee Government and from the widespread agitation and communal disturbances all over India.

Sylhet has seen many changes in its administration. In the British administrative reorganisation of India it was made a part of Assam, separating it from Bengal. It remained so until partition in 1947, following which, through a referendum, Muslims being in a slight majority, Sylhet became part of East Bengal (East Pakistan), later Bangladesh.

This historical connection of Sylhet with the UK has continued to the present time. In 1988, St Albans established a link when the local council sponsored a large housing project in Sylhet. In 1996, the Sylhet Municipal Corporation signed a twinning accord with the London Borough of Tower Hamlets in recognition of the fact that the borough is inhabited by a large number of Sylhetis.

As mentioned, the famous Shrine ('Dargah') of Hazrat Shah Jalal attracts Muslims from all over Bangladesh and beyond for the annual homage ('Urus'). They pay respect to the saint and spend days at the compound in heartfelt prayers. I have known some members of the Mufti family who are responsible for the upkeep and supervision of the shrine. Mufti Khosru, mentioned elsewhere in this book, was a close friend of my wife, Anna, and me. He was married to an English lady called Rosemary, whose family lived in Newmarket in Suffolk, England. Sadly he passed away recently. His love of Sylhet and the Dargah of Hazrat Shah Jalal was such that he took leave of his wife to return to Sylhet to pass his remaining days near the Shrine.

The scenic beauty of Sylhet, created by the winding Surma and Kushiyara rivers, is unsurpassed. They provide inland navigable waterways for trade and commerce. The tea gardens add to the beauty of the place.

The drive from Sylhet town to the border region of Tamabil is beautiful and breathtaking. The Khasi and Jointya hills in the north, separating Bangladesh and India, with their waterfalls are a major tourist attraction. Furthermore, two prominent landmarks make Sylhet very famous: Ali Amjad's 'Ghori' ('Clock') situated on the bank of the Surma, right below the second landmark, the Keane Bridge, built by the British. The bridge has served Sylhet for many years, but sadly its structure is weakening, so at the present time no vehicles are allowed over it. However, it continues to be used by pedestrians, rickshaws and scooter rickshaws, connecting one side of Sylhet town to the other. Both the clock tower and Keane Bridge are painted red and add to the historical character of Sylhet town.

Our area of Sylhet town, Sheikhghat, gets its name 'Sheikh' from Shaikh Sanaullah, the founder of the prominent mosque. Other significant things of interest in Sheikhghat were the imposing building of Jitu Miah's House, facing our house across the main road, and the nearby Ali Amjad's Field, which in my school days was a huge field where we played games – football, cricket and badminton – and held athletics competitions with local schools. Alas, now the whole field has gone into developers' hands for government officials' family quarters. When I visited Sylhet in April 2018, the area seemed lost under the pressure of the growing population of Sylhet as elsewhere in Bangladesh. Sylhet is no longer populated just by Sylhetis; people from other districts of Bangladesh have migrated into Sylhet because of its relative prosperity.

Sheikhghat and Khuliatoola neighbourhoods are attractive in wintertime. We used to play marbles with our age group, although 'class consciousness' played a part in the company one kept. There was the western part of Sheikhghat which was known as Pothua Bari (Street People's Home). But in playing games the youths were all together. There would be little quarrels and disagreements at times but we soon made up and we would be playing again. Some of my playmates I would like to name from memory: Kabir Bhai, Rafi, Shafi, Shahriar, Bazlu mama (my mother's youngest brother, he was my age), Mohi nana, Matin nana, me (Rana), Saleh, Mahmud, Gedu chacha, Sharo, his brother Nena, Kholku mama, Mokhoi mama, Bachchu mamna, Putul mama. We had 'inter-mahalla' (inter-neighbourhood) competitions in badminton, cricket, football and volleyball. In summer, with the onset of monsoon, the low-lying areas would get flooded by water from the Surma river and its tributaries.

Recently, when I visited Sylhet in April 2018, the whole of Sylhet, including our homes at Sheikhghat, seemed transformed, not for the better but for the worse. The population was bursting at the seams. But there was money circulating: from overseas aid (the World Bank, UN agencies, Asian Development Bank, bilaterally from the UK, Germany, Denmark, Sweden, the Aga Khan Foundation, etc.), home remittances and export earnings from the extremely successful garment trade. Seasonal crop production was good so Bangladesh did not have to depend on food from other countries. Barring natural disasters, the Bangladesh economy today is thriving. During our childhood we saw our servants did not have any footwear, now everyone in Bangladesh has something to wear on their feet; the population looks well fed and healthy. Bangladesh does not look like what Henry Kissinger once called a 'basket case' in the context of international aid.

One of my important fellow Rotarian contacts in Sylhet is Dr Monzurul Huq Choudhury, a Rotary scholar, past District Governor of the Rotary District Bangladesh, past president of the Rotary Club of Jalalabad, Sylhet, and chairman of the Jalalabad Disabled Rehabilitation Centre and Hospital (JDRCH). Through Dr Choudhury's influence I was able to visit the Kandryo Muslim Shahitya Shongshod (KMSS – the Central Muslim Literary Institution). I had heard from my father and others about Mr Muhammad Nurul Haque and his work in the establishment and running of this literary institution. Mr Nurul Haque was a literary giant. He was also the editor of the institution's journal, *Al Islah*, one of Bengal's oldest literary magazines, which continues to be published today. It is now in its eighty-fifth year of publication.

During a meeting with the present editor and members of the committee of the KMSS, I learnt how, on 16 September 1936, a group of distinguished Sylhetis had assembled to form the institution named the *Muslim Shahitya Shongshod* – later, because of its branch network, to become the Kandryo (Central) Muslim Shahitya Shongshod. That evening was to become a memorable occasion for me. I was presented with a number of publications, including *My Twelve Years in Sylhet* by Robert Lindsay. I learnt, too, that one of my classmates from Government High School, 1952 matriculation batch, Mahbubur Rahman, a successful businessman and an extremely generous philanthropist, had donated a very large sum for the rebuilding and renovation of the KMSS. I prayed for Mahbub: may Allah grant him health, happiness and prosperity for this act of outstanding benevolence. The library of the Shongshod has a rich collection of old newspapers, old copies of *Al Islah* and historical publications going back to ancient times. Today it attracts visitors and research students from all over the Indian subcontinent.

Family

I was told that when I was born my mother had a nervous breakdown. So I was brought up by one of my mother's younger sisters, my Aunty Dudu – 'Dudu moi' – who cared for and nurtured me until my mother became well again and I was returned to her. With the twists and turns that were to follow in my life, it almost seems as though her nervous breakdown was a significant omen for my later life.

My childhood was in the Khuliatoola, Sheikhghat areas ('parishes') south-west of Sylhet town. The neighbourhood was in a respectable part of Sylhet. Both my maternal and paternal grandfathers, Moulvi Abdun Noor ('Nana Saab', maternal grandfather) and Moulvi Safar Ali ('Dada', paternal grandfather) had retired from the Assam Government as personal assistants (PAs) to the British Revenue Commissioner of Assam (an Englishman, in the Indian Civil Service). My Nana Saab had inherited a huge compound of land in the town where he built houses. His mother (my great-grandmother, 'Boronani') had gifted a piece of land to my parents which was at the front of the compound adjacent to the main road. There my father built houses: the one inside was for the family and an outhouse was for meeting his clients and chess-playing friends, sometimes a children's playhouse; and a part of it was for my father's resident personal clerk (*mohrir*), Moulvi Asaddar Ali. We addressed him as an uncle ('Mori Chacha'). The gift of land enabled my father to establish himself in practice as a lawyer after giving up his studies at Shibpur Engineering College in India, much to the bitter disappointment of his father (that was in response to Mahatma Gandhi's call for non-co-operation against British rule).

My Nana Saab's inheritance included a mosque in the neighbourhood. One of my grandfather's ancestors, Sheikh Sanaullah, had built it (hence it is called the 'Sanaullah mosque'). It has been expanded to cater for a rise in the number of praying Muslims and is held in high esteem by worshippers. My Nana Saab was always a 'winner'! He always won arguments, domestic or external, orally or in writing; he was an intellectual. I remember two of my uncles, his sons, Uncle Tahir (a retired civil inspector – foods) and Uncle Toyyab (an advocate, later a public prosecutor (PP) of Sylhet courts), would get into trouble with their employers or need advice on their cases. My Nana Saab and uncles would sit down at high tables and chairs on his wide veranda wrapped in shawls in the wintry sunshine. Nana Saab would dictate responses in my uncles' cases; and more often than not disciplinary cases against them would be dropped, they would get reinstated or they would win their cases. The many 'battles' I have had to fight with my employers and others suggest that I must have got some of my Nana Saab in me. I think I have inherited from him the ability to focus on issues or cut through arguments to get to the nub of a problem. My colleagues in management consulting have called this my 'inimitable' style!

My paternal grandfather – 'Dada' – was a different kind of man. Unlike my Nana Saab, Dada was a small figure. He had retired from government service at the same time as my Nana Saab. He too had built two large houses on his plots of land at Thoigaon, our ancestral village (official name Dakkhin Raik Dara). Thoigaon is in Balaganj Thana (Police Station Area). Following new boundary demarcations due to population growth the area is now a sub-division (*upazila*). We used to call our paternal village home 'Barhi', our ancestral home. The Thoigaon houses were built traditionally in a row of detached in-houses – so that the ladies could maintain their dignity by observing 'purdah' – and outhouses, to sleep extra numbers of family members or visitors (mainly men). The row of houses belonged to my Dada and his brothers, also my 'Dadas': Borodada (the eldest Dada, a retired headmaster), Haji Dada (who had performed the Hajj in Mecca) and Hurudada (youngest Dada, who served on merchant ships or farmed).

Whenever my own Dada visited us in town, he would sit with all his grandchildren on the bed (at the time we were only four or five grandchildren), to tell us stories until dinnertime. He was a great storyteller.

Dada was a quiet, enigmatic person, busy with his prayers and readings, leaving the worldly chores to my very efficient and ingenuous step-grandmother ('Dadi'); she was quite a close relative – a sister of Nana Saab. My Dada married my Nana Saab's sister upon the death of my own grandmother – my father's mother – when both of them were working in Shillong in similar jobs. My Dadi was very clever in dealing with family matters. Her skills in persuading were unmatched; my Dada must have found her more than a match. She was able to get all my grandfather's properties in Thoigaon legally transferred into her name, thus depriving my father of any ancestral land inheritance in Thoigaon. This hurt my father gravely but he was not one for making a family row about it. He quietly decided to go his separate way, into his own farming ventures. Although clearly very hurt, my father never talked about this unhappy episode. Once Dada came to see my father. A crying Dada was heard to say, 'Aziz, please save me from her torments' – meaning save him from the torments of my step-grandmother who nagged him until he signed off all the property in her name! My father replied, 'Father, it's all your property. You do what you like, I won't mind but I don't want you to be worried or upset thinking about me.'

My father decided to set up on his own. He established a reasonably successful farm of over twenty-three acres of hilly grounds in Goalgaon. The farm produce included pineapple, jackfruit, sugarcane and rice. But with a young family to support and a daily trip to town for his law practice, all this exerted a heavy toll on his health. Futhermore, he had also set up a seasonal rice farm in Tamabil (translated, 'waterlogged copper field'), near the border with Shillong. The alluvial soil was immensely fertile but subject to extreme seasonal flooding, being under the waterfalls off the Khasi and Jointya hills. Eventually, due to a lack of resources and also due to his health (he was a chronic asthma patient) my father had to abandon Goalgaon and Tamabil. Some of my brothers and I have often talked about these unsuccessful ventures of our father and felt that he ought not to have struggled right up to his old age. He did it because he was deprived of his inheritance and he wanted to do something for us, his own children. But all was not lost. He had built his house in Sylhet town, and bequeathed it to us, his nine children.

My Dada and step-Dadi are no more in this world. But the actions of my step-Dadi have left behind a legacy of a divided family. But for this sad inheritance dispute overflowing into the present generation, 'the Safar Ali dynasty' (the direct descendants of Moulvi Safar Ali) had enjoyed a reasonably happy relationship! I was very proud to belong to my entire family and hardly recognised the difference between the descendants of Moulvi Safar Ali. There was love and affection all round.

But years later another disappointment struck: led by my step-Dadi's side, my younger Aunty Lucy, my youngest uncle, Joglu chacha, assisted by my cousin Towhid, aunt Lucy's son, and few others from that camp, and unbeknown to me or my immediate family, there was an attempt to sell our entire ancestral property in Thoigaon to a third party without my family's knowledge. Fortunately this was foiled when my uncle, Kamal chacha, decided to back off from that plan, and we came to know about the conspiracy. The plan was finally blocked by my family by a Court injunction to the effect that nothing relating to that property could be sold off until official demarcations had taken place under Court supervision, to establish who owned what before anyone attempted any sale in the future. The bitterness generated overflew into the current descendants of Moulvi Safar Ali with, sadly, no sign of reconciliation.

My upbringing was in humble circumstances. We were a large family and it was a big household to support. My father's job as a civil lawyer was freelance – a kind of occupation with which, as a retired self-employed management consultant, I am very familiar. We had to live within a fluctuating, unpredictable daily income. My father was known as a man of unwavering integrity, which meant that he was not tempted by anything 'on the side' in an otherwise corrupt economic and political environment. This meant that I and my siblings of school age had only one set of clothes for school; my mother would wash them at night ready (thankfully the generally warm climate helped!) for next morning – no need for ironing, except when getting them washed and ironed at the nearby washermen's home for special occasions such as Eid.

I did not have any suitable footwear for school. In the hot and rainy weather slippers were commonly worn. So my father and I decided on an affordable improvisation. There was a cobbler whose 'shop' was at the side of the steps to the Mukhtar Library. He was an elderly person, very kind and affectionate. We got him to make me a pair of slippers from the inner layers of vehicle tyres. They lasted a very long time.

On the way back to Goalgaon in the rickshaw, we would do some shopping at a regular shop – a sack of rice and other household necessities my mother had asked for. The rickshaw-wala would help with the stuff up the hills to our farmhouse. Everything would be put down on the floor. I would help my mother in unpacking the rice and shopping.

It's a sad episode that at a later date my father sold the Goalgaon farm at a throwaway price in order to finance my younger brother Raja's wish to come to England to work so as to follow in my footsteps (I had joined the navy and was coming to Dartmouth for naval training). His academic performance was such that he could not aspire to much in England. When he came to London he ended up living in a crowded house (three or four adults in a jumbo bed!) in depressed Aldgate of the late 1950s, with a job, with other Sylhetis, in a Jewish garment factory in Brick Lane. While working there, he took a sales course with the International Correspondence School (ICS). He completed the curriculum but nothing came of it. Eventually he returned home and got a job as a life insurance agent in a Pakistani-owned insurance company. Later on he set up a successful wholesale grocery shop in downtown Sylhet markets.

My father was an extremely bright student, obtaining outstanding results at school. He passed with distinction his matriculation of the Bengal Education Board and Intermediate in Science (I. Sc.) in the Calcutta University examination. Because of his academic achievements my grandfather had decided that my father should be sent to the world-renowned Shibpur Engineering College in India to study engineering. The college was predominantly for Hindus but my father's academic achievements helped him to gain admission.

It was the early days of the non-co-operation movement against the British Raj in the early 1930s. Mahatma Gandhi was leading the movement. My father decided to quit his studies at Shibpur in response to Mr Gandhi's call to what was to turn into the full Quit India Movement against the British. This route gave my father the freedom he wanted in order to play a full part in the Indian independence movement. Giving up his studies, however, was to cause my grandfather deep hurt. To be able to stand on his two feet, my father decided to study law in his own time to become a distinguished civil court lawyer (*mukhtar*), in an independent practice.

In his spare time my father wrote poems. His dramatisation of the Mughal period in India was published – *Bharotay Mughal* (The Mughals in India) – and stage plays were performed at many places in Sylhet and elsewhere. In 1947, after the Second World War, the Attlee Government in Britain sent Lord Mountbatten to oversee the independence of India. Done in some haste, and with little preparation, the result was the division of India into Hindu India and Muslim Pakistan.

In the context of the whole Indian subcontinent there was the 'little matter' of my home district, Sylhet, in Assam Province. With its unclear proportion of Hindus and Muslims, the question whether Sylhet should go to India or to Pakistan (East Pakistan or East Bengal) became a burning issue. It was decided that there should be a referendum. This took place in late 1947. The result was about 51% for Pakistan and 49% for India.

Sylhet joined East Pakistan with sixteen other former East Bengal districts. My father always supported an 'undivided India' following Mr Gandhi's declarations and the calls of some other leaders, both Hindus and Muslims. I am told that my father was selected as Mahatma Gandhi's man to lead the referendum in 1947 so that Sylhet would remain in India. This was kept so secret that even my mother did not know about my father's role in the Sylhet referendum on behalf of the Muslim section of the Congress Party (Jamat e Ulema Hind), until about five years after the referendum took place in 1952. After the transfer of Sylhet to (East) Pakistan, my father decided to retire from active politics. But he remained an astute politician, as evidenced by his pronouncements in debates and discussions amongst friends and relatives, including the volatile press of the time.

Prior to all this, my father did venture into local politics. He stood for election for membership of the Sylhet Union Board for our village seat. I saw the campaigning across the muddy paddy fields, checking and rechecking the coverage of voters by area. I tried to join in. All my uncles and village supporters had joined in. But sadly because of his political alignment with the Hindu-dominated Congress Party, he lost a lot of Muslim votes in the area, and a gentleman from the same locality, Dewan Abdur Rab, won the seat. After that my father didn't try for any other election or political recognition. I remember the excitement of electioneering. My whole family had migrated from our house in Sheikhghat in Sylhet town to our grandfather's village home in Thoigaon, fourteen miles south of the town. On the day of the election, I had decided to join the election day at the Tajpur Dak bungalow to see voting at the polling station. I needed to look smart, as the candidate, Azizur Rahman's, eldest son! I was only about eight or nine at the time. So the younger of my two paternal aunties (my father's two stepsisters), my dearest Aunt Lucy, decided to smarten me up. She gave me a shower and a rubbing-down at the steps of our private pond, to remove the dirt which had settled on me from the playing fields, before dressing me up.

Although most of our close relatives and friends supported Mr Jinnah's Muslim League for Pakistan, my father stood almost alone, except that he retained his friendship with leading people of Sylhet involved in the Non-Co-operation Movement against British rule. He had the courage of his convictions to stand alone in an adverse political climate, which resulted in threats to his life during and after the Sylhet referendum.

My family connections with British rule in India ran deep. My grandparents were well educated, highly respected and God-fearing people. As upper middle class Muslims, they brought up their children with good education and training. They both had large families; I had nine or ten uncles and aunties from each side and scores of first cousins. With no social security system, large families in Indian culture acted as 'pension policies' for providing care for elderly parents.

The impact of the Second World War was felt all over Sylhet. Up north in Assam, Dibrugarh, Guwahati and Manipur had been bombed by the Japanese as they advanced on Mountbatten's Burma. These were scary times! I remember one morning my Mum asked me to go to buy something (the snack called *muri* – puffed rice) for breakfast from a shop in Kazir Bazar. It was about nine o'clock in the morning. The siren went off, warning of Japanese planes approaching from Burma, which had already fallen. We were terrified that the Japanese were coming to bomb Sylhet. With many others I went down into the trench at the Kazir Bazar and stayed there for a couple of hours until the siren sounded to give the all clear. By the time I brought home the shopping for breakfast it was well near lunchtime. My father had gone to his court without breakfast, and my brothers and sisters had gone to school without breakfast.

Growing up in Sylhet, I had many friends in school and college. We were a small group who would play and picnic together. This closeness continued until some of us went our separate ways. A few went to the UK, others to the USA, Canada, Australia and Germany. Some married abroad like myself: I married Anna (English), Mufti married Rosemary (English), Rafi married Nora (Irish), Nurul married Mary (Irish).

We still keep in touch; we formed a group in the UK called the '1952 Batch' following the year in which we all passed our matriculation examination from the Sylhet Government High English School. The 1952 Batch met, along with our wives, for some years in and around London to keep in touch and reminisce about our younger days. We took it in turns to have lunch at our homes in England, until recently when we began to feel we were not getting any younger!

What direction: study engineering or 'join the navy to see the world'?

It was time to decide my next steps: should I take a job and start earning to help my father in supporting a large family? Or should I study medicine or engineering, or join the army or navy? It was a watershed moment.

I had already applied for a clerical job in the East Pakistan Government Secretariat where the husband of one of my aunts (Aunty Dudu referred to before) worked as a head clerk. To my mind the Secretariat represented the seat of the Government. I received a job offer as a clerk straightaway. Youth unemployment was very high in those days. So I felt encouraged to have landed a job. But then I felt a hankering for more. Other things were calling me! This feeling has played a big role in my life, a feeling that I must keep up with my ambition.

I was invited for interviews by Dhaka University Engineering College to study for a degree in one of the engineering disciplines. I travelled by overnight train from my hometown, Sylhet, to Dhaka, the journey of 120 miles taking about ten hours, on metre-gauge rails. I was in 'inter class'. (Inter class travel was for the respectable who could not afford the 'second class' preferred by the well-to-do. First class train travel was out of reach for the many; it was still for the whites such as the tea planters.) I had several maternal and paternal uncles and aunties living in Dhaka. I decided to stay with my Mum's younger sister, my Aunty Dudu. Her husband was deeply interested in educating his children, and I thought he would help me prepare for the interviews, which he did.

On the day of the tests and interviews I faced a three-member panel for the final interview. I was grilled for an hour or so. It was the first time in my life that I had faced an interview panel. I was nervous. One panel member asked me, 'What is the speed limit in Dhaka city?' I answered, 'Eighty mph.' That created a roar of laughter in the panel of professors! Clearly I had boobed. After the interview I asked someone the question. The reply was thirty mph! I thought that was the end of my aspirations to study engineering. But I was lucky. To my surprise, I was offered a place at Dhaka University Engineering College, to study mechanical engineering. I was also offered a scholarship, with all fees paid. My parents, my brothers and sisters and my friends were very pleased. I felt that while my father did not fulfil my grandfather's wish to study engineering at Shibpur, India, I would be doing so at Dhaka University – if God so wished.

But the other direction I had in mind was to 'join the navy to see the world'! Why? Well there's a bit of family history here! On my paternal step-grandmother's side I had five uncles and two aunties – my father's step-siblings. I was fond of all of them. The youngest of the uncles, 'Joglu chacha' – Mr Aminur Rahman (he had changed his name to something he liked from his given name, Asifur Rahman), was very keen to join the Pakistan Navy. He was my uncle but also very close to me, almost like a childhood friend. I was influenced by his plans and thinking. He had a third-division pass in the matriculation exam in his secondary education, so he managed only to enter the navy as a 'rating', to train as a stoker mechanic, which he duly became. But he had influenced me to join the navy. After my matriculation before enrolling to the MC College, I did try once to join the Pakistan Navy as an apprentice, in the technical side of the Pakistan Navy's non-commissioned branch. I took the apprentice recruitment examination held at the 'Sylhet circuit house' when the recruitment team was on a tour of East Pakistan. I passed and could have joined the navy as an apprentice, later specialising in any of the technical trades. But, providentially I think, I changed my mind and decided to continue my studies. So I enrolled for the Intermediate in Science (I. Sc.) course at Murari Chand College, Sylhet,

Dhaka University. But my craving to join the navy remained undiminished.

The Pakistan Government Ministry of Defence's programme for recruiting cadets for the army, navy and air force was an annual event. When the recruitment team came to Sylhet, I sat the examination, passed stage I, and was invited to a three-day Inter-Services Selection Board (ISSB) for stage II at the Military Cantonment, in Kurmitoola, Dhaka. That was in mid-1954, whilst I was at the MC College. I received a telegram from the Ministry of Defence giving me the news that I had been successful. But I had been assigned to the Pakistan Army, not the Pakistan Navy as I had wished! After discussing with my father, uncles and friends, I decided to accept the offer. An MoD telegram was later to arrive, asking me and seven others like me from East Pakistan to start training at the Joint Services Pre-Cadet Training School (JSPCTS), Quetta, capital of Baluchistan. I was asked to report there on 16 October 1954.

As an aside, Quetta has gained some notoriety! Baluchistan, the dry mountainous region of Pakistan bordering Afghanistan, is now in the grip of the Taliban. Quetta, its capital, was the place where the 'American Seals' found Wasama Bin Laden in hiding right near the Pakistan Military Academy, Kakul – close to the seat of the Pakistan Army. That was very near the JSPCTS where I was trained. Those interested in current affairs will recall the satellite TV scene beamed round the world from the Obama White House showing the killing of Bin Laden by the US Navy Seals.

There must have been about 150 pre-cadets divided up in four 'houses' – Khaibar, Tochi, Gomal, Bolan – named after mountain passes. Each house was under the supervision of a military house master. There were Pathans, Punjabis, Beluchis, Sindhis – all from West Pakistan; I was the sole Bengali from East Pakistan. There were also some Bihari cadets who were not Bengalis but had crossed over from Bihar in India, to Muslim East Pakistan at the time of partition in 1947. All the cadets got on well together. But the disparity in the proportion of West and East Pakistani cadets was obvious. Out of the total of some 150, there were only eight Bengalis (including the four Biharis) from the East; the rest, may be close to 140, were from West Pakistan. The dominant group was the Punjabis.

After my Quetta training of four months I passed out as a cadet. Army cadets went to the Pakistan Military Academy (PMA), Kakul, near Quetta,

Baluchistan Province; the naval cadets went on to the Pakistan Navy Ship (PNS) *Himalaya*, a shore establishment, in Manora Island, off Keamari, Karachi, Sindh Province; air force cadets went to Risalpur, in North West Frontier Province (NWFP). I had spoken to my house master, a flight lieutenant of the Pakistan Air Force, and expressed my wish to transfer from the Pakistan Army to the Pakistan Navy. A few weeks later I was told that my application to transfer to the navy had been approved by the Ministry of Defence. As mentioned earlier, in my batch there were eight Bengali cadets in the group; I was the only actual Bengali from East Pakistan (population at the time about 110 million) and seven were from various parts of West Pakistan and Bihar, India. The population of Pakistan at the time was about 70 million. The disparity in recruitment between East and West Pakistan was striking.

PNS Himalaya

I headed for PNS *Himalaya* on Manora Island, Karachi. The training was to last about eight months and cover studies in English, history, mathematics, navigation, physical training (PT), seamanship and sailing.

I have mentioned my Uncle Joglu who had become a naval rating – a stoker mechanic. I heard that he was planning to leave the navy. He told me that he was seeking discharge on medical grounds. Years afterwards I was to discover that his main reason for wanting to leave the navy was different. It was that when I myself became a sub-lieutenant, he would have to salute me as an officer! An uncle having to salute his own nephew! This was not a done thing in our culture. His self-esteem wouldn't allow him to do it. He used to gleefully tell us how he had fooled the navy to get his discharge. As our lives moved on, I was to discover that my Uncle Joglu had other issues. I could not understand why he nursed a resentment. Sadly, in later years, he spread lies to defame me but to no avail. I felt hurt because I treated him as a friend.

The Pakistan Army action against the Bengalis in late 1970/early 1971 leading to the creation of Bangladesh is well documented. At the time East Pakistan had a majority of Muslims, about 56%, while in West Pakistan they were about 44%. East Pakistan was led by Sheikh Mujibur Rahman, Bangladesh's nationalist leader of the main political party, the Awami League.

West Pakistan was led by Mr Zulfiqar Ali Bhutto (father of Benazir Bhutto, later to be Prime Minister) whose Pakistan Peoples Party (PPP) had the support of the Punjabi Army. He wanted the general election result to be set aside or ignored so that he (Bhutto) would be Prime Minister of the whole of Pakistan. This was not acceptable to the Bengalis who felt that Sheikh Mujib, having a majority in the whole of Pakistan, should be the Prime Minister. So, as *The Guardian* (London) wrote at the time, 'the Generals reached for the guns'. Army action followed; many Bengalis were killed or migrated over the border to India as refugees. Mrs Indira Gandhi was Prime Minister of India at the time. She did not want disturbances at India's eastern borders, so close to China. Being a democrat herself, Mrs Gandhi supported Sheikh Mujib. The Indian Army moved into East Pakistan and the Pakistan Army surrendered without a fight. Thus Bangladesh was created under the leadership of Sheikh Mujib with the support of Indira Gandhi's Congress Government in India.

How two groups of people bound by one common religion, Islam, came to be so hostile towards one another is a sad episode of Pakistan's history. But it reflects the fact that religion could not hold the two parts of Pakistan together: two different people by culture and languages, separated by a thousand miles of hostile India. As *The Daily Telegraph* reported at the time: 'It was an un-natural marriage'! The British political and administrative basis of division of India by Lord Mountbatten on the basis of religion thus became untenable. Economic exploitation of the Bengalis by the army-backed Punjabis was also a decisive factor in the break-up of Pakistan and creation of two countries: Pakistan (formerly West Pakistan) and Bangladesh.

Bangladesh, born out of the conflicts and bloodshed of 1970/71, is still in its formative years as a new country. Politics is relatively stable but squabbly. Leaders have been assassinated. Democracy is taking root slowly. The economy is showing promise and strength, with a steady rate of impressive GDP growth of 6-7%. Bangladesh still has Talibans, and Muslim fundamentalists are claimed to be there.

Back to my story: Pakistan Navy Ship Himalaya, Karachi

As well as the studies I have mentioned, we were taught English social etiquette and what to expect about life in England when we entered

Dartmouth Naval College. There were monthly formal dinners with the Cadet Training School commander or our instructors, and on one occasion, we had Captain and Mrs Tyminski and his pretty young daughter Donia as our dinner guests. Captain Tyminski (of Polish origin) was an officer on loan from the Royal Navy commanding PNS *Himalaya*, with responsibility for all training.

Commodore Bailey was also on loan from the Royal Navy to assist with the operational side of the Pakistan Navy.

At the monthly dinners we were told stories about what to expect of social life in England. Some of my fellow cadets from West Pakistan were fair-skinned and thought they would pass for 'whites' in England. As a Bengali, I was a relatively darker shade. At one dinner, when our CTS commander was the dinner guest, we were discussing racial prejudice and racial discrimination in England. I recall our guest, Lieutenant Commander Anwar Sayeed, himself very fair-skinned, rather curtly reminding us, especially the fair-skinned cadets, that 'various shades of skin colour do not mean much in England, they are all treated as "black or coloured"'! That was the first time I heard about colour discrimination in England. It was to feature much in my later life in England.

Some aspects of time on *Himalaya* I remember well. At a seven-a-side football match between the CTS and a ratings' training batch, we won by a single goal scored by myself. At the subsequent monthly dinner a post-mortem was in full flow. The CTS commander said, 'Suhail was there to put the ball in!' I looked round the table to see how this appreciation of me went down with the rest of the cadets round the table; I was struck by the lack of enthusiasm.

Lieutenant Commander Khatib Uddin – a very learned gentleman, a fair-skinned Pathan, slim, very smart in naval summer outfit of shorts and short-sleeve shirts with his lieutenant commander lapels – taught us English. Some of the cadets in my batch came from various school backgrounds in West Pakistan. Some had studied in English medium schools following the GCE O- and A-level curriculum of Britain; others standard secondary or intermediate level education from Pakistani Universities and Boards of Examinations. In my case it was the Dhaka University-passed Intermediate in Science (I. Sc.) examination, equivalent to GCE O-level plus a bit more.

The cadets' standard of English therefore differed. Commander Khatib Uddin was trying to bring us up to the same level in English in preparation for entry to Britannia Royal Naval College Dartmouth. He always asked us to 'read'! He used to say, 'Try writing something and see how difficult it is. Authors, writers, poets, philosophers are learned people. They have written books, assembled their thoughts into books, written stories, essays, prose, poems, literature, and became famous, even Nobel Prize Laureates. So read. Learn what they have said, how they have said it, practise it. Reading is so important.' His assertions stuck in my mind; I remember him with deep respect.

While at *Himalaya* I made a point of searching out Sylheti and Bengali people living in Karachi. There were not many to be found! During weekend shore leave, I would visit friends and acquaintances, eat rice and curries and see films, and try to make myself feel at home. (I was missing home a lot, being away for the first time for such a length of time.) At the time of our passing-out from *Himalaya*, we were told we could invite guests to the farewell party and dinner. I invited a very well-placed Bengali couple in Karachi. I used to go to their house to eat brilliantly cooked Bengali dishes. But I made a boob in writing the invitation card. Instead of writing Mr and Mrs…, I just wrote Mr…, and left out the Mrs. My guests understood the mistake but gently told me it should have been: '… request the pleasure of the company of Mr and Mrs'. I argued with them, with hindsight stupidly, that 'request the pleasure of the company of' meant that the Mr could bring the Mrs as his 'company'! How smart and illiterate could you get?

At the end of the eight months' training at the CTS, PNS *Himalaya*, our batch was to proceed on a few weeks' leave prior to departing for Dartmouth, England, for naval training at the Britannia Royal Naval College. I was enormously proud to be going to such a prestigious and historic institution where royal princes had received training. Before proceeding on leave we were all medically checked. All my fellow West Pakistani cadets were found fit and were able to go home on leave in parts of West Pakistan. Sadly, I was not allowed to go to my home in East Pakistan (a flight of 1,000 miles across India) because they found a calcified node in my chest X-ray, which needed to be investigated and treated. I was held back for a week or so, for tests in the Naval Hospital, Karachi. Then there was not enough time left for me to go to East Pakistan, as the departure date for Dartmouth was getting close. So I decided to spend the week or so left of my leave undertaking some travels in West Pakistan. Fortunately I had an uncle, a first cousin of my father, in the Pakistan Army; he was an infantry major, who was stationed in Abbottabad, Baluchistan. I went along to stay with him in his officers' mess quarters. From Abbottabad, I was able to visit the Pakistan Military Academy (PMA) in Kakul, also the Pakistan Air Force cadet training college in Risalpur, and other places like Nowshera Cantonment etc. That was the first time I learned something about the history and geography of West Pakistan, and understood a little about the predominantly military culture and tradition prevailing there. During British rule in India, this part of what is now West Pakistan provided most of the manpower for the crack military of the British Raj. It still provides the backbone of the formidable Pakistan military.

This cancellation of my leave to go home also meant that as I was going to Dartmouth for three years, it would be four years before I would see my family and friends back home in Sylhet again. I was about eighteen. It was a long time for someone who had never been away from home before. I had already been home sick at the JSPCTS, Quetta, and PNS *Himalaya*, Karachi. Another long period away was bound to intensify my homesickness. I was particularly missing my mother. I couldn't forget the way she cried all day when I was leaving home. I recall tears flowing down her face while she prepared food for a special family farewell dinner on the eve of my departure.

My sister Ruby, professor in politics at the Government Women's College in Sylhet, had presented me with a book; she had written inside the front cover in Bengali in her beautiful handwriting, a quote from the Bengali poet, Rabindranath Tagore, the Nobel Prize Laureate (I translate): 'Go forth ye the conquering hero, at the dawn of a new life, you have the sceptre of new hope in your hands' ('*Hay Bijoyi Beer Nobo Jiboner Pratay, Nobino Ashar Khorhgo Tumar Hatay*'). I hope what followed in my life would not have disappointed my late sister. Sadly she passed away with a brain haemorrhage some years after I returned to West Pakistan to commence my service life; she never saw me in my naval uniform with the bright gold stripes.

Chapter Two

Britannia Royal Naval College Dartmouth

Meeting Anna – how it all began

Britannia Royal Naval College Dartmouth

After an overnight flight from Karachi with PanAm airlines via Beirut, I arrived in London Heathrow Airport, on an extremely cold night at the end of December 1955. Christmas was just over but the lights and the decorations were still up to welcome the New Year. I was met at the airport by an official of the Pakistan High Commission, who took me by taxi to a B&B in Bayswater Road. I was to rest the following day and then go to visit the naval adviser at the Pakistan High Commission, 35 Lowndes Square. I woke up early, about 6.30am (10.30am Pakistan time), not being able to sleep due to jetlag. I got myself ready. I saw a member of the staff. He asked, 'Can I help, sir?' I said I wanted to go to a shop to buy myself a jumper. He said, 'Sir, we don't start life here until after nine o'clock! You'd better have some breakfast and then go out.' I felt I was truly lost. But I was to get my bearings.

That December in 1955 in London was bitterly cold. I could see snow and ice everywhere. Although I had some warm clothing in expectation of the cold weather, I felt I needed a jumper. So I took a cab and asked the driver to take me to the Army and Navy Stores in Victoria. I had heard the name before. I knew nothing about the Tube, and had not the faintest idea where I was. At the A&N Store, I asked for the jumper and sweater section in the men's clothing department. What they showed me were all loose-fitting. We were not used to wearing loose jumpers. So, following what I was used to wearing back home in Sylhet, I asked for a tight-fitting sweater. The staff member was puzzled. So he asked me to go down to the children's section. There I bought a tightly fitting blue full-sleeve woollen jumper; I took a taxi back to the Bayswater Road B&B. I hung around the hotel lounge and slept in the middle of the day to shake off the jetlag.

On the third day after arrival, I went to the Pakistan High Commission to see the naval adviser; he was Lieutenant Qizilbash, PN. I went into his office, dressed in my cadet uniform – all black navy 'winter rig – No. 5'. He took my salute even though he was in civilian clothes. He stood up, shook hands and then without a word took my cap off my head, pulled off its white drill-cloth cover, then handed it back to me. I remembered what I had been told about 'winter rig': it was black uniform throughout the winter. He gave me some briefing, some advice on do's and don'ts; then I was given some cash and a one-way train travel warrant.

The following day it was Paddington station and the train for Dartmouth. They were pre-Beeching days, so the trains went to Kingswear, where one took the ferry to Dartmouth railway station. The train soon arrived at Kingswear. It was carrying all the cadets who were starting the Easter term at the college – January to April. We disembarked and were led to the waiting ferry. We crossed the River Dart. As we disembarked, we were met by two chief petty officers, very tall and smart. They told us to fall into lines, three deep. Soon it was 'turn right' and 'quick march' up the hill to the college. It was extremely cold. The winding road was icy and slippery, with snow all over the grounds. We arrived and took shelter in the covered area by the side of the parade ground. We were issued with kit bags to carry our issue of new uniforms, shoes and other items of kit. Soon we were heading for our cabins (rooms). I was allocated to St Vincent Division, the farthest of the buildings up the hill at the back of the college. I shared the cabin with Cadet Shelton-Agar, an English boy of my age. We were all seventeen to eighteen years of age, the entry age for Dartmouth.

Devon has been described as heaven if one wants a country life. Dartmouth, in South Devon, is world famous for the Britannia Royal

Naval College, where kings and princes of Great Britain and cadets from several Commonwealth countries received naval training. Set on a hilltop overlooking the harbour of the River Dart, with Kingswear on the other side and the sea beyond, the beauty of Dartmouth is unsurpassed and unmatched in the world. But more about Dartmouth later.

Britannia Royal Naval College opened on 14 September 1905. Sir Aston Webb was the architect of the college; he also designed the façade of Buckingham Palace and the main buildings of the Victoria and Albert Museum. Thousands of naval officers have passed out from the college after their officer training, amongst whom were two former kings of Great Britain: King Edward VIII and King George VI. Among the recent royals are Prince Philip, Prince Charles and Prince Andrew. It is recorded that during a royal visit to the college in July 1939, the young Princess Elizabeth (later Queen Elizabeth II) first met Prince Philip. The Royals have honoured the passing-out parades of officers on many occasions. These royal connections of the college continued into the future.

For me, soon it was to be the start of college life at the Britannia Royal Naval College Dartmouth. The St Vincent divisional officer was Lieutenant Staveley. I was to discover later that he was a bright star of the Royal Navy. He rose to become an admiral of the fleet. He came from a naval tradition; his father was also an admiral. We were duly addressed by Lt Staveley, welcoming us, telling us about do's and don'ts, what was expected of us, etc. A senior cadet was appointed from amongst us. But the senior midshipmen in the division laid down the rules for the new arrivals – rituals, custom and practice! We were issued with books, class routines, shown round the college, what was to be found where, and so on. Quite a lot of the initial information went over my head!

It was a tough routine in the coldest of winter seasons. Early morning we would be awakened at 6am by the boatswain's (bos'n) pipe, in the dark January mornings. Out of pyjamas, into shorts, vests, socks and gym shoes; run out to the back yard for exercises; following the senior midshipman, jump up and down, swing arms and shoulders, run on the spot, lift the legs and knees – warm-ups. Fifteen minutes' exercise finished, it was back to the cabins, for showers or quick baths in the communal bathrooms, then dress in the 'rig of the day' (No. 13): thick blue full-sleeve shirts, navy jumpers, blue winter trousers, blue, thick long woollen socks, polished black shoes with thick soles. Then we ran down to the dining hall and sat down at long tables for hearty breakfasts: porridge, eggs and mushrooms, sausages, tomatoes, a glass of cold milk, tea or coffee. I and my fellow Muslim cadets could not eat 'eggs and bacon', so stewards were soon organising alternatives: two eggs, or an omelette.

One thing was difficult in the dining hall. There was a very motherly, tall, brawny lady called Miss Bullah who oversaw the dining hall, and saw that we were fed well. I was having difficulty drinking a cold glass of milk. I was not used to this English custom. I had never drunk cold milk back home, I was used to drinking warm milk. Miss Bullah would be saying, 'Come on, boys, drink up your milk!' I just could not take a liking to drinking cold milk!

With the change of diet and coming into a cold climate almost at the start of the term, I became unwell, with a pain in the upper abdomen. I was unable to be very active in my training – indoors or out. I was admitted to the college sick bay for a few days before being transferred to the Royal Naval Hospital Devonport. I was there for about two weeks under the care of a Royal Navy surgeon captain and a Queen Anne's Royal Naval Nursing Service (QARNNS) matron. The nurses all looked after me extremely well. With their affectionate care I was made to feel at home. I was diagnosed as having a duodenal ulcer. I remember asking the surgeon captain, 'Sir, I still suffer from wind in the tummy.' The captain said, 'Don't worry, Suhail, I too get wind.' That shut me up in front of the very prim and proper superintending sister from QARNNS!

One important thing was to happen while I was at the Royal Naval Hospital. The head of QARNNS, Princess Alexandra, was paying a formal visit. I had been allocated a cabin, a room to myself because even as a cadet I was to be treated as a naval officer. I was not forewarned, though the nursing staff had ensured I was looking smart and made my cabin shipshape. Suddenly the door opened and there was Princess Alexandra, accompanied by the surgeon captain and the matron. I was so surprised and shocked at being introduced to the Princess by the captain: 'Your Royal Highness, this is Cadet Suhail Ibne Aziz, from the Royal Naval College Dartmouth. He is on training there from the Pakistan Navy.' Princess Alexandra shook hands with me, engaged in some small talk (Was I liking the college? Was I settling in alright?) and departed with a beautiful smile and a nod, the entourage following her out of the cabin. I was young, and didn't know much about the background of the Royals. I was shocked at the surprise visit, but so thrilled at my first encounter with a princess of England.

Soon after, I was discharged from the hospital and went back to the college. Because of the illness I missed classes. So, after informing the naval adviser at the Pakistan High Commission, London, I was told I was being put back a term. I realised my academic subjects needed a great deal of work to catch up. However, to be put back a three-month term right at the start of my Dartmouth training seemed an unfortunate setback. Happily, my duodenal ulcer was cured, enabling me to continue my training.

The college was organised with a naval and a civilian hierarchy. At the top was a four-ringer captain (Capt.) with overall administrative and operational responsibility. Under him was a three-ringer commander (Cdr) responsible for administering the college. A training commander looked after the operational aspects of all training. Below them were officers of lieutenant commander (Lt Cdr) and lieutenant (Lt) ranks. Then there were chief and petty officers (CPOs and POs – we addressed them as 'Chief'), including some retired chiefs who would provide practical seamanship and other technical training. When I entered the college, at the top was Capt. Crawford. Soon afterwards it was Capt. Munn who remained at the college throughout my training from 1956 to 1958. I remember both Capt. Crawford and Capt. Munn as officers with serious demeanours, impeccably dressed, taking the Sunday salutes from the 'bridge', with their telescope smartly tucked under their left arm, engaging our eyes as we saluted, eyes right, at the march-pasts. They set very high standards, an impression that was to last my whole life.

The civilian training staff were organised like a public school, with a headmaster at the top and all the civilian academic training staff under him. They were more stable than the naval staff, who changed every three years. While I was at the college, the headmaster was Mr Stork. His office was next to the captain's, on the large landing up the steps from the main hallway. I didn't see Mr Stork much but a chance meeting with his wife, Mrs Stork, was to cause quite an event at the tail end of my time at Dartmouth – as will be seen later!

The parade ground routine was not too difficult. But we had to run from one class to another or between the parade ground and the classrooms. We were allowed five minutes between classrooms or to the parade ground, so 'run' and 'run faster' were the urgent calls. On one occasion on the parade ground we were practising various drill manoeuvres. One of the Pakistani or Malaysian cadets was marching away in the opposite direction to the rest of his platoon. The drill instructor, Chief Petty Officer Long, halted the platoon. The lone cadet stood to attention some yards away. CPO Long went over to him, and with a serious face, asked, 'Sir, do you understand English?' The cadet said, 'Yes, Chief.' CPO: 'How nice you understand English.' Then with a fierce shout he said, 'Then do it!' On another occasion, there was a tinge of suggestion of a 'race problem' which the CPO had to deal with. His mastery of the situation was truly noteworthy. He went over to the cadet, his face close to the cadet's and said, 'I do not care if you are black, brown, yellow, green or white! What I want you to do here on the parade ground is do as you are told. If you don't then you will run round this parade ground until you fall. Is that clear?' We dreaded these two or three CPO drill instructors. But I believe that for the character-building of young cadets, the lessons given by the CPO drill instructors were robust and invaluable.

College routine after breakfast would be classroom instruction: seamanship (including learning how to tie various knots as used in the navy), physics, mathematics, naval history, navigation, theories in gunnery, torpedo and anti-submarine warfare, and so on. These classes were usually up to lunchtime. After lunch, we spent a bit of time reading newspapers in the gunroom or cabins. Then it was change of rig to sports gear and various activities during the afternoon: football, swimming, hockey, cross-country running, down the hill to Sandquay for dinghy sailing, whaler and cutter rowing. I enjoyed the cross-country runs, about five miles up and down the hills, on narrow tracks – ending huffing and puffing.

Our academic instructors were all learned in their subject disciplines. But one or two had other hobbies. Our physics/electrical subject tutor was a very keen birdwatcher. I think his name was Mr Burchill. On some Monday mornings after his weekend of birdwatching he would project the pictures of some unusual birds on the screen and explain their special features. We Commonwealth cadets listened to Mr Burchill out of politeness but birdwatching, with all the trouble of walking through jungles, mud and marshy lands or river banks at low ebb, and having the patience to sit out in cold, freezing weather, not knowing when a quaint bird might be sighted, was not for me or other Commonwealth cadets!

At weekends it was time for shore leave for most of us. On Saturdays we visited Dartmouth, Paignton or Torquay, seeing a film or having a drink in a small group. Some weekends were 'outward-bound weekends' on Dartmoor; I could be leading a group of sailors, map reading and walking on the moor, rain or shine. Not infrequently we got 'lost' – but we were told to keep walking in any direction and eventually we would reach 'civilisation'! Escapees from Dartmoor Prison could also be seen by chance during our exercises! Some weekends I would stay in – time to do some washing by hand, or to write letters to my father, mother, or my sisters Ruby and Mina back home. I would get upset writing home. I was missing them a lot, also my school and college friends – including girlfriends.

Meeting Anna

After the somewhat restricted life of the first (Easter) term at the college while we got some idea about life in the forces, and what was expected of us while out mixing with civilians, we were allowed to go ashore to Dartmouth and other neighbouring towns: Torquay, Paignton, Totnes, Plymouth.

Anna's full name was Elizabeth Ann Pyne. I switch between 'Anna' and 'Ann' depending on who I am talking to; most of her relatives, friends and acquaintances called her Ann. We met one beautiful Saturday evening in the summer of 1956 at a dance at the Guildhall in Dartmouth. She was with a group of girlfriends; I discovered three of them were also called Ann (with or without an 'e'). That Saturday evening a number of cadets and midshipmen from the naval college were enjoying themselves at the Guildhall. I and a couple of my close friends from the Pakistan Navy and Royal Malaysian Navy were there to dance. Cadets and midshipmen were allowed 'shore leave' on Saturdays from after lunchtime to 10pm – 'pipe-down' time.

I gathered some courage and walked across the floor to the group of girls who were sitting and laughing. I approached the girl with golden blonde hair and a gorgeous smile.

'Hello, would you like to dance?'

'Yes, of course.'

'I am Suhail. I know it is difficult to say it first time. It is "Su" then "hail", but not "Su" on its own, you see! Don't worry, it gets easier with practice! What's your name?'

'I am Ann, Ann Pyne.'

Then the age-old question: 'Do you come here often?'

'Yes, most Saturdays. But some Saturdays I have to help my mum as she has friends to visit. She likes me to look after Dad, he is not very well, you see, and also the cat to stop it going all over the beds and chairs, or out on the street.'

We both laughed.

'Very nice to do all that, you must be very caring and considerate.'

We talked and danced. Anna's radiant sweet smile was enthralling. I don't think anyone else partnered her the whole of that evening. She seemed focused on me. I thought I monopolised her! I felt I hit it off with Anna – a strange feeling of being at ease with her. She seemed so sincere and beautiful, with that innocent smile. I took to her! She was very reserved, not 'common'. She seemed so genuine. I decided I had to meet her again.

It was getting close to 10pm, pipe-down time. The walk up the hill to the college, to my cabin at the westernmost end of the St Vincent Division, the topmost building on the hill, took about twenty-five minutes from the town centre.

'Will you be here next week? May I see you again next Saturday?'

Without hesitation Anna said, 'Yes.'

'I was wondering, as the dancing starts about eight o'clock, if I may invite you to have a meal with me? You must know nice places?'

'Oh, that will be nice. I will see you at the Butter Walk, a hundred yards up that way, at six then.'

'Fine, thank you, I would very much look forward to that.'

The following Saturday evening I arrived at the Butter Walk a few minutes before 6pm. It was a beautiful warm summer evening; across the River Dart, Kingswear was dazzling in the sun. Exactly at six, the bus from Townstal pulled up, stopped at the other side of the road, the passengers got off and the bus pulled away.

Anna saw me.

'Oh hello! How are you? Nice to see you again.' That 'Oh hello' remains deeply imbedded in my memory.

Anna was looking stunning, glorious, eye-catching, engaging, beautiful, with her curled-up golden-blonde hair shoulder length, and blue eyes. She was tall, slim, with perfect body features, dressed in a tight skirt to below the knee and a white blouse, buttoned near to the top, low-heeled shoes and wearing fashionable sunglasses – like a glamorous Hollywood star. I said to myself an emphatic, 'Yes!'

'Very nice of you to come down, nice to see you again. You are looking great. Where shall we go to eat?'

'Yes, there is a restaurant, called Amidships, just by the upper ferry. Shall we go there, give it a try, you might like it?'

'Yes, fine.'

Amidships was by the upper ferry. 'What would you like to eat and drink?'

'I think I would like half a lager shandy and fish and chips, please. This place does good fish and chips.'

'Yes, me too, fish and chips. I am sure the fish has just come up the river this afternoon!' We both laughed.

'I will go and order.'

Chatting and small talk followed – about my family back home, her family, her job as an artist and painter at Dartmouth Pottery. The meal ended. We headed back to the Guildhall for dancing the rest of the evening.

Our dating continued at a regular pace. Anna soon invited me to meet her family: her mum and dad; her brother, David, younger than her; and her sister, Lynda, the youngest. Just the three of them. Frequently I would get invited to join Anna's family for traditional Sunday lunch. Mrs Pyne was a very good cook so the meals were delicious.

That's how it all started, over sixty years ago on that memorable August afternoon in 1956. I would see her most Saturdays or Sundays which meant that my commitment to the college activities in my spare time was less than it should have been. I was falling in love. My lack of interest in college activities was of course noted by my divisional officer, Lt Nelson. I recall once towards the end of my training in Dartmouth, he said to me, 'Suhail, I know you help us on occasion but not a lot. You should spend more time in the college, to participate in college activities.' I noted that comment, but didn't do much about it. I was too much in love. Every moment of my spare time I wanted to spend with Anna, especially because I would soon be finishing my training and returning home to the Pakistan Navy. But my serious focus also remained on my training and studies so that I would pass out, doing reasonably well. This I did; I managed to pass out with three months ante-dated seniority, commissioned as an acting sub-lieutenant. My love affair with Anna didn't cause much setback to my training.

Our practical training meant running down the hill to Sandquay for marine workshops, launch and picket-boat handling, dinghy sailing, etc. We had a host of single-screw launches and twin-screw picket boats which were used for practice in boat-handling, and dismantling and reassembling boats' engines. The picket boats were also used to teach us ship-handling, in preparation for handling larger ships.

The Dartmouth Training Squadron comprised: HMS *Caron*, a destroyer; *Vigilant* and *Roebuck*, frigates; and the minesweepers, *Jewel* and *Acute*. They were to give us training at sea in navigation; gunnery; minesweeping; torpedo and antisubmarine (TAS); ship-handling; atomic, biological, chemical and damage control (ABCD); warfare; and safety training. Then there were the practical aspects of looking after a ship. Cadets would be put over the ship side, sitting on suspended planks, with life belts on, given pots of paint and brushes and ordered by the petty officer in charge to paint the ship's side. I remember painting the shipside of HMS *Vigilant* in a foreign harbour and singing, 'Cindy oh Cindy, don't let me down, write me your letter soon and I will be homeward bound...'! While I sang I would be thinking of Anna and how soon I could be back in Dartmouth to see her again.

Life on the *Vigilant* was great. Sea training took us to Den Helder in Holland, Vigo in Spain, Gibraltar and Malta, Lorient in France and Hamburg in Germany. In ports of call we got invited to admirals' houses for dinner dances. We met many pretty girls. Good thing I had some dancing lessons at the college. Ms Gladys of Kingswear had taught us foreign cadets and midshipmen basic ballroom dancing – waltz, foxtrot, tango, cha cha

cha – so we were able to impress the young ladies at parties in the naval bases!

On return to Dartmouth, my first objective was shore leave to see Anna. But we had midshipmen's duty watches. So unless I was able to find a substitute midshipman I could not go ashore. And after finding my substitute, the next big hurdle was to hang around the wardroom to get the attention of my divisional officer, Lt Grant RN, as the Officer of the Day (OOD). He was kind but fiercely mindful of duties. To get him to agree to my shore leave with a substitute arranged would be a daunting task. But I was very pleased when I was able to go ashore by the 6pm boat and return by the 10pm boat. Ashore I would take Anna to dinner, then go for a walk; if there was a dance at the Guildhall, we would go dancing. We would visit her home and see everyone. It was great fun. That's how my courting of Anna went while I was on the *Vigilant*. I treated those few hours ashore with Anna as my 'quality time'.

One thing I may note here in respect of racial prejudice or racial discrimination: for the entire time at Dartmouth, never did they manifest themselves. There might be an occasional feeling of 'strangeness' or 'foreignness', but that's all. Whether amongst the cadets and midshipmen, college staff, the drill instructors or from anyone else in downtown Dartmouth, I did not encounter or feel any form of race problem. It might be that local people were so used to seeing black and Asian people from overseas countries coming to the college that they were broadminded and welcoming. In the late 1950s, these problems were not as overt as in more recent times. I recall only once reading in *The Daily Telegraph*, in the cadets'/midshipmen's gunroom, that coloured immigration was becoming a political issue. At that time (1956), a Tory government was in power. Home Secretary Rab Butler was thinking of bringing in legislation to control coloured immigration from the Commonwealth – mainly from the West Indies and the Indian subcontinent. The British people wanted control of numbers. Legislation was planned. I recall his statement to the House of Commons as reported in *The Daily Telegraph* at the time, that immigration controls would be applied 'benignly'! We have come a long way both in terms of living in a generally tolerant British society, with legal sanctions in the background to combat racial discrimination in its various forms, while at the same time discussions on the subject have become more open and frank. That is not to say that racial prejudice has diminished, but its overt expression is illegal.

Dartmouth

Dartmouth has strong links with the Britannia Royal Naval College. The town has a rich history going back centuries. Every year in August at the time of the Royal Regatta the college proudly takes part in the mayor's parade through the town, to the delight and pride of the spectators. The college band participates in the march and plays at the bandstand in the Mayor's Park.

There is a lot to see in Dartmouth. The town is packed with historical buildings, shops, galleries, pubs and restaurants. The view from the college of the winding river, its boats, the steam train, the ferries, and the houses tumbling down the hills have engaged school children in drawing a busy little port, and attracted serious artists. Boats take visitors up the river to Warfleet and the interesting village of Dittisham.

To name a few of Dartmouth's attractions: the Boat Float and the Royal Avenue Gardens; the house on the corner of Fairfax Place built in the seventeenth century; the Royal Castle Hotel with its history going back to 1639, which featured in two of Agatha Christie's books, *The Regatta Mystery* and *Ordeal by Innocence*, as the 'Royal George Hotel'. The present owner of the hotel, Mr Nigel Way, is a charming man; I had great pleasure meeting him. Other buildings are York House at the corner of the Boat Float; the Station café, previously the British Rail terminal; the bandstand; the Royal Avenue Gardens in various seasonal flowers and colours; the historical seventeenth-century Butter Walk building on Duke Street (named after Prince William, Duke of Clarence who visited Dartmouth in 1828, now housing Dartmouth Museum); and the historical Foss Street which was a dam across from the river with water wheel and the creek reaching right up to Victoria Street. Foss Street today is full of shops with artists' displays, shops and cafés. Before it was converted to its present-day use as a betting shop, we used frequently to visit the corner café between Foss Street and Duke Street.

St Saviour's church, at the end of Anzac Street, stands above the centre of Dartmouth. The Anzac name recalls the Australians and New Zealanders who came to Dartmouth as survivors from Gallipoli in the First World War. Walking up from the church there is Higher Street with a lovely walk past the Seven Stars pub and the shops, arriving at the Cherub Inn, also called the Cherub Club by my friend Keith Whitmore. The Cherub Inn is a historical building, originally built as a warehouse around 1380; I was fortunate to visit this place with Keith on more than one occasion. Other places around town are Bayard's Cove, with its flowers in season, leading on to Bayard's Cove Fort, originally built during Henry VIII's defences of the English coasts; and Dartmouth Pottery where Anna had worked as a pottery painter along with her friends (I would teasingly call them the 'Ann mafia'!).

Anna used to take me for walks in and around Warfleet Creek and Dartmouth Castle, right down to Castle Cove, with steps to the sea – a treacherous spot when the sea was high.

Turning round you reach the relatively newly built Dart Marina and carry on to the restricted area of Sandquay, the college's pontoon, with boats alongside and workshops for introductory training on marine engineering. The walk along South Embankment, although crowded, is beautiful, with boats and ferries crossing the river, and people sitting at the edge of the embankment hanging their legs, fishing or crabbing.

The Dartmouth Regatta started in 1822. It was renamed the Port of Dartmouth Royal Regatta during Queen Victoria's time when, in August 1856, the Queen and Prince Albert visited Dartmouth in the *Royal Yacht*. The Regatta is the largest in Britain after Cowes, with hundreds of boats participating. I have regularly visited Dartmouth at Regatta time with our daughters and grandchildren. Meeting our relatives and friends was a regular feature – a meal or a drink at the Royal Castle, the funfair in the Royal Avenue Gardens, or a boat trip to see the activities on the river, with competing yachts sailing out for the Start Point Race, and whaler racing. Usually a Royal Navy ship would be present in the harbour at Regatta time, acting as a 'guard ship' – a frigate or a minesweeper usually open to the visitors. The highest point of excitement was the show put on by the Red Arrows of the Royal Air Force. On the Thursday and Saturday evenings fireworks marked the occasion.

Agatha Christie's holiday home, Greenway, is a must for visitors. It can be reached by road from the top or from the river from Greenway's own jetty on the River Dart. It must be one of the most beautiful places in the world with its large gardens, the views of the River Dart and the hills beyond. We have enjoyed listening to the history of the place, about Agatha Christie herself, her life and work; we have bought Agatha Christie's books; we have sat on one of the benches in the gardens enjoying the quietness and had high tea at the café.

*

Outside Dartmouth we have been to Blackpool Beach and Slapton Sands many times. The fish and chips shops at the beaches are famous for dishes with the daily catch. The village of Stoke Fleming is very pretty; we have stayed there at B&B guest houses and fixed caravan sites. Once we hired two fixed caravans next to one another for our two family holidays together – ours and Lisa's. It was a truly Devon holiday with grand outings, walks, never ending chit-chat.

*

After three years' training I was commissioned in July 1958 as an acting sub-lieutenant. Lord Mountbatten of Burma was the guest of honour at the passing-out parade of our batch of acting sub-lieutenants, our arms sporting single gold stripes, as we embarked on careers in the navy.

I had got through the passing-out examinations with credit. Congratulatory telegrams were flying around from back home – parents, uncles, relatives all happy with my news.

I invited Anna and her parents as my guests at the parade. I cannot forget the smile of pride on Anna's face that day. Her parents, too, were very happy for me, as were her friends in Dartmouth. But there was sadness also, as it meant I would soon be departing for home. It might be I would be leaving Anna behind for a while until she could join me in Pakistan.

For the occasion I had collected my brand new uniforms from Gieves in Dartmouth, the famous Savile Row uniform makers. My boots for the parade had to be polished until I could see my face clearly in the mirror on their toes. My patent shoes were all ready for the dinner-dance that evening.

On the morning of our passing-out parade, the drives going up both sides of the parade ground up to the 'bridge' were full of college guests – friends and families of newly commissioned sub-lieutenants and others, Anna's family amongst them. We were fallen into platoons. First was our batch, the newly commissioned officers, with a new gold ring on their arms, followed division by division by the rest of the college midshipmen with their white patches on their collars, then the cadets. The Royal Marines Band played familiar tunes for the march.

At the end of the parade the sub-lieutenants assembled inside on the quarterdeck for the farewell address by Lord Mountbatten. His speech was brief, no more than ten minutes, but full of advice about the future we would face, the challenges of life at sea and ashore. I remember one powerful piece of advice he gave: 'Keep in contact with your civilian friends, they will prove to be very useful and important.' Little did I know at the time what he meant. That piece of advice was to prove so useful in my later life, working with civilians to get things done!

I joined Anna and her family afterwards to walk back to their home just outside Dartmouth for a celebratory glass of sherry. Then Anna and I went out for lunch. The town was full of visitors, friends and families. Lots of 'Hi's', 'Hello's' and 'Greetings'! Great feelings of pride and warmth.

Anna was always fond of walking. She would say, 'Let's go this way or that.' Reluctantly I would agree as I was not that fond of walking. So on that beautiful summer day we walked!

'Well, Anna, I have got my commission, what next? What about our engagement?'

Before she could answer, I decided to tell her something about life in Pakistan that she would be launching into if she decided to marry me.

'Anna, I must tell you about the life in Pakistan you will be letting yourself into. It won't be easy. On a sub-lieutenant's pay life will be tough. I come from a reasonably well-to-do family, but not rich. I suppose you could take a job in Karachi, where the Pakistan naval base is, at the British High Commission. So between both our incomes we should be OK. Pakistan's lifestyle and culture will be different but nice. Having known you over the past three years, and seeing the way you related to my cadet and midshipmen friends from Commonwealth countries, I feel you would take easily to the people of Pakistan. The climate is hot, dry, the evenings are pleasant and you will be comfortable in the mild "Indian summer" winters. You will need to take light clothing, not your Harris Tweed suits or too many woollens. You will meet my people. My parents, as you know, have given their blessing to our proposed marriage. They are looking forward to meeting you. But I have still to get the navy's permission to marry you, as they have restrictions on marriages of Pakistani officers with foreign nationals. And if it does not work out and should you not be happy, London is only sixteen hours' flight away!'

Having heard all this, I could see Anna was undaunted, quietly determined, smiling.

'Thanks for telling me all this. Sounds exciting. I should be happy.'

'OK. I am glad I got it off my chest, I feel lighter!'

Back to the passing-out from Dartmouth – the razzmatazz! Prior to the parade each division in the college – Blake, Drake, Exmouth and St Vincent – had to decorate one of the classrooms surrounding the quarterdeck with a particular theme, where guests could sit, stand and relax during the evening of the passing-out ball. I was asked by Lt Nelson, my divisional officer, to do something for my division – the St Vincent Division. I chose the theme of an Arabian harem. With my mates we got the room ready – with mattresses and sheets, large pillows and cushions, colourful mats and curtains, and Arabic paraphernalia, ready for the evening's competition.

Later on, the chairman of the judges' panel said to me and my mates gathered in the harem, 'Suhail, I am delighted to tell you that judges declared your harem as the second best. For your prize you get a bottle of fine champagne.' It was heartening to come a close second!

The college ball was always a great traditional event sustained over many, many years. Anna was my personal guest. For the occasion Anna wore a beautiful dress, a rust-coloured dress with one shoulder bare, mildly provocative for those days, more so for my Muslim culture. With her shoulder-length blonde hair, simple jewellery and happy sweet smile, Anna was looking very attractive and radiant. We danced the evening away to the music of the college marines band playing popular old classic dance music, Sinatra's amongst others. Occasionally we sat in the St Vincent Division's 'harem'.

During my three years at the college Anna had not seen my cabin – right at the back at the top of the hill, near the fire escape at the west end of the building frequently used by me to 'escape' from the college after ten o'clock 'pipe-down' to go and see Anna. She wanted to see how I had lived all these years in a single cabin, sleeping, studying, laying my clothes and shoes tidy for regular inspection. Fortunately the cabins were cleaned and beds made up every day for us by college stewards/stewardesses. For Anna's visit the cabin was nice and tidy, so I felt relaxed. Anna was impressed. While in the cabin of course we kissed each other but that's as far as it went. She wouldn't have liked us to go further; and also in case one of my mates might put his head round the door!

The evening ended very late; we were tired and happy. I was glad that our divisional effort for the 'harem' got some recognition from my divisional officer, Lt Nelson, especially because he thought I was spending all my spare time dating Anna and not participating in college activities except the compulsory athletics, sports, cross-country running, swimming and dinghy sailing.

An encounter with Mrs Stork!

One evening while on a date with Anna I was coming back to the college from her home. It was late. I was worried that the house senior midshipman would catch me out not being in my cabin or in bed by ten o'clock during his inspection. I would then end up in front of the commander getting some punishment like clearing up the leaves on the roof of the college canteen! I was rushing back, half running. I was perhaps lucky. That evening the headmaster's wife, Mrs Stork, was driving back to the college, probably from some dinner with friends. She saw me walking fast. She stopped and saw I was breathless. She asked, 'Are you alright? Do you want a lift? You're late returning, aren't you?'

'Yes please.' I got into the car.

I could not say much. But Mrs Stork must have guessed that I was dating a girl. I did not know that she would be telling the college's commanding officer, Capt. Munn. Anyway, rumour spread among the higher echelons of the college.

It was about the time our summer term was coming to an end. Lt Cdr (newly promoted) John Nelson was still my divisional officer. He called me into his office out of the blue. I thought, *Goodness what's up? What have I done?* A concerned Mrs Stork must have told her husband, Mr Stork, the college headmaster, and word had reached the captain. The captain must have told the college commander and he instructed Lt Cdr Nelson to see me about my affair!

In his office, I sat down, nervous, as Nelson said to me, 'Suhail, we have come to know that you are seriously seeing a young lady from Dartmouth. I wanted to have a chat. Look, Suhail, you are a very young officer [I was twenty] just starting on a career with a great future. Do you think it's a good idea to get involved with a girl at this stage of your naval career?'

'Sir, I am getting engaged, she would come out to Pakistan afterwards. My parents have agreed and given their blessing.'

'Look, Suhail, let me tell you my story! I used to have a beautiful red-haired girlfriend when I was a young sub like you. I was deeply in love. But in the interest of a career in the Royal Navy, with a life ahead of me, I was persuaded I could not go on, so with a lot of upset and heavy hearts, we parted. I let her go. It was painful for both of us but I had to do it.'

Then Nelson came to the important bit.

'I understand the girl is from Dartmouth. Are you sure she would fit into your lifestyle as a naval officer?'

I got a bit annoyed.

'Are you referring to her class? Sir, let me tell you, she comes from a very respectable family of Dartmouth. Her uncle has been my instructor at the college. Another uncle has been a mayor of Dartmouth. Anna's parents, her brother and sister, I have met them all, they are nice people. That she is from the working class is irrelevant. Above all, I am happy with her, I love her, she loves me, that's all that matters.'

Nelson gave in. 'OK, Suhail. If you think she would be happy as a "navy wife", that's fine. I wish you the best of luck.'

'Thank you, sir.'

*

I was to encounter 'class' in my own family. Some years later when I was back home after leaving the navy, I was visiting my parents' house in Sylhet.

I picked up that Raja, my younger brother, had visited my in-law-to-be's' house in Dartmouth and seen my father-in-law in working overalls. When Raja was back home from London he gave out that I was getting married into the working class. He didn't mention that Anna's uncle was a mayor of Dartmouth and another uncle was my instructor at the naval college as a chief petty officer. Nor in later years Raja felt able to acknowledge his own or his wife's side of relationships or shortcomings! But happily he was to become very fond of Anna – his 'Bhabi' being his elder brother's wife. When I was at Lever Brothers in Chittagong, Raja stayed with us while working as an insurance agent at a Pakistani life insurance company.

Ending the speculation!

What next? I was about to go back home to the Pakistan Navy. After finishing at the college, I stayed for a few days with Anna's family. One day we went for a day out to Torquay by bus from Kingswear. We sat upstairs at the front, enjoying beautiful views on a sunny day of Torbay and the English Riviera.

Quite suddenly I asked, 'Anna, will you marry me?'

Without hesitation she said, 'Yes.' We kissed.

Well, that was done! We spent the day in Torquay strolling along the seafront, talking but also in deep thought. At the other end of the harbour front, we found a jewellery shop. We went in and Anna examined the rings on display.

'Look, come here. I think I have found one.'

It had a turquoise-colour stone, aquamarine, and was within my budget. I bought it. I put the ring on her finger. We were engaged! We returned to Dartmouth. We saw her Mum in the sitting room, knitting. Anna and I stood in front of her mother, Mrs Pyne, our elbows locked into each other, with the happiest of smiles, and I said, 'Mum, we have got engaged. I want your permission to marry Ann.'

Anna looked at her Mum with a beautiful smile and nodding as if to say, 'Well, there you are then!'

Her Mum said, 'Well, dears, we knew it was coming. Of course you have our permission and we hope very much that you will be happy.' Those touching words brought immense happiness to me; I was quite emotional.

Ours was a very small engagement party with close friends (including the 'Ann mafia' – Ann King, Anne Chase, Anne Cud, Ann Pyne (i.e. my 'Anna'), June, Julie, and their partners, and a few of my close friends from the college – from other navies. We celebrated, drank champagne and wine, pictures were taken, good wishes given.

Soon, it was time for me to go to London to get ready to return to the Pakistan Navy.

We were talking about things when suddenly Anna said, 'I am coming with you to London to see you off.'

'That will be great. But how will you do that? What about your work? Would you get time off?'

'That should be no problem, it would be arranged.'

'OK then, but you will have to share a large room with me. It will be in the Earl's Court area because that's all we are used to renting during holiday breaks from the college. It will have cooking facilities, a shared bathroom – not expensive.'

'It's alright. I don't mind sharing a room with you, it won't bother me. I know how to be careful!'

I knew I would get that reply from Anna. After our engagement she told me more than once in unspoken words, 'I will remain a virgin until I am married and am able to offer my virginity as my wedding gift to you.' Anna gave me that precious gift after our marriage in Karachi; I was so proud to have married someone of such purity.

In London, we rented a large room with a double bed. We ate out anyway – breakfast, lunch and dinner at nearby cafés. We enjoyed London – sightseeing, eating and dining. We both loved dancing. Our favourite place during our earlier trips to London was the Astoria ballroom, at the junction of Tottenham Court Road and Oxford Street. The band played the type of dance music we liked: waltz, foxtrot, Latin American music – rhumba, samba, cha cha cha. We were not experts but we enjoyed dancing very much.

Anna told me, 'After you have gone, I'll stay a few days in London with Julie and Colin.'

The day before I was going to leave for Pakistan, I telephoned one of my very close friends, Mufti Khosru, a childhood friend from my hometown, Sylhet. My father and Mufti's father were very close friends too. There was a close family affinity between us. Khosru had come to England to work about the same time that I entered Dartmouth. He was a dependable friend. He lived in Newmarket, Suffolk, with his English wife, Rosemary, and their children.

I called him. 'Khosru Bhai, I am going back to Pakistan. Anna is with me. She is not very familiar with London. She wants to spend a few days with her friends in New Cross Gate. I want you to accompany her to her friends' house after I have left. I should be very grateful if you could come down in the morning and meet us about ten o'clock?'

[Note: The word 'Bhai' means 'brother', it is a custom to address friends cordially like this out of fondness and respect.]

Khosru Bhai readily agreed: 'Of course I will come down to take Anna to her friends' house after you have left.' I gave him the address of the place in Earl's Court.

He came down the next morning.

I was going home by BOAC – British Overseas Airways Corporation. Those days BOAC's offices were located in Buckingham Palace Road, Victoria. The building, with its driveway, is still there, refurbished but unchanged. We arrived at the terminal building on time. We were both very sad. There was very little to say to Anna except small talk. I kept saying to her, 'See you in Pakistan soon.' We couldn't say much more in front of Khosru Bhai – 'not the done thing'! I explained to him how they would travel to New Cross Gate: by train from Victoria to New Cross Gate, then to Julie's house which was just over the railway bridge – 23 Trout Beck Road. It was time to board the coach for Heathrow. Anna and I were crying in each other's arms, in a goodbye embrace. We were far away from this world, when the driver tapped my shoulder. I saw everyone in the bus staring and smiling at us. We released each other. I said, 'Goodbye, Anna, I love you, see you soon in Pakistan.' Anna said, 'Goodbye, Suhail, I love you too, and see you soon. Be careful.'

I got onto the coach. Anna, with tears flowing down her face, was still smiling as she and Khosru waved goodbye. The coach started pulling away towards Ebury Bridge Road. I saw them walking away, waving, until they drifted into the crowd.

I was departing comforted and sustained by the thought, *It is only for a time!* Then she would join me in Pakistan. A history and narrative of our life together, with all its ups and downs, for the next fifty-four years, still remains to be told!

Anna had decided to save up for her fare to join me as soon as she could. I knew with a sub-lieutenant's pay I was not going to be able to do much by way of preparation to receive her. But both of us knew that we would both work to set up our home in Karachi and our life together.

Getting to know British families

While at Dartmouth, the college used to make arrangements through the Royal Overseas League (ROSL) and the Royal Victoria League, for cadets and midshipmen to stay with British families in England, Scotland and Wales for a week or so during Easter (three weeks), summer (six weeks) and Christmas (three weeks) breaks. I was fortunate to stay with several British families: Mr and Mrs Edwards (a retired major of the British Army) in Horsham, Sussex; Mr and Mrs M. L. Lewis, also in Horsham – Mr Lewis was a director at the multinational company Hawker Siddeley; a professor from Exeter University and his family (their names escape me); Dr and Mrs Bell in East Lothian, Scotland – Dr Bell was a brain surgeon at an Edinburgh hospital. I also stayed with Mr and Mrs Grefka, a Polish family in Lincoln. The college would send us to stay for a few days at a time with these families 'to learn the British way of life'. We would be paired up, usually two cadets/midshipmen at a time. For instance I was once paired with Anwar Qureshi to stay with Mr and Mrs Lewis in Horsham. The Lewises had two little lovely children: Philippa, about nine, and Stephen, about six. That was in the 1956 Easter break. Today Philippa would be seventy-two, her little brother about sixty-nine. How time has flown!

We got to know the families well. We would help with some of the daily chores – laying tables, washing and drying up dishes, putting them away, and so on. Sometimes, there would also be one or two female student guests staying with these families. We would sit and watch TV with the family, play scrabble, chess or monopoly with the children. Occasionally we would even date the girls to go to London or nearby towns. I remember going to London for the day with Maria (Austrian), Lilly (Dutch) and Françoise (Belgian). In London I enjoyed dancing at the Astoria ballroom at Tottenham Court Road. Most host families would not accept any money from us for our keep but one or two did.

While at the Cadet Training School in PNS *Himalaya*, Karachi, cadets were encouraged to have pen friends in the UK, so that we could get to know people and through correspondence try to polish up our written and colloquial English. I had a pen friend, Margaret Hepburn, aged about sixteen. She lived with her parents in Skegness, a seaside holiday resort in Lincolnshire. When I was on my first holiday, Easter 1956, and long before I met Anna, I chose to go to stay with Mr and Mrs Grefka in Lincoln – solely because Margaret lived in Skegness nearby. I had written to Margaret telling her that I wanted to meet her when I arrived in England, to put faces to our letters. I arrived by train in Skegness, walked from the station, asking people along the way where was Melrose Avenue. Eventually I turned up at Margaret's front door. I was to have my first shock in trying to socialise in England. No one came to open the door, although I felt sure there were people inside!

The families we stayed with were well educated, broad-minded, well-travelled and knowledgeable in world affairs. So engaging in discussions in British homes, sitting by the fireside with the hosts, was also part of our training and the broadening of our outlook. I became quite close to Mr and Mrs Lewis in Horsham and Dr and Mrs Bell in East Lothian, where I stayed on more than one occasion during breaks from Dartmouth. They became my dear friends for many years to come, especially Michael and Diana Lewis and their two children. I was going to visit East Lothian to see my dear friend Mrs Isobel Bell after my return to England but before I could do that her son Bill wrote and gave me the sad news that his mother had had an accident – a fall – and died. I was fortunate that some years before, while I was at the CRE, I visited Scotland once and was able to see Isobel at her East Lothian home; they had downsized since I saw them last in their family home in Scotland. She was fit and well. It was a beautiful day in East Lothian. I remember we went out to a lovely scenic spot by a little river and a bridge and had lunch at a nice restaurant. We chatted. Her two children had got married following distinguished careers. Mrs Bell listened with interest to my account of my life with Anna. I would like to find out about Mr and Mrs Lewis and their children, Philippa and Stephen; they must be traceable in Gloucestershire. I have asked Lisa, my daughter in the media to help me locate them, as she is familiar with the Cotswolds.

Chapter Three

My dismissal from the Pakistan Navy

Upon arrival back in Pakistan I reported to PNS *Dilawar* to complete formalities, then went straight to my home in Sylhet on two months' leave. After four years away (October 1954 – July 1958) I saw my family again. It was an extremely happy and joyful occasion. I visited everyone and chatted to them about my training in Dartmouth. My maternal grandfather and my uncles were keen to hear about my training in England and asked a lot of questions, which I answered as best I could. I had to be very careful not to divulge that I was already engaged to Anna. Any questions from relatives had to be circumvented somehow into generalities. I thought I did a good job of keeping my secret! It was only for a time. My cousins of marriageable age were circling round me but of course they didn't know that I was already engaged. My mother's eldest sister, my eldest maternal aunt, Boromoi, was keen that I should marry her daughter, a first cousin of mine, Dolly, a very pretty girl of amiable nature and fine manners. So when my mother told her that I was 'no longer on the market', my aunty wrote to me a lengthy letter asking, much as the navy had done, 'Would that kind of marriage be OK?' I had already returned to my ship after my leave. I read the long letter, trying to persuade me but holding back from disclosing that she was interested in me for her daughter Dolly. I was a 'suitable boy'! I could not find words to write to her. It was a tricky situation, and I didn't want to hurt or upset her. I was very fond of her, my Boromoi.

Similarly, upon arrival in Dhaka to start my leave, my favourite (paternal) aunty, Borofufu, and her husband, my most affectionate uncle,

Mr M. M. Samad, a distinguished citizen and politician, welcomed me at the airport and took me to their lovely house. After I had been shown my room and settled in, I walked into their bedroom for a chat. I was taken by surprise when my uncle turned round to ask my aunty, 'Well, Rana [that's me] is back, he has got his commission as a naval officer, now we must look for a bride for him!' Needless to add, there were two cousins of mine in his own family, both 'eligible'! I don't remember what my aunty said in reply. Clearly I was again seen as a 'suitable boy'!

My father was acutely observant. He had of course noted during my holiday in Sylhet, whenever I was in, that one or two eligible bride cousins would be circling round on our front lawn, visiting our house uninvited, pretending to want to see my sisters – my elder sister, Ruby, Mina or Nargis. One day he was having his wash, preparing for his prayers on the veranda. He saw me passing and called out, 'Rana, don't forget you have given your word to someone there!' I quietly acknowledged what he said in agreement and turned away.

*

Many years after that, when Anna was unwell during 2014 and we were driving back from Guy's Hospital, London, after one of her chemotherapy sessions, I told her of my father's reminder. Quite seriously she turned to me and said, 'You never told me that!' I felt she was quietly happy to learn of it. I didn't know why I hadn't told her my father's comment. There was nothing I kept from her. We had a relationship of total trust. I suppose I just felt that the time had come to share what my father had said.

*

At the end of my leave I joined my first ship, PNS *Khaibar*, a battle class destroyer, formerly HMS *Cadiz* of the Royal Navy, to complete my sea training and obtain my certificates of competence, bridge watch-keeping and ocean navigation. My commanding officer, Commander Awan, was a distinguished commander of the Pakistan Navy, a natural leader – tall, handsome, quite big and brawny, a professional naval officer. He was from the Punjab, a very decent, likeable man. I joined his happy ship. His No. 1, Lt Cdr Rifat Shaikh, was a pleasant, helpful person.

Officers on the ship were particular in their etiquette and behaviour in the wardroom, although some officers were quick to pick on me and other sub-lieutenants because we were freshly commissioned. I recall one day, Lt Rashid Taj (a relatively senior lieutenant) pointing out to me: 'Look here, subby, you are supposed to be seen but not heard, do you understand?' But it was all in good fun and naval tradition.

There was no cabin available for the four newly arrived ex-Dartmouth acting sub-lieutenants. So improvisation was to follow. Under the foc'sl, just aft of the storage of the anchor cables, there was space. So berths with drawers underneath were fitted, meshed against the two sides. We were issued with bedding; in the morning we had to roll up our beds and stow them away – a good thing we had been trained to sling up and stow away hammocks on the frigate *Vigilant* and the minesweeper *Jewel*. This was to be our living space on the destroyer. But we could enjoy the officers' washing facilities and the use of the wardroom during the day and well into the evening. I had a framed picture of Anna which she had had taken to give to me when I was leaving Dartmouth. It was a side view of her, looking beautiful. Other subs knew of my 'affair' and respected my feelings. I don't know what has happened to that picture – gone with the numerous moves during our lives together with all my other navy belongings, uniform etc. in that big long trunk!

Lt Taj had an Italian wife, a lovely lady called Rosanna. They became good friends to us. Taj too came over to England after leaving the Pakistan Navy as a full captain. We kept in touch for some time. He helped me a lot in my early days in the Pakistan Navy. Taj too was a Punjabi, a nice, brotherly friend.

*

A year after leaving England, in 1959, Anna was to follow me out to Pakistan. I was nervous about her arrival. I was only a young sub-lieutenant, with that rank's pay. I had done no preparation. I was already serving on ships and had made no accommodation arrangements. As she was about to leave England on a BOAC flight, I was still hesitating about whether I should tell her not to come to Pakistan yet. There was no one in Karachi to turn to for advice. I even went to McLeod Road central post and telegraph office to send a telegram asking her to delay her departure. At the veranda of the crowded post office, I said to myself, *No, that would be letting Anna down, she would be upset.* So I turned round and returned to my ship. Providentially, I felt I did the right thing. I never told Anna about this hesitation!

Anna arrived at Karachi late one evening in November 1959. From the viewers' gallery at the airport I watched the plane's exit door to see when she emerged. Almost all the passengers had come out of the plane, but there was no sign of Anna. Eventually, Anna, the country girl from Devon, emerged, one of the last few passengers out of the plane; she must have been upset. Friends have said she was very brave to come to Pakistan, a strange, foreign place on her own; she was only twenty-one. I received her at the airport, collected her baggage and took her in a taxi to a Karachi city centre hotel where I had booked a room for her. She was quiet, upset at leaving her family and friends, and tired after a long flight. Next morning I took her to the flat of Lt David Rafi Uddin and his English wife, Sheila, who lived in the Pakistan Employees Co-operative Housing Society (PECHS). Rafi Uddin and Sheila warmly invited Anna to stay with them for a few days as she settled into her new environment.

We planned to get married. We were both only just twenty-one. In a strange country, Anna knew only me – a sub-lieutenant, not of substantial means. It was to be a tough start to our life together. After staying the first few days with Lt David Rafi Uddin and his wife, Anna stayed for a while with Lt Azhar Ali Shaikh, my class fellow in the navy, and his wife, Laura, an Italian lady. Their help in Anna's very early days was much appreciated. They were kind, hospitable and supportive. We always valued that friendship dating from the early days after Anna's arrival.

But staying with Azhar and Laura was not really comfortable or appropriate; it must have been an inconvenience to them as well. So, after a search, we found a suitable flat. We rented a one-bedroom flat in Block 4, Nazimabad, a residential area of Karachi. My parents had given their blessing to our marriage. We were ready to get married and I was going to do my best to get the navy's permission to marry a 'foreign wife'.

In 1958 General Ayub Khan took over the country through a military coup. He and his generals declared martial law in Pakistan. The constitution was abrogated. I was informed that the 'Government of Pakistan is averse to marriages with foreign nationals' and warned that if I went ahead I would be liable to dismissal from the service. This new rule under martial law directly affected me and another colleague, Lt Ali Khan, who wanted to marry a German. The rule was brought in during martial law, an arbitrary action by the Punjab-dominated fundamentalists in the Pakistan military. In their view, too many officers were going abroad for training to the UK, USA, Germany etc., some marrying abroad, and, in the authorities' view, such marriages did not work out. This new rule had no parliamentary or constitutional basis. In fact the Martial Law Government had abrogated the constitution. It was left unsaid that they regarded such marriages as against the interest of girls from Pakistan!

I tried very hard to get the Government's permission. My commanding officer, Commander Awan, involved his friend, one of the best, UK-trained high court barristers in Pakistan, to try to get me permission, but it was not forthcoming. I remember well that meeting between Commander Awan and his lawyer friend and myself in the wardroom of PNS *Khaibar*. In his submission to the Government, amongst other things, the lawyer friend had articulated a powerful appeal on my behalf. It said, '*Denying permission to this young officer will leave him disgruntled for the rest of his life.*' How providential those words turned out to be! My father also wrote to the navy chief, Vice-Admiral A. R. Khan, but sadly to no avail. My father was told that in the Government's experience such marriages with foreign nationals did not work out. But the hypocrisy was that many West Pakistanis in the three services, and in Pakistan foreign and civil services, were already married to 'foreign wives'! And it was not true that all Pakistani marriages were successful or 'worked out'! As mentioned, one of my classmates from Dartmouth, Azhar Ali Shaikh, had an Italian wife. She was not even from a Commonwealth country but, being a clever Punjabi, he pulled strings and preserved the marriage. Ali Khan and I just got caught up in the 1958 Martial Law Government's new arbitrary and hastily concocted unconstitutional 'rule', undermining the UN Convention on Human Rights, to which Pakistan was a signatory.

At a later date, when he was commanding a minesweeper and his ship was visiting Chittagong, Lt Cdr Firdaus, who knew me from his time when he was the navigation officer on the PNS *Khaibar*, told me that 'the decision to dismiss me and Ali Khan was taken by officials at a much lower level down the line'. I suspect Ali and I were the victims of the influence of some Muslim fundamentalists. Later, this lower-level decision-making was to become apparent when, upon reaching the highest echelons of the Martial Law Government – the President and Governor no less – both Ali and I were invited to return to the navy if we wished.

As far as I was concerned, I had got my parents' blessing, I was engaged to Anna, she was already in Pakistan to get married to me, and my conscience and heart could not allow me to ask Anna to go back to England because the navy was not giving me permission to marry her. I was clear that I had to sacrifice my career in the navy for my marriage. I realised that in life one has sometimes to value material things less than moral or ethical issues. By the Grace of God, things worked out for me. Anna and I had a contented and happy life together spanning fifty-eight years: three years of courting and fifty-five years married – quite a record in this day and age!

On one occasion, recently commissioned sub-lieutenants – about ten or twelve of us – were invited by the naval secretary to the C-in-C, Cdr U. A. Sayid, to afternoon tea at the Officers' Club in Elphinstone Street, Karachi. It was a beautiful autumn evening. We sat in a circle in chairs outside in the garden, chatting about our time in the UK and the careers we looked forward to in the Pakistan Navy. Quite out of context, and suddenly, Commander Sayid turned to me: 'Suhail, you go and see the C-in-C privately at Admiral House.' Naval Intelligence must have told the NHQ that Anna was already in Pakistan, and that we planned to get married soon. For some reason, it didn't dawn on me that I should have acted on the naval secretary's suggestion and gone to see the C-in-C in his residence immediately that evening. With hindsight I felt that had I gone to see the C-in-C, most probably the permission to marry Anna would have been given. I put it down to my inexperience at the time of how things worked. But as events unfolded in Pakistan I believe it was providential. Pakistan was soon to break up. Luckily I was out of the navy, otherwise the Punjabi-controlled military might have 'bumped me off' as they did many Bengali personnel in posts in West Pakistan. What God does, He does it for the best. Things worked out for the better.

Years later in England when working for Lewisham Council in London, my council committee chairman, Cllr Ron Stockbridge, and his deputy Cllr Dave Harker, who knew a bit about the break-up of Pakistan, said to me, 'Suhail, if you were still in the navy you would be a dead admiral by now!'

After obtaining my naval certificates I was transferred to one of the recently acquired wooden-hulled minesweepers, PNS *Mubarak*, received under military aid from the Eisenhower administration in the USA. As a member of the Southeast Asia Treaty Organization (SEATO) and the Central Treaty Organisation (CENTO), Pakistan received a large amount of military aid. The *Mubarak*, which I joined as navigation officer, was the flagship of the minesweeping squadron, under the command of Cdr I. H. Malik. The other three ships in the minesweeping squadron were the *Mujahid*, *Muhafiz* and *Munsif*.

A word about the Punjab and the Punjabis. At the time of partition in 1947, the Punjab province of the British Raj was inhabited mostly by Punjabi Muslims in the western part of the province, and predominantly by Sikhs in the eastern part. The Punjabis had a strong tradition of military service. Upon partition, following the 'drawing of the line' by Sir Cyril Radcliffe, West Punjab went to Pakistan while East Punjab went to India. When I was at the Joint Services Pre-Cadet Training School (JSPCTS), Quetta, there was a very strong presence of Punjabi pre-cadets in each of the four houses. They were strong, fit and athletic, and had a domineering attitude towards the Pathan, Baluchi, Sindhi and Bengali pre-cadets. On one occasion we were on a camping weekend. A Punjabi, Khaledul Huq Mia, turned to me and quite angrily said, 'Suhail, it's good you are transferring to the navy!' Whether out of jealousy or spite, I didn't know.

Apart from myself – a recently promoted lieutenant – there was another officer on the *Mubarak*, Lt Mirza (a Punjabi), with a foreign (English) wife. I could feel that Mirza was not kindly disposed towards me, perhaps because he was not Dartmouth trained. But my life on the *Mubarak* was satisfying. The ratings were pleasant, and it was a reasonably happy ship under Cdr Malik.

I had arranged for Anna to stay temporarily with Azhar Ali Shaikh and his Italian wife, Laura. They created a makeshift bedroom for Anna on their wide veranda. I rented some furniture and Anna was happy to be put up for a time. When in harbour, the rule was that unmarried officers like me were required to live on board, whilst married officers could live ashore. So I would go ashore to see Anna and do things together in town from our base at Shaikh's flat. Some evenings I would leave Anna quite late, then get a bus to the dockyard to sleep on board before the married officers, Cdr Dr Malik and Lt Mirza, came on board in the morning.

My commanding officer, Cdr Malik, was transferred, and was replaced by a Lt Cdr Nasir, an officer from other ranks, also a Punjabi. I was soon to discover that I was not going to get on with him! He was never close enough or interested in me. In a minesweeper life is intimate, even between ratings and officers. But Nasir never tried to get to know his ship's company. Having come up the ranks, he probably felt that he had to make an extra effort to keep his distance.

Lt Mirza was clearly of 'officer class' but he was full of Punjabi pomposity! I knew I had to show him respect as a senior lieutenant. Whenever our ship was in harbour, Nasir and Mirza would live ashore with their families while I was expected to live on board.

Once I had a brush with Lt Mirza, which revealed how 'un-officer-like' he could be. I was present at a defaulters' parade, representing one of my ratings. The rating was called, I stepped up and his charge (a minor one) was read out. After the rating had said something, it was my turn to say something in his defence. I thought Mirza was not listening. So I was a little insistent. Quite out of the blue in full temper he shouted, 'Look, Officer, if you carry on like this, I will put you under arrest!' I looked at him fiercely. It was hugely embarrassing to be insulted in front of so many ratings, most of whom were Punjabis. I left the defaulters' parade, changed into civvies and left the ship. Out of the dockyard, I went on a scooter rickshaw and to the defence officers' housing society, found Cdr Malik's house and narrated to him what had happened. He was most understanding and told me he would see Mirza the following morning. I duly returned to the ship. The following day the captain arrived. He summoned Mirza into his cabin. The door was shut for a while, and I could sense that things were not going right for Mirza.

But not long afterwards occurred the transfer of Cdr Malik and the arrival of Lt Cdr Nasir. I would frequently see Nasir and Mirza chatting chummily, in Punjabi. They were oblivious to the fact that, as a Bengali, I might not be able to follow their discussion.

Our marriage in extreme secrecy

Anna and I felt that in the Islamic culture of Pakistan, it was wise to get married rather than invite the criticism of 'living in sin'. I was not sleeping at the Shaikhs' but I departed for my ship late in the evenings. Azhar Ali told me that it was getting noticed by the landlord and his family and staff that I was leaving their flat late at night, thus generating gossip. He said it would be best if I started looking for alternative accommodation. I agreed. Azhar and Laura had been very helpful but it was time we found somewhere else.

Anna and I started searching for a flat, passing word to friends and acquaintances that we were doing so. We did the searching on days when both of us were available, normally at weekends when my ship would be in the harbour and Anna would be off work. Not long after, we found a flat in the rear part of the first floor of a building, in Nazimabad, Karachi. The rent was affordable. I being in the navy and Anna working at the British High Commission helped us to get over the initial formalities quickly. I hired some basic furniture for the flat: a double bed, dressing table, stools, bedside tables, a dining table and four chairs, some other chairs, a coffee table, stuff for the bathroom. We bought some kitchen utensils and a gas cooker (there was ample supply of gas from the nearby gas field). So our kitchen was fitted out. I got all the stuff delivered on a Saturday afternoon. So we were all set up to start a new life.

But we had still to find a cook/servant. Word began to circulate amongst unemployed people in the neighbourhood. Soon we were extremely fortunate to find a young Pathan of about eighteen or nineteen, called Bostan Khan. He wore a loose-fitting *shelwar*, a long shirt (*punjabi*), a round woollen Pathan cap and a heavy-soled pair of *kabuli* sandals. Interviewing him was a few minutes' job for Anna and me. His English was very basic but Anna felt she could manage the communication. We felt happy to hire him; his wages were reasonable. He would eat with us and sleep on the floor of the veranda outside the kitchen, a very amenable arrangement all round. He would take Anna her lunch in a 'tiffin carrier' to the High Commission by bus.

Nazimabad was a distant northern development of Karachi, still relatively uninhabited, where the infrastructure of roads, water supply, shops and market was slowly being developed. Our flat was in the building of a girlfriend, Ms Shahnaz, of Mr Ghulam Ali Talpur, a former minister of Sindh, and a member of the landed gentry in the Sindh Province of West Pakistan. Talpur and Shahnaz took us out with them to show us his underground club, a most mysterious place, and to dance at a hotel in a posh area of Karachi.

The wedding ceremony was extremely simple and sombre, humble in every way. We invited only six or seven very close friends, including some from my training batch at Dartmouth. An Imam (a Muslim priest) witnessed the marriage ceremony after Anna had willingly converted to Islam. Everyone knew that 'confidentiality' had to be safeguarded. I understood that naval friends could be fearful of attending an 'unapproved marriage' lest the naval authorities found out.

Anna and I sat on a floor mat on a red mosaic floor to go through the rituals with the Imam. Anna wore a simple pink silk sari for the occasion. The wife of one of my Pakistan Air Force friends, Flt Lt Raquib, made her up. Anna looked most beautiful, happy and radiant. I had bought a simple gold wedding ring to go with the engagement ring we had bought together in Torquay in the summer of 1958.

Our wedding ceremony was soon over. Friends wished us well and departed. Anna and I went to celebrate; we ate a meal at a very quiet Chinese restaurant in Karachi, and then saw a film – I think it was *Peyton Place* or *Love is a Many-Splendored Thing*. No honeymoon followed! Anna continued with her job at the British High Commission, and I went back to my minesweeper, taking it upon myself to sleep ashore whenever in harbour, even though it was officially not allowed for 'single officers' to do so. No doubt I generated a lot of gossip and resentment from the Muslim fundamentalists of the Pakistan Navy and government officials. The secrecy in which our marriage ceremony took place didn't last long. Naval Intelligence found out that I was married. Both Lt Cdr Nasir and his No. 1, Lt Farook, began pressing me hard to officially declare that I was married.

I couldn't take this pressure for too long. I told Anna that I was going to let the navy know officially that we were married. One afternoon when the ship was in harbour, while I was officer-of-the-day, I called the leading telegraphist to the ship's communications room, and asked him to type a letter from me to the C-in-C on his typewriter as I dictated it. My message covered less than a third of a page. The gist was: I was married because the girl I loved, and was engaged to, was already in Pakistan. I could not ask her to go back because the navy wouldn't give me permission to marry her; that would not be me, I could not do it. My parents had given their blessing. I was therefore informing the C-in-C, through my commanding officer, that I was already married to Elizabeth Ann Pyne and was submitting myself to his 'mercy' and begged for permission to remain in the navy. I handed that letter to my CO the following morning and hoped for the best. As soon as he got my letter, Lt Cdr Nasir could not wait to run out of the ship in extreme glee, heading for the naval headquarters to give them the news that he had secured my 'confession'.

On 14 February 1961 (Valentine's Day – not a day recognised by the Government of Pakistan or by the naval headquarters) I was at sea, on PNS *Mubarak* with the rest of the minesweeping flotilla engaged in a minesweeping exercise. I was on the bridge on my own, as officer-of-the-watch. The leading telegraphist, who had typed my letter to the C-in-C mentioned above, came up to the bridge and said with tearful eyes, 'Sir, I am very sorry to give you this signal.' He looked upset and very sad. I took it from him and read it. The signal read:

MESSAGE FORM

Priority: UC
From: NHQ
To: PNS Mubarak Himalaya
Info: Dilawar COMPAK Comkar Navy Pay
1) **Government have decided that PNo 573 Lt A. A. M. Ali Khan and PNo 666 Lt S. I. Aziz be dismissed from the PN with immediate effect for disobeying government orders concerning marriage with foreign nationals.**
2) **Both officers appointed Dilawar additional forthwith and dismissed from the PN with immediate effect.**
= 141143
Cc N PC TSR1256 Ha 14/2/61

Minutes after, the commanding officer came up onto the bridge. He called up the duty signalman and dictated a message to the COMPAK (commodore in charge of the Pakistan Navy flotilla) thus: 'I have a passenger on board. Shall I return to harbour to disembark him?' The COMPAK, a Royal Navy commodore, A. P. W. Northey RN, on loan from the Royal Navy, signalled back, 'Carry on with your exercises, return to harbour on completion.'

My blood ran cold. I left the bridge, completely traumatised, went down to my cabin, lay on my bunk and wept bitterly. I prayed and sought God's help for justice. All sorts of things were flashing through my head: a foreign wife in a foreign land, myself thrown out on the street, out of a job, no money – what was I going to do? I stayed in my cabin, ate no food and wept. Neither Nasir nor Mirza, the Punjabi with a foreign wife, two heartless human beings, came to speak a word to me. I felt very lonely, helpless, at sea, with no one to talk to. I couldn't think. Confused, I sought Allah's help.

Upon arrival back in Karachi harbour, I walked off PNS *Mubarak*, and out of the Pakistan Navy. No proper goodbyes to the small ship's crew. I was too upset.

When I got back to our flat in Nazimabad, Anna was yet to arrive back from work at the British High Commission. I lay on the bed wondering how to put it to her that I was out of the navy because of my marriage to her. Soon it was time for Anna's arrival. I went out onto the narrow veranda of the flat, saw her, and asked, 'Have you heard?' She put on her smile and asked, 'What?' I put it as softly I could: 'I have left the navy!' The rest is history. Anna didn't say much, there was nothing that we could say. We knew it was coming. That evening we were completely traumatised. What was to happen?

But Allah heard my prayers. I was lucky. Unbeknown to me, two former high-ranking naval officers who knew what was going on were working behind the scenes. PNS *Dilawar*, the shore station to which Ali and I were attached after dismissal to complete formalities, received a telegram for me calling me to fly to East Pakistan for an interview for a senior position as an assistant conservancy and pilot superintendent (ACPS) in the East Pakistan Inland Water Transport Authority. Anna and I acted quickly. One-way air tickets by Pakistan International Airlines (PIA) were issued at Dilawar. We returned the rented furniture, sent a telegram to my uncle and aunty in

Dhaka to tell them we were coming and asking if we could stay with them. We said goodbye to Bostan Khan, who cried bitterly; he was very fond of Anna because she treated him so kindly. Anna too was quite upset.

We promptly flew out to East Pakistan. I got the job lined up for me by my friends – both former senior naval officers – Capt. C. S. Ahmed and Cdr Erfan Ahmed. The job interview was a mere formality.

I got my first posting to a remote station, Sirajganj, on the bank of the River Jamuna in early 1961. I was told by my chief executive, Capt. Ahmed, that arrangements had been made for me and my wife to stay with Capt. King, the pilot and conservancy superintendent who lived in a very large, comfortable bungalow, with guest rooms. The bungalow was built during the British Joint Steamer Company time when pilotage superintendents would be stationed to oversee the navigational safety for vessels and steamers plying the Jamuna River. The house was very comfortable, with high ceilings and all the comforts, including its own diesel generators to cope with the frequent power cuts.

My duties included charting the depth of water from my pilotage launch, to mark the safe navigable channels for tugs with barges and vessels plying up and down the Jamuna. Capt. King was a fine Englishman, very understanding that I had an English wife just arrived from England. In those pleasant wintry days, Anna and I used to go out for walks in the evenings along the bank of the Jamuna. Frequently Anna would be pleasantly surprised to notice a little procession of the village kids, some without clothes, following her, smiling and giggling, gently saying, 'Mam Saab' – reminiscent of the children's procession in *The Pied Piper of Hamelin*! Anna took to liking the smiling, laughing kids even though they were covered in sand from the riverbank.

Could two Brits have done more?

Commodore A. P. W. Northey RN was on loan from the Royal Navy to the fledgling Pakistan Navy and was commodore in charge of the Pakistan Navy flotilla – 'COMPAK'. Anna and I decided to visit him one afternoon at his naval residence upon receiving a naval signal from his ADC (aide de camp) asking me to see him. It read, 'U c Me.' Noting that it was from COMPAK I thought it was to see Northey, but I got it wrong. It was supposed to mean that I should see the ADC. Anyway, Anna and I went along to Northey's residence. We were met by his staff, seated on the cane sofa on the veranda and offered tea. Because Anna was with me that afternoon, Northey's wife also came out to meet us; they must have been having their afternoon rest, which we had disturbed. I showed Commodore Northey the signal inviting us. He looked puzzled but kept quiet. Most diplomatically they did not make us feel I had made a mistake! It seemed as if he didn't know. Naval headquarters must have asked the flag lieutenant to see me, cutting out COMPAK. We had a cup of tea, and after some small talk we left. On the way back in our scooter rickshaw, Anna looked at me and said, 'Well, that wasn't much use!' Anyway, we both felt that when Ali Khan's and my dismissal were being planned at the naval headquarters, Commodore Northey could have intervened – unless of course he was cut out from the decision-making apparatus.

The other person who might have intervened was the UK high commissioner in Pakistan, based in Karachi where my Anna was working in the passport section. I do not remember his name. It did not occur to any of us to talk to him. I was just too inexperienced to do any 'lobbying'. But his 'intelligence people' must have kept him informed that an English girl called Elizabeth Ann Pyne was working at the High Commission, was in Pakistan to marry a young Pakistan naval officer and that his dismissal was on the cards in the light of the ruling that the Government was averse to marriages with foreign nationals. He could have intervened to protect the interests of a British citizen.

Invitation to go back, no rancour!

Following about two years of strict martial law, General Ayub Khan, now a Field Marshal, declared himself President of Pakistan. Some semblance of civilian rule was returning. A constituent assembly was functioning in Karachi, West Pakistan. Elections were held in East and West Pakistan. Members were elected; they were called Members of the Constituent Assembly (MCAs). My uncle, Mr Mohammad Muhibus Samad (M M Samad), my aunt Nesa's husband, himself a former Member of the

Provincial Legislative Assembly (MLA) of East Pakistan, had a friend in the Constituent Assembly. Through my uncle's friend's immense efforts our two names (Lt Ali Khan and Lt Suhail Aziz) were raised at a session in the constituent assembly. The question was asked why two Bengali naval officers had to be dismissed from the Pakistan Navy for marrying foreign nationals, while officers from West Pakistan continue to serve in the civil and military services of Pakistan with foreign wives? News about our dismissal reached the president Field Marshal Ayub Khan. Consequently, the Governor of East Pakistan, Lt Gen. Azam Khan, was asked to find out if Ali Khan and Suhail Aziz wanted to go back to the navy?

Upon being directed by the Governor, our respective company chairmen contacted us to find out if we wanted to return to the navy. I was called up by my chairman, Syed Masud Hussain, from my duty station, Fenchuganj in Sylhet, to the Dhaka head office of the East Pakistan Inland Water Transport Authority. I duly met him. He asked me, 'Suhail, the Governor [that is Lt Gen. Azam Khan] wants to know if you want to go back to the navy.' Of course this came as a shock! I asked for a bit of time to discuss this with my family. I spoke to Anna, consulted my uncle, Mr M. M. Samad, who had always been a pillar of support to me, and a few others. I did not speak to Cdr Erfan Ahmed or Capt. C. S. Ahmed as I thought, mistakenly, my chairman and I were the only ones in the know about the enquiry from the Governor. After some soul-searching and taking account of political aspects and things that had happened to me in my time in the Pakistan Navy, I decided to decline the Governor's offer. I met my chairman on the following morning to tell him: 'No, sir, I have decided to decline the Governor's invitation and stay on at the IWTA.' He said, 'Of course it is up to you. But here, as you know, we treat people like dogs!' I took no notice of this. Later I came to learn that Ali Khan had also declined the Governor's offer made via his chairman at ESSO. It turned out to be a providential decision, given that the break-up of Pakistan was in the offing.

Obviously the Martial Law Government of Pakistan saw its mistake in denying us natural justice, denying our human rights, in a blatantly discriminatory practice against two Bengali officers, while Punjabi officers remained in Pakistan's services with foreign wives. I regarded the Government's enquiry as to whether Ali and I wished to return to the navy as an 'apology'. *So, I bear no rancour!*

So to conclude: our marriage didn't have to be in such secrecy. It could have taken place in public with drums beating and trumpets blaring! There was no need for the secrecy as it didn't help me or Ali to keep our jobs in the navy. But it was just as well, given that Pakistan was to break up.

I had many friends amongst the people I had been trained by and served with during my time in the Pakistan Navy. I was deeply disappointed that none of them bothered to enquire where I was or what happened to me. After some years I met a few of the former naval officers in London. Our natural naval friendship was still there. But not one of them spoke favourably or happily about the Pakistan Navy, nor with any pride.

A sad story

Admiral (Retd.) Mansur ul Huq and I had passed out together from Dartmouth as acting sub-lieutenants in the summer of 1958. We were quite close during our training in Pakistan and at Dartmouth. I was proud that he rose to become a full admiral and C-in-C of the Pakistan Navy. But reportedly he got embroiled in a corruption case for receiving some US$7.2 million (Wikipedia news) in kickback at the time of the Pakistan Navy's procurement of a couple of submarines from the French Navy. He had left Pakistan after his retirement in the 1990s to go and live in Texas. But upon another martial law being declared by the army chief, Parvez Musharraf, who toppled Nawaz Sharif's premiership, Mansur was extradited back to Pakistan, put on trial and jailed, and stripped of his rank and all retirement benefits. Reportedly he paid back the money to the navy. Eventually he was released from jail. Later he sued the Government of Pakistan and got his rank of admiral restored, but not his retirement benefits. Mansur tried to change his facial identity and decided to live with his family in Dubai, as he was too well known in Pakistan. I heard that he died of a heart attack in February 2018. My own disappointment is that during his entire career not once did he get in touch to enquire what became of me. I tried to contact him, as I still held him in some affection as my old classmate on PNS *Himalaya* and at Dartmouth. I prepared a letter to send to him but before I could find a way to reach him at his address in Dubai, I heard that he had passed away.

My posting to EPIWTA Sirajganj was to be interesting. On a routine inspection of Shell Oil Company operational depots in East Pakistan, my friend Cdr Erfan Ahmed dropped by to see how we were doing in remote Sirajganj. But on his visit to my 'loo', he must have noted that the toilet facilities were very basic! On his return to the capital he must have spoken to Capt. C. S. Ahmed, chief executive of IWTA, and told him, 'Get Suhail out of Sirajganj, he can't be expected to be there with absolutely shameful toilet arrangements for his English wife!' Almost immediately after his visit I got my posting to another remote station in Sylhet – Fenchuganj. This time we had a lovely bungalow from the old British Joint Steamer Company days, a conservancy and pilotage base by the Kushiyara River, and with very satisfactory bathroom facilities!

Fenchuganj was a lonely village, even though it was only five miles from Sylhet town by train. There was nothing there except the long railway bridge over the Kushiyara River. There was hardly any food – fish, meat or vegetables. At the market, the only vegetable our servant could get was *mukhi*, a smaller version of yam-yam. All the good quality fish got shipped to the prosperous Sylhet town, so what remained in Fenchuganj bazaar was leftover stuff. After a few months, Anna and I decided that perhaps she should return to England for a while until I could get a better posting in a city like Chittagong. I took her to Dhaka. In Karachi she was going to stay the night with my cousin Dolly and her husband, Flt Lt Mazhar, of the Pakistan Air Force. But Anna didn't go to London. She cancelled her booking, and returned to me. I asked her what happened: 'Why didn't you go to London?' Anna replied, 'I couldn't go, leaving you here all on your own in Fenchuganj!' I deeply appreciated her love and her concern for the wellbeing of both of us. We were back together again in the bungalow on a little island, the size of the island in the BBC series *Desert Island Discs*, surrounded by flood waters in the monsoon climate of Bengal!

I was very grateful to my cousin Dolly and Mazhar for looking after Anna in Karachi and helping her to return, back to Fenchuganj, and to me. Sadly Dolly, too, died from the dreaded disease of cancer.

Fenchuganj was only five miles from Sylhet town where my family – my parents and most of my brothers and sisters – were living. Anna and I would frequently visit them. It was a bit of a journey: from the bungalow by a little boat, walking up the railway embankment to the tiny station where waiting time could be indefinite as trains on the metre-gauge rails ran slowly. But that didn't matter; we were not in a hurry! We would go to my parents' house, eat, rest and chat. My elder sister, Ruby, was very observant. Once or twice she noticed that I was unfairly picking on Anna or commenting that she did not understand the cultural nuances. Anna, of course, took it all quietly, not engaging in an argument. But my sister Ruby would tell me off: 'Rana, you must control your temper with Anna!' At Fenchuganj, I followed my routine of measuring the river levels each morning with a line with a weight at its end so as to allow the river traffic – the tug boats, paddle steamers and large sailing boats with big masts – to pass under the bridge without obstruction.

Fenchuganj was as remote a waterlogged station as one could wish for. It was better than living in Sirajganj, my previous IWTA station where, on the bank of the Jamuna, you might go to sleep and by next morning the bank would have collapsed into the river and that would have been it!

One morning Anna said she was feeling a bit 'sick'. I called the *chowkidar* (the night guard) and asked him to call the company doctor (of the joint steamer company based next door). The doctor came. Anna was taken into our bedroom for a check-up. When they came out, both sat down on the porch cane chairs. Before I could ask, the doctor announced, 'Mr Aziz, I congratulate you both. Your wife is expecting!' I rose from the chair, kissed Anna and said, 'Well done, darling!', then shook hands with him. 'Thank you, Doctor.' Anna and I discussed what came next. We decided she would like to be with her family during her pregnancy. So not long after, Anna left for England. She and I went to stay in my Aunty Nesa's place in Dhaka for a few days before she flew to England.

I met my two high-level mentors in Dhaka, my supporters and fixers, Capt. C. S. Ahmed, ex-PN, chief executive of IWTA, and Cdr Erfan Ahmed, ex-PN, now Shell chief in East Pakistan, former naval secretary to the C-in-C PN. (Sadly both have passed away since, and to both I remain eternally grateful.) I told them the news and asked if something could be done for me to be in England at the time of Anna's last months of pregnancy and her first childbirth. It happened! I was sent for training to Trinity House. I was appointed to the Trinity House vessel based in Harwich where we took a flat and spent a couple of months together while I went out to sea on daily trips fixing the lighting systems. Then as Anna's final couple of months arrived before the birth, I was kindly transferred to the Trinity House Vessel (THV) *Vesta* based in Penzance. Again I would be on board during the week, learning about buoyage and lighting systems around the coast. In the evenings there was socialising with the officers and invitations to dinner with their families. I drove to Dartmouth in my new yellow Ford Anglia, a two-hour drive (with no speed restrictions of fifty mph on A-grade country roads in those days). I recall one Monday morning I could not report back on the ship as the baby's birth at the Bromborough Hospital, Totnes, was imminent. Later, I was told that the captain of *Vesta*, not seeing me on the bridge, had enquired, 'Where is Suhail?' An officer had replied, 'He is not here, sir, his wife is about to have a baby.' The captain said, 'He is not having the baby, is he?'

In June 1962 our first child was born. We decided to call her Lisa – my wife's choice of name. After four months' training with Trinity House depots in Harwich and Penzance and their ships, I returned to my job, leaving Anna and Lisa to join me a little later. A few months later they sailed from Liverpool on board the Anchor Line ship, *Cilicia*. Also on board was another Devonian, a navy wife, Hilary Farookh, who was returning to join her husband in Karachi. Their child, Kim, was about the same age as Lisa. Anna and Hilary became close friends and remained so for a long time.

There came another turning point. Lever Brothers Pakistan Ltd, a Unilever company, was setting up a brand new factory for their expanding market in East Pakistan for soaps, detergents and edible oils. They advertised for a personnel manager for their proposed factory in Chittagong. Following a Pakistan-wide competition I got the job. I served for almost four years from early 1963 to late 1966. During this time Levers' East Pakistan factory was acclaimed as a showpiece of the Unilever world (see testimonial from my manager Alan Jones).

Chapter Four

Back to England: 'drop like a brick' and the hard slog upward

After about four years at Lever Brothers (Unilever) in Chittagong, in about 1966 my feet got itchy again. Having gained recognition for my achievements in the Levers' East Pakistan factory, I had requested a transfer to their larger operations in Rahim Yar Khan, West Pakistan. But they refused, saying, 'Bengal is for Bengalis!' Lisa was about four and not in good health. Once she had a very high temperature. My company doctor diagnosed it as pneumonia and prescribed antibiotics. The temperature wouldn't come down. We sought a second opinion. That doctor said Lisa had malaria (commonly found in that part of the world) and prescribed baby paludrine. Lisa's temperature then came down. Nevertheless we were concerned. After a lengthy discussion we decided to weigh anchor and return to England. We knew it was a big jump into the unknown, but we had relatives and friends in England, and, as a result of my years at Dartmouth, I had some high-level connections.

My departure from Lever Brothers was quite emotional. Alan Jones, my manager at the factory, had given a glowing personal testimonial for my services (see Annexe A). The opening ceremony of the new factory had been led by the Governor of East Pakistan, Mr Monem Khan. It was attended by dignitaries from Chittagong and Dhaka, and directors of Lever Brothers from their head office in Rahim Yar Khan. The police chief came over to me to warn me that if any incident took place harming the Governor, then he 'would arrest the lot of us'! Happily the opening ceremony ended joyfully with sweets, eats and drinks.

For my departure, the staff had organised a farewell gathering. They gave me two framed farewell messages, which they read out to the assembled staff. They were deeply touching to hear. Some tears were shed. The framed messages adorn my picture gallery at home in England. The affection and respect I enjoyed from the staff of Lever Brothers were memorable. Leaving Chittagong was not easy. We had made many friends. It was sad leaving it all behind.

The afternoon we left Chittagong for Dhaka by road, I was driving the Lever Brothers' Land Rover. The journey turned out to be potentially quite dangerous.

*

A memory recalled

Chittagong is situated on the eastern side of Bangladesh (then East Pakistan), bordering Burma (now Myanmar). It was October 1966, the monsoon season had just ended and it should have been the stable weather of autumn. We thought it would be a pleasant, new experience, to travel by road to Dhaka (then called Dacca), the capital, about 160 miles north west. Anna asked me, 'Are you sure you want to be driving all that way with a child on board?' I was able to persuade her. We both knew early autumn weather in the Bay of Bengal region was pleasant but could also be unpredictable.

It was a bright day. I had borrowed the company Land Rover for the journey. We set off late that Saturday afternoon, avoiding the hot sun. I had not bothered to check the weather forecast or to seek advice. There were no mobile phones in those days.

Rush-hour traffic was ending, but the roads were still busy with slow-moving city buses, pedal rickshaws, scooter rickshaws, bullock carts and unruly pedestrians. The tarmacked part of the road was narrow; on either side was soft earth, often muddy. Although it was a busy trunk road, the Asian Development Bank-funded road was too narrow, accidents were frequent and road deaths numerous. Oncoming trucks and buses had to stop to let one another pass, but not always carefully! Systemic corruption meant that vehicles were not always roadworthy, and drivers were frequently found to be unqualified. With heavy rain the roads were full of potholes.

As we began exiting Chittagong, I noticed that the weather was changing. The air began to feel cooler. Was it the calm before the storm? The car radio was giving forecasts of changeable weather conditions in the Bay of Bengal. Strong wind and rain, and low-pressure areas over the bay began to be reported. Cyclones, floods, even tsunami-like conditions had always prevailed in coastal areas of the country. So villages in the coastal belt had cyclone and flood shelters, and transistor radios allowed people to listen to weather warnings and to take shelter.

About thirty miles out of the city, about 4pm, we stopped to have a cup of tea and snack. Then our real drive to Dhaka began. The weather conditions still seemed fine but with a cool, strong breeze developing. Far on the distant horizon, a cumulonimbus cloud was gathering. The sight was ominous, indicating a storm.

I kept driving. Anna and Lisa were calm, Lisa busy drawing something on her pad. Then Anna turned to me: 'Can you see all the people in the distance?' I said, 'No!' She didn't say anything for a minute or two, and then she said again, 'Look, they are running across the paddy fields, leaving their homes and villages behind, running towards the roads and traffic.' But it was all still far away. I kept driving; the crowd were getting closer. Closer, they were shouting and gesturing at us: 'Turn round, turn round, water is coming, there is a storm, a tsunami is coming, turn your car round, head back, head back, it is dangerous.' The black cloud was swirling with the wind and rain, the wind gaining speed. People were close to us now. We stopped and they crowded round our vehicle, telling us, 'You face death, turn round, go back to Chittagong, no way you can go to Dhaka by road, you will be killed, you face danger.'

We turned our Land Rover round and started driving back. People were running in their thousands, along the road, along the roadside, frightened for their lives. The tidal bore was advancing fast, houses and villages were going under water. A real calamity was taking place. There was absolutely no help in sight, no rescue boats. Fishing boats were being torn from their moorings. A howl of helpless human beings filled the air. The sight of a calamitous disaster with black clouds and whistling cyclonic wind and rain was frightening.

We arrived back at Chittagong fairly quickly. In the city area the ferocity of the cyclone was much less, as the buildings provided protection. The wind and rain were easing. I knew the last express train to Dhaka went at 10pm. There was still time to leave for Dhaka. We ate something at a café, went back to the flat and got the company driver to drop us at the station. We were lucky to get a first-class cabin to ourselves. The train departed on time. We arrived in Dhaka safely next morning, to spend a few days at the house of my Uncle Joglu before we took the flight to London. When we narrated our experience to my relatives in Dhaka, my uncle quite angrily said, 'You must be mad, trying to come to Dhaka by road with your family in the vehicle. You are very lucky to be alive.' Anna joined in: 'I told him not to drive all this way to Dhaka in this season of unpredictable weather conditions but he wouldn't listen!' Looking back, I admit I was reckless; I exposed my family to unnecessary danger.

Years have gone past. We are in England. But still I feel nervous at the sight of black cloud, wind and rain in England's wintry conditions. They bring back the sight of appalling weather, swirling black cloud, wind and rain, the howling of the crowd, the cries of 'help, help', hapless crowds running for their lives, seeking shelter, people being swept away in their thousands by tidal bores – human suffering from natural disasters.

*

We arrived in London, penniless, entirely dependent on the goodwill of our friends and relatives. Because I was coming back so soon after my last trip to the UK, the governor of the State Bank of Pakistan, even though a fairly close relative, could not permit any foreign exchange because of currency restrictions. So I did not have any pounds in my pocket. Luckily my friend Kolomdor Ali met me at Heathrow Airport and lent me £35 for expenses. We were put up by friends who were our neighbours and friends in Chittagong – Mahboob Ali and Annette Khan. They were most kind and helpful in our very early days in England. But soon after, we moved to a flat in Pelham Road, Wimbledon, owned by a Pakistani couple. I found the husband rather difficult, probably because I was married to a 'foreign' wife. We then found a nice place with an Italian landlord, Mr Capozzi, in Alverstone Avenue, Wimbledon, followed by a more amiable landlord, Mr Yusuf, at 54 Pretoria Road, Mitcham Lane, in Streatham SW16. It was not easy in those early days, with both of us working and little Lisa, only four, having to be taken to childminders by Anna. It was quite upsetting to leave Lisa at these places, crying.

I tried for jobs. First I had started in the civil service as a clerical officer. At the same time a hundred applications via an executive search firm produced not one interview – such was the extent of racism, racial prejudice and employment discrimination in England in those days. The mere sight of a foreign name – Aziz – on my CV was enough for personnel managers to bin it.

One would search for accommodation and read ads at the Earl's Court tube station: 'Double room available with all amenities. Regret no black or Asian or Irish, no dogs.' Undaunted I applied to the local employment exchange in Wimbledon. The manager said to me, 'Mr Aziz, we have only two vacancies: one sweeping roads in Wimbledon; the other will entail telling a lie!'

I smiled and said, 'Tell me the one with the lie.'

He said, 'It's a job at a small British Rail station as a booking office clerk selling tickets. But you have to say that you would love a career at BR, you see a bright future in BR, etc.'

I said I would go for BR!

I was duly interviewed and got the ticketing clerk job. Those days, tickets were arranged in alphabetical order in pigeonholes – no computerised ticket sales yet.

So my career hit the ground like a falling brick! From personnel manager at Unilever, one of world's largest companies, to booking office clerk at a small BR station, Motspur Park, in Surrey.

I ought to mention that, although I was leaving my personnel manager job with Lever Brothers in Chittagong, nevertheless I retained a strong interest in suitable job opportunities in East Pakistan. I had enquired about job opportunities with Shell. The director there said to me he did not have anything but he kindly picked up the phone to the director of Burma Oil

Company (BOC), Chittagong, and asked him, '... would you like to meet an upstanding Bengali for anything you might have?' I was told to go to meet the BOC chief, which I did. After our discussion he said that he was going to England on company business and would let me know on his return. But then I was in the advanced stages of preparation to depart with my family for England. I made a last call to him when he said, 'Let me let you know.' After I had arrived in England, I received a letter from the personnel director, Mr Carnell, from BOC, Chiswell Street HQ at Moorgate, saying that it was the East Pakistan director's intention to contact me on his return but he discovered that I had already left for England. Mr Carnell asked me to go and see him. I went along for an interview. I duly got a job offer to return to Chittagong with top-of-the-range terms and conditions. After discussion and some soul searching, Anna and I decided not to return to Chittagong.

Although things were beginning to work out in England, it was going to be uphill, not easy. I had to face discrimination, humiliation, disappointments, frustrations and tears. With frequent job changes, studies in the evenings, both Anna and me working, holding down two jobs sometimes, we just about managed to keep our heads above water. I decided I would make my own approaches to employers. The executive search firm showering companies with my CV, drawn up by them, had produced no results. The CV lacked the personal touch. Some friendships from Dartmouth days proved useful. Mr Lewis was extremely helpful. When we arrived back in England, Anna and I were twenty-nine, Lisa was four. Mr and Mrs Lewis wanted to meet us. We stayed with them for a night. We were put up in their beautifully arranged guest room. Anna and Mrs Lewis – Diana – spent the morning together in the kitchen, Anna helping her. Later that morning Diana said to me, 'Suhail, isn't she sweet? A lovely choice, we are very pleased to meet her...' Those words from Mrs Lewis meant a lot to me because she was a fine, highly educated lady.

We had a sumptuous English breakfast. Mr Lewis – Michael – knew that after arrival in England the first thing I would need was a good job, if possible befitting my qualifications and experience. So after breakfast, Michael called me: 'Suhail, let's have a walk in the garden.' We walked up and down the garden for about an hour. He knew my background of training at Dartmouth and Trinity House, and my work experience with Unilever. He gave me his advice: 'Suhail, it's not going to be easy. What you should do is make a list of management search firms in London and systematically knock at their doors. Tell them you are here, what you can do, etc. It will be a frustrating process. And I will also look out for any opportunities.' Those words meant a lot to me, reflecting, as they did, the situation of 'a foreigner in a foreign land'. I got a glimmer of what I had let myself in for by way of racial prejudice. At that time, under the leadership of The Rt Hon. Roy Jenkins, Home Secretary in the Harold Wilson Government, the first of the Race Relations Acts was passed by Parliament in 1965. The background was the determined pursuit by the stalwarts of race relations in this country: Mr (later Lord) Mark Bonham Carter, John Little, Mr (later Lord) Anthony Lester, Mr (later Sir and a QC) Geoffrey Bindman, solicitor, Mr Rose, Mr Frank Cousins of TGWU, and some distinguished black and Asian leaders: Lord Leary Constantine, the cricketer, and some other leading black and Asian persons. With the passing of the Race Relations Act 1965, the Race Relations Board (RRB) was established under the Home Office. The country was by no means ready to be told by an Act of Parliament that discrimination in public places like pubs, hotels etc. was not permitted. People said you could not legislate to dictate attitudes, how people should behave or how they should think. Mark Bonham Carter made the profoundly important statement: 'Legal sanction in the background is a vital persuader.' Basically the 1965 Act, called sometimes, 'the Pub and Grub Act', allowed black and Asian people to have a drink at their locals without being kept waiting to be served or facing similar discriminatory treatment, and to obtain accommodation with no discrimination. The Act was by no means a success but it was a start. It was followed by successive Race Relations Acts – 1968, 1976, 2000. Step by step a fairer society, free from overt discrimination, was to emerge in Britain. By and large all forms of discrimination became illegal, although there was still some way to go. Racial prejudice was difficult to eliminate, being privately held deep in an individual's mind.

I saw the RRB advertising jobs in *The Guardian* for assistant conciliation officers (ACOs) for the RRB's conciliation committees up and down the country. I had applied, unsuccessfully, for one of these posts. But two things happened. One morning I was pleasantly surprised to receive a letter from Mr Bonham Carter telling me that after seeing me at the interview for the

ACO jobs, he had written to Unilever head office in Blackfriars, London, telling them, 'Mr Aziz, having served in Lever Brothers in Pakistan, is now here and is looking for a job. It might be useful to them to see him,' and that I should expect to hear from them (Unilever). I duly received a letter from the Unilever HQ personnel director, inviting me for an interview. I felt honoured to visit Unilever House. It was beautifully set on the bank of the Thames in Blackfriars. The atmosphere in the Unilever office was exhilarating. I had my meeting with the director. He started our discussion by asking me, 'Decided to make your home in England, Mr Aziz?' In a bit of a panic, I gave a 'stupid' answer: 'I don't think I can ever make my home in England!' He didn't show any reaction. He asked me about my background and experience. At the end he said, 'It is going to be difficult to find something suitable for you. What I am going to do is to ask some of my colleagues in various operating units and see what happens.' Later on I was to hear from him that he had asked Wall's Ice Cream, Birds Eye and a few other operations but regretfully they could not find anything. This was a symptom of racial discrimination, even though I had a lot to offer. I recalled what Alan Jones, my manager at Lever Brothers, had told me at the time of leaving: 'You may have to take a job like Zain did, wrapping Wall's ice creams.' (Zain ul Abedin was my colleague at Levers', a UK-qualified civil engineer.)

The second positive thing that was to come out of my approach to the RRB was that I was invited to join the North London Conciliation Committee of the RRB as a member under the very able chairmanship of Dr Fred Bayles, a renowned professor at a UK university. One does not come across many great and good people easily. I was fortunate to begin to make contacts at a high level, and I learnt that I must take any job I could get, get started and climb with patience. The support I got from Anna during this time was to prove important. She was a pillar of support. With little Lisa we had made a start to our life in England.

My father Moulvi Mohammaed Azizur Rahman, mother Lutfunnessa Khatun, and little Shameem, my sister Mina's son

Anna with my parents, sisters Nargis and Mina, and her husband Feroz Bhai (wearing a tie), and my brothers (right to left): Nripa, Molik, Raja, and Koysar

My brothers (left to right) Koysar, Nripa, Molik, Raja and Lama

*The Sanaullah mosque
in Khuliatoola – our
neighbourhood*

*Anna and me
in Sylhet*

*My elder sister Ruby
with her husband
Matin Bhai*

*A young Anna with her whimsical look
at her house in Dartmouth*

*Anna's little sister Lynda trying her
hands at the piano.*

Above: Anna's parents Mr Alfred and Mrs Betty Pyne

Below: Anna with her brother David and sister Lynda

Above:Cadets and Midshipmen from the Naval College on parade
in Dartmouth during the annual Royal Regatta

Below: Her Majesty the Queen during a visit to Britannia Royal Naval College, Dartmouth

I am with Midshipman Phang of the Royal Malaysian Navy after a Sunday morning parade at the College

With Midshipman Yusuf of the Pakistan Navy

On the bridge of my training ship passing orders to the wheel house

The passing-out batch of midshipmen with our divisional officers just before being commissioned as acting sub-lieutenants from the Britannia Royal Naval College, Dartmouth, by the British Board of Admiralty, Summer 1958

One of the ships of the Dartmouth Training Squadron, HMS Vigilant, a Type 15 Frigate, where I received my sea training as a cadet and midshipman

Above: Anna with her mates. Seated from left: Anna, Anne King, Anne Chase, and Anne Cudd (standing), at their lunch break near the Dartmouth Pottery where they all worked. Anna did pottery painting, some of the items became very famous.

Below: Anne Cudd and Anne Chase at our engagement party in Anna's home, Dartmouth

Above: We are about to go off to the BRNC Passing-out Ball, July 1958.
Here sharing something intensely funny!

Below: Dancing the evening away

With some of the British families
I got to know while at the BRNC
Dartmouth:

*Left: Mrs Isobel Bell with her son,
seen here at home, The Hermitage,
Roxborough, Scotland. I kept in touch
with Mrs Bell for some years. Soon
after my return to England in 1966 I
learnt she died from an accident*

Below left: Me, Kuthan with Bill and Cynthia Gorrill and friends in the Lake District

*Below Right: With our host Mrs Gorrill – me (Pakistan Navy), Nettur, Kuthan –
Malaysian Navy cadets, the Lake District, Cumbria.*

*Below left and centre: Mrs Diana Lewis, children
Philippa and Stephen, in their home in Horsham, Sussex*

*Below: On the beach with
Mrs Lewis, little Stephen,
and friend Mrs Edward.*

Chapter Five

Joining the Royal Air Force and Return to Civvy Street

I was always interested in economics, and this later developed into my interest in management consulting. Somehow I felt it was my innermost desire to study economics, even though at the time I did not know much about the basic workings of the 'demand and supply curves'! As I gained experience in life I became more interested. But first I had to gain some qualifications. People considering giving me a job would want to see that I was on the same wavelength and frequency, that I understood something about the job market, the organisation of work. To fulfil my ambition to study economics and to gain educational qualifications which people in this country would recognise, I had to study for degrees and diplomas, while at the same time gaining experience in job situations in the fields I wanted to enter – such as economics and management consulting. Without these basic ingredients I could not hope to succeed in anything.

Soon after arrival back in England in 1966, I made enquiries how to launch into undergraduate study at the University of London. I was told by the senate admissions office that they would equate my Dartmouth studies in maths, navigation, English, naval history, naval warfare, etc. to GCE A-level in two subjects: maths and English. So they wanted me to obtain one more A-level. Then with three A-level passes, I would be eligible to register for a BSc Economics Part I (External).

As we were living in Wimbledon, I registered for a part-time evening class in economics at Wimbledon College. As I have said, I didn't know much about basic economics. My knowledge was limited to what I had picked up from reading newspapers, seeing TV and listening to radio. I began attending classes a couple of evenings a week from after Christmas 1966. I registered to sit the A-level Economics papers (I think it was in two parts), in June 1967. I was pleasantly surprised to get a grade C pass. I felt quite encouraged by the amount of common-sense economics I knew. So I fast-tracked myself into registering as an external student at the University of London to begin my studies in earnest for a BSc(Econ) degree, studying in my own time while holding down my day job as a clerical/temporary executive officer in government departments.

Anna and I worked almost all day long. We had to keep our heads above water with a young family; Lisa was barely five. Our weekly expenses were relatively high; we had to be comfortable and the rent of the flat was taking away a big chunk of our weekly wages. There was a lot of running around in a day: Anna had to take Lisa to the childminder, then rush to one job, then to the next, collect the child, do the cooking, with some relaxation and bit of watching TV thrown in. I had my studies in the evenings. It was a lot to do but we took it in our stride. We accepted that it wasn't going to be easy finding our feet in England.

The grounding I had from Dartmouth helped me to study in the rigorous British educational environment. After three years of part-time study involving homework, tutorials, summer schools, e.g. at Churchill College, Cambridge, and so on, eventually in 1970 I managed to pass Part I. I was ready to launch into Part II Economics, which would take two years more, part-time. Thus, altogether the external degree took five years. Completing these two parts filled me with joy. The 'external' and 'internal' degree courses were of the same rigour and quality. An internal economics degree of the University of London obtained studying full-time took three years. My ambition had been to get the BSc(Econ)(Lond); I had now got it.

Anna agreed our efforts and sacrifice had paid off. I could have just taken mundane jobs and carried on but I felt that for both Anna and me, it would not be a happy situation. I know Anna wouldn't have been happy if I was performing below what I was capable of. We both were quietly ambitious, keen not to fall behind what we might have attained had we not come back to England. We knew there would be a price. We were mentally prepared to pay it.

My BSc Economics degree unfortunately was only a Third Class Honours because, as I said, it was hard going for us. But I was happy with the achievement. I was determined to keep pushing.

During the period 1967 to 1972 I managed to make some progress in career terms. I sat the Civil Service Commission (CSC) clerical officer open competition (I was too old at twenty-nine for the executive class recruitment which had an upper age limit of twenty-five); I came fifth out of 5,000 candidates who sat that examination in 1966. After working as a ticketing clerk at Motspur Park British Rail station in Surrey for a few months I moved on. Having passed the CSC clerical grade examination, I was assigned to Her Majesty's Factory Inspectorate (HMFI) – now the Health and Safety Commission – acting as assistant to two factory inspectors, Mr Thomas and Mr Moleneux, two very fine gentlemen of the British Civil Service genre. My job was to assist the two HM inspectors with their appointments for visits to factories, minuting files, bringing forward cases, talking to them about particular cases of factories, etc. Having worked at Lever Brothers' factory in Chittagong this job proved quite interesting to me. More importantly, I was able to talk to them, especially Mr Moleneux, about my outside interests. He was very interested in what I told him about my background. I felt that he recognised that with my Dartmouth background, a naval career, plus service in the private sector – Inland Water Transport, Lever Brothers in East Pakistan – I was in an unsuitable job at the HMFI, and that I could do more. I knew that. It was good to get that recognised by someone of the calibre and experience of a British factory inspector. That was enough for me. I used to tell Anna about my work at the HMFI. She was quietly happy that I was beginning to feel content in England.

After some months at the HMFI, I noticed the announcement in the press about the setting up of the National Board for Prices and Incomes (NBPI) by the Harold Wilson Government, under the chairmanship of Mr Aubrey Jones. The mission of this body was to exert some sensible control over both prices and incomes which were escalating out of control, thus fuelling inflation, to the detriment of the economy and the standard of living. I appreciated George Brown's idea of setting up the Department of Economics Affairs (DEA) and creating the NBPI; and also the increasing role of the Ministry of Labour under Mrs Barbara Castle to try to tame the unions. What was of interest to me was the economics of all these initiatives.

Simultaneously with my Economics Part I studies, I had also enrolled myself for a Diploma in Management Studies (DMS) at Kingston Polytechnic (now Kingston University). I felt that having done some management jobs in Pakistan – Dartmouth-trained Pakistan naval officer, Inland Water Transport, Unilever – I should get a DMS, which would take three years, from 1967. So, studying part-time, I should get the DMS in 1970 – which I did. The desire to progress my career as fast as possible to the level I would have been had I continued in Pakistan naturally meant that I was in some hurry. All along Anna was supporting my ambition, but it was not easy for her. It meant a lot of work and the sacrifice of our quality of life. Sometimes I would wonder if I was being selfish. Why this unstoppable desire to keep pushing to succeed? What about our family life?

But deep inside me I felt that to achieve more would make Anna and me happy, and it would also mean that as my career progressed Lisa would get better opportunities for education. We would be able to put her into good schools, in better areas, with benefits for her mind and mental development. Anna and I never neglected Lisa's education. We did whatever was possible for us to do for her educational development and wellbeing. We would have liked to do more and give her a private education. But despite our good intentions, we were constrained by our limited means.

My DMS course at Kingston Polytechnic was running in parallel to my Part I BSc Economics course. I recall being interviewed for enrolment to the DMS course by the principal lecturer, Mr Mogford. I had given him my CV, showing my background. Whether he had read it, I didn't know. His first question was, 'What do you want to do with a management studies course?' I answered as best I could, stating that although I was presently doing a clerical officer job, I would like to get back to the level of work I had been doing in Pakistan – at management level. But I reflected on Mr Mogford's question. In those days of the late 1960s, the extent of racial discrimination in employment was severe. For example, London Transport did not have black or Asian bus drivers, they were allowed just up to conductor level. Banks did not employ black people at the counters lest the customers, especially elderly white ladies, should dislike being handed pound notes by black hands! Ladies' lingerie sections in department stores did not have black staff because the white lady customers would not like to be served by black girls or women. One did not see coloured junior-level staff at large employers like local authorities, publicly owned utilities, or at their reception desks. This was the extent of racial discrimination in employment in lower grades, not to mention management-level jobs in government, public authorities, industry and commerce. So I could see what Mr Mogford at Kingston Poly was getting at: given the rampant scale of wholesale racial discrimination, what indeed did I want to do with a Diploma in Management Studies! In other words, was I being very naive to have such an unrealistic ambition in the Britain of those days?

Mercifully, our communities have come a long way in Britain. Today our boys and girls are doing extremely well in education and employment and fulfilling their ambitions, within a culture of reasonable acceptance and tolerance. We are not completely there, but our communities' achievements so far have been noteworthy.

After moving out from our friends' place in Wimbledon, we lived more permanently in a small flat in Streatham; our landlord, a Pakistani gentleman, Mr Yusuf, a widower, was a very nice gentleman. We had one large bedroom, a kitchen and bathroom in the middle, and right at the back of the flat was our little sitting room. The cleanliness was very poor when we moved in. So Anna had to invest a lot of time to get the flat nice and clean. The sitting room furniture was a couple of light chairs, a small table and a couple of side tables on a maroon-coloured carpet. It seemed old but had to do for us for the time being.

Our daily life was: up early, wash, breakfast, off to work; Anna would drop Lisa to her childminder, then go to her first job at a sweet manufacturing factory, then lunch and a second job, pick up Lisa and home to cook supper. I would walk to Streatham Common BR station, about ten minutes' walk, then to Victoria, and be in the office at NBPI by nine o'clock. Fortunately my DMS course and BSc(Econ) studies were supported by the NBPI for some fees, books and travel and some time off when I had classes. On my college days at Kingston, I was allowed to leave an hour early so that I could attend DMS lectures from 6pm after a snack at home, then catching the No. 57 bus from Mitcham Lane to Kingston. I would be home by 10pm. Lisa would be in bed. Anna might be watching some TV. We had some chat about what sort of day we had had. Then we were tired, so it was off to bed, to be up early for next day's rituals. Not much else! Weekends were mostly free for shopping, and visiting friends and relatives.

In the flat there was not much room for my studies or keeping the books I bought and borrowed from libraries. I decided to be my own carpenter and put up a shelf in the bedroom for the books. Mr Yusuf's flat's walls seemed not to be strong. I fixed the shelf duly with rawl plugs and screws. I put all my books on it. Behold: shortly afterwards the whole lot came crashing down! A shriek of laughter ensued from Anna and Lisa. Of course I was embarrassed by my poor carpentry. Anyway, my books were stowed away here and there.

After nothing had come of a recruitment consultancy firm's circulation of one hundred CVs, I decided to do my own job search. I approached a few potential employers who I thought might give serious consideration to my application. I was really lucky and felt I should have done this before. This approach was strictly in line with what Mr Michael Lewis, my friend and well-wisher, had recommended. I should have taken his advice rather than wasting those few years in low-grade jobs.

A little story here from my Dartmouth days: one Friday afternoon, HMS *Vigilant*, a converted type 15 frigate, one of several ships at the Dartmouth Training Squadron, was on a training exercise in the Bay of Biscay – famously known as one of the roughest of seas at times. I was standing on the bridge (for bridge watch-keeping officer training), next to a four-ringer captain of the Royal Navy, Capt. Morgan-Giles RN. I was learning how to steer a destroyer/frigate, exercising, when it was not just rolling and pitching, but being lifted up and dropped. I forgot about seasickness! The following morning I could be slung out on a plank over the shipside washing and painting. That training was to make me flexible and adaptable. I was able to do whatever came my way; it taught me how not to be obsessed or be fixed on something. It was important to be flexible in coping with life's experiences. So, truly, I was not showing arrogance or pomposity to my elderly British Rail colleague, my boss, at the ticketing office at Motspur Park station, nor did I feel humiliated selling a ticket to an elderly, elegant-looking English lady! As one industrial tribunal judge told me when I had lost my racial discrimination claim against the Tower Hamlets City Challenge: 'You can,

I am sure, take it in your stride, Mr Aziz.' I believe my training in the Royal Navy has largely contributed to my ability to work at all levels comfortably: standing next to an RN captain one minute, painting the shipside the next! This attitude helped me, I believe, with Anna, in our efforts to rise in Britain from the bottom of the pile.

However, with hindsight, I feel I did not have to go so far below my abilities in jobs I had to start with. Had I taken Mr Lewis's advice and persevered in knocking at the doors of management consultancies or recruitment consultants a little longer, I would have started at management cadre and cut out some of the time wasted toiling at the bottom. But then I have to admit that I did knock at a few doors of big firms. I did get an invitation from McKinsey & Company, the renowned international management consultancy, and saw Brigadier (Retd.) Langstaff, who interviewed me. It most probably could have resulted in my entry to management consulting but unfortunately, I messed it up. I had taken a double dose of anti-allergy tablets in the morning of the interview to control my hay fever attack and sneezed during the interview with Brigadier Langstaff. I had a good interview, but on the way out I walked straight into the glass wall of the reception area. The impact cracked the glass wall. The security guard asked me, 'Are you alright, sir, should we call an ambulance?' I thanked them and said I was alright and left. Later I wrote a letter apologising to Brigadier Langstaff. That was the end of a chance to enter management consulting!

A BP interview made me feel proud. I went to BP Tower in Moorgate to be interviewed by a senior-level personnel manager. The job was a first rung of the management ladder as an 'assistant'. Training was to follow at BP. It would have been a great opening. It would be almost at the same level where I left things in Pakistan: a young lieutenant in the Pakistan Navy, a pilot superintendent at Inland Water Transport and a Unilever personnel manager.

Another job offer from Constructors John Brown (CJB) was interesting. When we came to England we were on an Aeroflot Russian Airlines flight from Dhaka via Moscow. (It was the cheapest for us.) When the plane took off from Moscow, I had next to me a large, distinguished-looking Englishman. We got talking. He was the personnel director of a company called CJB. He gave me his card. He was Mr Bilsland. The company was involved in laying a gas pipeline from Russia to Europe. I suppose he was doing recruitment and selection of high-level people for jobs in Russia and Europe. I was quick to start talking about my background and experience: Dartmouth, naval training, service as a lieutenant in the Pakistan Navy, Lever Brothers. I must have said it all in one breath! I might have impressed him. But I didn't mention that I would be looking for a job. Although I felt comfortable talking to him, recalling what Mr Alan Jones had told me that I might have to do a mundane 'ice cream wrapping job at Wall's' ice cream factory in Grimsby, I probably felt it was too much to be asking Mr Bilsland for a job. Besides, his was a construction industry outfit, hardly a firm with a job for me. The flight landed in London Heathrow and that was it: 'Goodbye, Mr Bilsland.'

Because I had his card I sent off an application to Mr Bilsland, personally addressed to him, reminding him of our meeting on the Aeroflot flight from Moscow. I didn't hear any more from CJB. But by then we had moved from Mahboob Khan and Annette's place in south Wimbledon to a flat in Pelham Road in Wimbledon. It was a flat with a Pakistani landlord who was quite rude, insensitive and selfish. Poor Lisa was still four, so she couldn't be started at the nearby primary school. She had to be left with the landlord's wife as our childminder. It was heartbreaking to both of us to see Lisa crying her eyes out sitting at the top of the stairs as we left. I will never forget how hurt I felt at seeing Lisa like that and the carelessness of the landlord's wife. She was useless as a childminder, though charging quite a high hourly rate. She was unkind, with no feelings for the child in her care. She did not even telephone me or Anna to tell us that Lisa was upset! I felt very sad and responsible for causing this upheaval to Lisa's childhood but hoped that soon things would look up for us in England, *Inshallah.*

After a week or so, I went to visit the Khans' house to check with them if there was any mail for us. Annette Khan was in. Most intriguingly Annette said, 'There is something.' 'What?' Then she got a long stick, pushed open the manhole door to the roof, stood up on a domestic ladder and fetched a large brown envelope. I saw on the outside of the envelope stamped CJB! I felt elated, as it must be as a result of my writing to Mr Bilsland. Apart from some CJB company information and its activities, there was a letter from the company personnel manager to contact him for an interview for an opening – again as an 'assistant' – at management level.

I went along. Mr Bilsland saw me. He said, 'Quite a coincidence. We flew together. You could have told me you would be looking for a job upon arrival in England. I would have offered you a job there and then!' He told me a bit more about CJB company activities on heavy construction projects in the UK and overseas. What would be my role as an assistant? It was a management trainee-level job, with many opportunities in the company's business worldwide. I was so happy. Anyway, the job offer soon followed, to start immediately. So that was my job offer No. 2, after BP, searched for and found by myself without the exorbitant expense of recruitment consultants!

The third job interview was at the Trades Union Congress (TUC) at Congress House, Great Russell Street, central London. Mr Vic Feather, a stalwart in the trade union movement in Britain, was the assistant general secretary and the general secretary was Mr George Woodcock. It was quite an office Mr Feather had. It was soundproofed, his door was heavy and leather-cushioned, no doubt lest confidential discussions with union leaders got overheard or leaked to nearby Fleet Street! Mr Feather started: 'Welcome. I have read your CV. I would like to hear from you a little more. Tell me bit about yourself. What you have done, your career, why are you here, what would you like to do? I hope you have gathered something about what we do at the TUC. Mainly we are here to assist unions in collective bargaining with their employers so that workmen get good wages and working conditions for their wellbeing. We assist in resolution of industrial disputes, strikes and so on. Now you tell me something.' I gave my prepared piece. I could see he was interested in my naval background, my work with Lever Brothers, Trinity House etc. I told him about my young family and why I was out of the Pakistan Navy. After about twenty minutes, Mr Feather said, 'Well, the job we have is as an assistant in the social security section. It will be an interesting opening for you with a future within the TUC. I would urge you to take it.' I had already received information about the TUC and found the prospect very interesting. The pay was less than that offered by BP or CJB, but the assurance of a good future was there, especially because at that time, the late 1960s, the trade unions were increasingly getting more and more workers from black and ethnic minority communities into their membership, with associated claims of rampant racial discrimination. Collective bargaining and industrial relations in Britain were taking on a new dimension, with regular media coverage, mostly negative. I felt honoured to have had a thirty-minute interview with the assistant general secretary of the TUC. He was waiting for his turn to become the general secretary succeeding Mr Woodcock when he stepped down. I thanked him. He said, 'Let me know. As I said, it will be a good opportunity for you at the TUC.' I felt lucky with another job offer: 'assistant' – first step to management at Britain's TUC.

I had also approached the Ministry of Defence. I told them I was here, sent them my CV and asked if I could join the Royal Navy, as my training at Dartmouth was the same as that of British Royal Navy cadets and midshipmen, leading to the award of a Queen's Commission. I had a letter from the second sea lord's department (responsible for naval personnel) stating that there was an age limit. At the age of twenty-nine I could not join the Royal Navy, given the career break of almost six years. What was most probably left unsaid, and I hope I am not being unfair on the navy, was that the Royal Navy did not have any black or brown people! So I drew a blank with the Royal Navy.

However, the Royal Air Force was different. It had a tradition, going back to the Second World War, of employing Commonwealth citizens. In fact there were senior officers up to the rank of air commodore in the RAF from the West Indies or the Indian subcontinent, not necessarily in flying but other branches – technical support, administration, etc. I received an encouraging letter from the MoD (Air) telling me that the RAF would be interested. They asked me to go to RAF Biggin Hill, Kent, for two days of written, psychological and physical fitness tests. If I got through these, then I would be considered for a commission in the RAF – with antedated seniority for my Dartmouth training, Pakistan Navy service and relevant civilian experience, such as personnel management at Unilever. I went to Biggin Hill, did the written tests and interviews, including jumping over obstacles, swinging on the ropes, as indeed I had done at the time of joining as a pre-cadet at the JSPCTS, Quetta, all those years ago in 1954, twelve years previously. On the final day I was told at the final interview that I would be hearing from the MoD (Air) soon. I got a letter offering me direct entry to flying officer rank, in the secretarial branch of the RAF (personnel/administration work). I drove to pick up Anna from her work one morning in August 1968 and joyfully told her of the offer of a commission. Anna was pleased that my background was being recognised. She asked, 'What next?' I told her it would entail some 'reorientation' training followed by posting to a real job in the Royal Air Force.

So it was decision time!

I was sitting on job offers as 'assistant' from (i) the British Petroleum (BP), (ii) Constructors John Brown (CJB), (iii) the Trades Union Congress (TUC) and finally (iv) a Queen's Commission in the Royal Air Force as a direct entry flying officer. All these were first class job offers in full recognition of my career so far. Each would offer me the opportunity to make a life in Britain. Coupled with my progress in studies in economics and management, any of these jobs would give me a good grounding to become a macroeconomist and prepare me for a management consulting career.

Naturally we pondered. I asked Anna's opinion about what I should do. I knew she would be happy with whatever I wanted to do, she would support me. Anna said, 'These are all good job offers for you. You decide. I will be happy, as it would also be good for Lisa's education.' After a lot of soul-searching, and in view of the recognition being given by the Royal Air Force to my Dartmouth training, PN service and to my management career, I decided to accept the MoD offer of a job in the RAF. My only qualm was that as a Pakistan Navy lieutenant, I would have been a lieutenant with eight years' seniority in 1968. I would be a lieutenant commander (equivalent to a squadron leader in the RAF). So as a flying officer in the RAF I would be two ranks lower. But it was the best I could hope for at the start of my life in Britain with a young family. I had to find my feet, fast and quick! The other attraction for the RAF was that terms and conditions would be good: good housing – a squadron leader-level three-bedroom fully furnished house, with a garage and cleaning service; social life as an officer of the RAF; job security of a permanent commission, with a future to look forward to.

But with hindsight the RAF might have been a great mistake. The BP, CJB or TUC jobs discussed above could have offered me a grounding in practical economics and prepared me better for a career in management consulting. The RAF, on the other hand, would take me away from business into the narrow and, in a way, isolated life of an officer in one of the armed forces. However, the decision was made. I took the plunge. I resigned from the temporary executive officer job in the Economics and Statistics branch of the National Board for Prices and Incomes. I wrote off to the MoD (Air) accepting their offer as a flying officer in the secretarial branch. And, a bit sadly, told BP, CJB and TUC that I would not be accepting their offers.

Thankfully it was beginning to look like I had a 'lift-off' in Britain. But after three years – October 1967 to October 1970 – I had gained an insight into the service. I felt that I was languishing in a junior-ranking job when my British compatriots from Dartmouth in the Royal Navy, or from the Pakistan Navy, were already lieutenant commander (squadron leader equivalent in the RAF), two full ranks above. The quality of job I had in the RAF was very basic, not challenging at all. Challenging were the jobs of operational flying officers and flight lieutenants flying the planes. I was not doing that – too late! Also, Anna and I felt there was a very subtle undercurrent of serious racial prejudice and discrimination. For example, once when I was the station duty officer, doing my rounds to check all was well, I put my head into the officers' mess. I was embarrassed and indeed shocked to discover that a senior squadron leader was hosting a wedding reception for his daughter. Both he and some of his guests, who were still looking sober, quietly interrupted their chatting for a moment, stared at me and seemed startled. I could not have been quicker to shut the door and leave. Later I discovered that the white couples at the station had all been invited to the reception, but not Anna and me. I spoke to Anna about it. She said, 'I knew this all along. In fact I do not see why I should be looked down upon by these men and women. I am not less than them in any way.' I knew Anna was unhappy with what we were experiencing – subtle, conscious or unconscious discrimination, call it what you like. It is incidents like these, bit by bit, which eventually form into a big picture of what goes on in the privacy of white people's lives in England. This you can never get rid of with lectures or speeches or legislation. It's historical, deeply held. Actually I am not complaining about deeply held prejudice. We all have a degree of prejudice. The whole Indian subcontinental society – Hindu, Muslim, Sikh, Buddhist – is layered according to birth. We still have a quarter of Indian society who are called 'the untouchables' ('the scheduled class' during the British time). But prejudice is private, a privately held view. It is the overt expression of prejudice, discrimination, which is illegal. This is what the late

Lord Bonham Carter and his colleagues tried to rectify with legislation, with their firm commitment and belief that 'Legal sanction in the background is a vital persuader' – not to allow your personally held prejudice to flow into acts of discrimination in housing, employment, provision of goods and services. If one takes account of the achievements of the law in this field, undoubtedly Britain has come a very long way in becoming a tolerant society.

At the time of 'passing out' from RAF Upwood, a senior officer from MoD (Air) joined us for dinner at the officers' mess. We were having an after-dinner drink with him. Little did I know that such meetings were also used by the MoD (Air) for talent-spotting and recruiting of officers for appropriate assignments in the future. Two or three of us were chatting with him, when he suddenly asked, 'Is there someone in your group who really stands out?' I remember telling him at once, 'Penny Haag.' Penny struck me as a young flying officer who was destined to go on to do higher things in the RAF. She was bright, likeable, diligent and top of our class. I don't know how far she progressed in the RAF or if she decided to leave to get married and raise a family.

While in the RAF, I was still feeling as if I was a civilian, free to say what I liked. I did not feel so much governed by the air force discipline, rules and regulations. I would write to newspapers such as *The Economist*, *The Times*, *The Guardian*, with strong views but telling the editor not to print my name and address but my *nom de plume*!

After three years I had decided to leave the RAF. But as I was holding a permanent commission, it wasn't going to be easy. First, my immediate boss, Sqn Ldr Ford, knew that I was unhappy and that I definitely felt underutilised at the relatively junior rank of flying officer. One morning I was in his office to ask him something; we were chatting. Suddenly he asked, 'Suhail, would you like to transfer to the education branch of the RAF?' I had of course already passed the promotion examination to become flight lieutenant and, in due course, squadron leader. So that pre-qualifying side was clear. Also, from discussions and dinners at his home with him and his very able wife, he knew that I sought something intellectually challenging and perhaps the education branch of the RAF would give me the challenge. I told him, 'Let me talk to my wife and consider this interesting suggestion.' I talked it over with Anna. Once again she left it to me to decide. She wanted me to be happy, for us all to be happy in England. She left it to me. I pondered for a few days. During the RAF reorientation course at RAF stations Henlow and Upwood, I saw some of the educational instructors in action, a batch of men and women, some university graduates or Master's degree holders, teaching us war history, RAF disciplines and regulations, do's and don'ts in the RAF, and so on. Frankly that was all quite basic, but of course one had to learn that to become knowledgeable about the job and life in the RAF. But it certainly did not seem challenging or intellectually stimulating.

I gave my reply to Sqn Ldr Ford: 'Sir, I have discussed this with my wife. I feel that having tasted industry [I had in mind my time at the EPIWTA, Trinity House, London, Unilever in Pakistan, and having seen a bit of life in industry in England – BR, HMFI, NBPI] I would like to go back to industry.' Ford: 'Alright then, Suhail, if you are sure, if that is what you want. I will speak to the station commander.' The latter, Group Captain Iuan Thomas, wrote a note of testimonial saying that he agreed that I would flourish in industry. He wrote something including: 'Suhail was always a diligent officer, impeccably dressed and a credit to the Royal Air Force.' (see Annexe B).

On leaving the RAF I became a permanent member of the Royal Air Force Club. As I progressed into civilian occupations the value of this membership became clear. Living in London, I frequently used the club for business meetings, meeting friends and for my family. Events were held for engagement and wedding celebrations for our two daughters. I was instrumental in organising gala fundraising dinners for Rotary Clubs in the UK and Sylhet in Bangladesh (the Rotary Club of Streatham, Rotary Club of Tooting, Rotary Club of Jalalabad, and the Jalalabad Disabled Rehabilitation Centre and Hospital in Sylhet).

Friends would ask me, 'How does a naval officer come to be in the Royal Air Force Club?!' I would start by saying, 'That's a short question which has a long answer!' This generated a little laughter and interest, but then I would narrate a summary of my life's history up to that point in my life. My friends who had heard my story would quite often say, 'Suhail, you have a story to tell, you should write a book.' Those little encouraging words sowed a seed.

Life in the RAF had given me a lot of spare time. So, apart from corresponding with the responsible press – *The Economist, The Sunday Times, The Guardian* – I was strategically looking out for life and jobs on

Civvy Street after the RAF.

My posting at RAF Swinderby, as officer in charge of clerical services flight (OCCF) – personnel administration work – meant that I had the opportunity to keep tabs on the press, including magazines like *The Economist*. I tried to be a regular reader. *The Times, The Guardian, The Daily Telegraph* were all available in the officers' mess, which enabled me to keep an eye on developments especially in government, the public sector and job opportunities for my life after the RAF.

One important development was keeping me very interested. The 1970 Wilson Government, especially the energetic Mrs Barbara Castle, was keen to reform industrial relations and the collective bargaining system with a view to reducing the extent of wildcat strikes, flying pickets, etc. which were disrupting production and distribution of manufactured goods. Reform of industrial relations was a priority.

So the Government decided to set up a royal commission under the chairmanship of Lord Donovan with the brief to come up with recommendations for the 'Reform of Industrial Relations in Great Britain'. The membership of the Donovan Commission was drawn from the highest level of both sides of the industry. In due course the commission reported to the Government with specific recommendations for implementation. One recommendation was to establish a commission on industrial relations (CIR), with powerful, heavyweight membership. The chairman was the recently retired general secretary of the TUC, Mr George Woodcock. The commission included Mr Will Paynter, the general secretary of the National Union of Mineworkers, and the director of industrial relations at Ford Motor Company. Barbara Castle was determined to introduce legislation based on the White Paper, 'In Place of Strife'.

While at RAF Swinderby I had time to start corresponding with the personnel director of the CIR, a senior civil servant, Mr Cliff Senior. The upshot was that he asked me to go and see him once I had left the RAF. He knew I had something to offer: Dartmouth, Unilever Pakistan and some job experience in Britain, plus my studies in economics and management. I felt sure that Mr Senior was satisfied that I had enough to build on. So the indications were that I could be appointed as an industrial relations officer.

The job, as I understood, would be interviewing, listening to the unions and management in selected firms and unions, analysis, consideration and making recommendations for reform. That was my broad-brush understanding of the nature of the job. Of course it was not that simple. Britain's best brains were assigned the task of reform of collective bargaining. It was going to take time. But as far as I was concerned I could see that the nature of the work would be just what I felt I would be good at: fact-finding, analysis, recommendations and implementation – the tools and methods of management consulting which I had picked up from my reading of a very important book on the subject by Milan Kubr of the UN International Labour Office (ILO), in Geneva.

Before I left the RAF, I was asked to go to see a group captain at the MoD regarding my wish to leave. At that meeting at Adastral House, the group captain asked me, 'Why do you want to leave? You are on a permanent commission. We see you retiring at least as a group captain.' I felt I could negotiate but I didn't want to. I had already passed the examinations for promotion to flight lieutenant and squadron leader. So I said, 'No, sir, having tasted industry I want to go back to industry. I have decided to leave the RAF. Thank you for your kind words. I am most grateful to the RAF for giving me the chance.' Upon return from London to Swinderby that evening, Anna and I discussed the next steps, like joining the CIR, buying a house and returning to what I wanted to do.

I was lucky to have been able to leave one job and walk into another. I was appointed an industrial relations officer at the CIR. I was assigned to a unit under a principal grade officer, Ms Coombe. To improve my understanding of industrial relations and collective bargaining in Britain, I was gratified by Ms Coombe's interest in me. She gave me files to review, books to read; her guidance meant that very quickly I was moved on to the operational side of the CIR, working on the Government's 'references' for reform. Successively, I worked on the following references: (i) disclosure of information by employers to trade unions for the purpose of collective bargaining; (ii) Williams and Glyn's Bank – recognition of unions for collective bargaining. Disclosure reference was fascinating. I worked in a team led by a senior industrial relations officer (SIRO – a lady) and three IROs. In order to review how collective bargaining and trade union relations were conducted in certain countries of Europe, our team, led by Peter Carr (later to become labour attaché at the British Embassy in Washington, D.C.), visited Belgium, France and Holland. Another team visited Germany, Italy and Luxembourg. Our team interviewed many people from both sides of industry in these European countries, collected evidence, analysed it and then formulated recommendations. The delivery of disclosure reference took more than two years to completion and publication of the CIR's report to the Government. This got extensive coverage in the press. All through the process, the responsible commissioners steered the study to what was to be seen as a monumental piece of work. My work with the team on the Williams and Glyn's Bank union recognition reference was less glamorous. It was mainly completed in the City of London, in the space of one year, culminating in the very conservative bank giving recognition to its union. The other reference I was involved in was trade union recognition in the banking, insurance and finance sector. Very similar in genre to the Williams and Glyn's Bank reference, this much larger reference in the banking insurance and finance industry brought landmark reforms in that sector.

The work in the CIR gave me an understanding of how you do fact-finding and analysis, and develop recommendations for implementation. One of my bosses at PA International Management Consultants, Brian Shaw, said to me when we were working on a World Bank-funded PA assignment for the Government of the Sudan, 'Suhail, can you find out some information from Syed Tawfiq in your inimitable style?' Tawfiq was the managing director of the Mechanised Farming Corporation, the head office organisation in the rain-fed agriculture sector of the Sudan. The process gave me experience of interface work with senior people in industry and commerce. I found my naval and RAF training, and my time in CIR, gave me insight into human relations, working with people at all levels, providing acceptable outcomes for consultancy assignments.

In all these situations I interfaced with senior managers, directors, trade union officials and shop stewards. I felt I won their acceptance; my self-confidence was building. I could see my future in Britain was going to be good for me and my young family. There is no doubt that the commissioned service in the RAF gave me a lift-off in Britain. With that foundation I could move on.

I worked at the CIR from the time I left the RAF in 1970 to 1973. Then I moved on to Ford Motor Company, first in the Forward Planning and

Policy division, dealing with central labour relations under the leadership of Paul Roots and John Hougham, very senior labour relations managers who reported to the director of industrial relations, Mr Bob Ramsey. My immediate line manager was Peter Matthews, a very bright labour relations man. I was once asked by Paul Roots to go over to the trucks and tractors plant in Slough and help the local managers over the problem of providing prayer facilities for the large number of Pakistani Muslim workmen at the plant. After some months, I was sent to the hot frontline of Dagenham body plant, always in the national news for the presence of strong shop stewards, the most famous being Mr Jack McCray, the shop steward at the body plant. I was a personnel officer with four others, reporting to the plant personnel manager, Jack Scrutton, a fine young, very capable IR manager. Once Jack McCray came into my office and said, 'Suhail, the carousel has been stopped. Until we have resolved the problem in hand quickly, the whole plant will stop.' This was the nature of Ford Dagenham's industrial relations; witness *The Daily Telegraph*'s banner headline: 'That lot are out again'. The importance of the Labour Government's strategy for the reform of industrial relations and collective bargaining through the Donovan Commission and Barbara Castle's White Paper, 'In Place of Strife', was becoming evident.

My preparation for entering management consulting

My preparation continued when I was almost headhunted as a personnel officer (information and research), at the Pedigree Petfoods division of the Mars Group, based in Melton Mowbray. I reported to David Drennan, an accomplished personnel professional. The first piece of work was to research pay and conditions in most of the major companies in the Midlands and the North – Shell, Lever Brothers Port Sunlight, Metal Box – and many others in our sample. I formed my team of two with a colleague of mine who had a background in production, rather an enigmatic person, but very open in his rapport. He was called Dennis Toon, an elderly personnel convert. We drove to all these companies to collect data in order to ensure that Pedigree Petfoods' position remained well above the median of wages, terms and conditions of service in the region. Later I was asked by Drennan to compile a history of wages movement in the company going back to the establishment of the Melton Mowbray plant. When I finished this work, contained in large blue hard-cover ledgers, Drennan was heard to say with great satisfaction, 'I knew he would do it!' But just before that, hardly a year into my job in Melton Mowbray, Drennan called me into his office and asked, 'Suhail, how would you like to become personnel manager at Mars' new Kenco coffee-making plant in Slough, next to Mars' UK chocolate-making operations [Mars Bars' production facility]?' The suggestion was made because I was a Muslim. The job was relevant for me because of my personnel management (now called 'human resources' – HR) background and the very large number of Asians, predominantly Pakistani Muslims, in Mars' Slough employment. I talked it over with Anna. We had just bought a lovely house in a nice part of Nottingham – Trevor Road, West Bridgford. Every morning my fourteen-mile drive to work to Melton took me through the beautiful Vale of Belvoir. Lisa was attending a nice primary school. Anna was happy setting up our home in a beautiful detached house with a large garden in a very quiet residential area. We thought about the Slough job offer but decided to decline. It would have been too much disruption after such a short time after the move.

Again, looking back, was it a mistake? I don't know. It was a personnel manager job, at a new plant of Mars. Not accepting definitely slowed me down on catching up on my career, because my later experience at the Petfoods plant took me on to night shift. Night shifts were dreadful. I felt demeaned. Performing as a personnel officer on a night shift producing cat and dog foods was humiliating. I took to drinking pints of beer, sleeping during the day, leaving home at 9pm, getting to the plant at 10pm for the night shift to 6am. I did it for a few months, then felt enough was enough. It seemed I generated some unfortunate aggravation amongst my personnel and production line colleagues. The resentment had, I think, a racial aspect. The shift supervisor told people I was not showing an interest in night-shift work, and that I was not seen on the production floor with the workmen. He was not far wrong, though I participated as much as I could. My line manager, Roger Chatterton, a very bright manager of the Mars Group, called me in for a chat. He had written down a number of 'concerns' about me. I interrupted his narrative. I was quite upset. I told him that the night-shift work was harmful to my family and me. I requested a move. The next morning I was moved to a 'non-job' in an office with another personnel officer who had also come off night shifts. Our job was to review the daily press cuttings being sent every day by an agency, consider which were relevant to any aspect of the business and then send them on to the directors concerned. It was extremely boring and probably a bit of a punishment!

Shortly after, my interest in the race relations field was bearing results. These activities gave me exposure to job opportunities in community and race relations following the new legislation on these race relations. I applied for a job opportunity I saw in *The Sunday Times* for a director, General Services Division, at the newly established Commission for Racial Equality, with David Lane, a former Home Office minister. His board comprised white, Asian and black commissioners. Out of more than a hundred applicants, white, brown and black, eight were shortlisted. I beat off the competition and got the job. It was a completely new field except that I had suffered some subtle racial discrimination, and was aware of the complexity and uphill struggle in the achievement of good race relations in the UK. There were friends amongst the commissioners: the late Pranlal Sheth, a top executive in an American insurance company in the City of London, and Mrs Anowara Jahan, a fellow Bangladeshi lady involved in community and social work, and some others I knew or had heard of such as Councillor Bashir Maan, from Glasgow. His resentment of me was obvious; he had wanted a Pakistani to be appointed.

I was shortlisted for the position of director, General Services Division, at the Commission for Racial Equality. I travelled from Nottingham, was interviewed and offered the job the same evening.

On the following morning I had a longish chat with David Drennan, the Mars personnel director. We chose the factory canteen for our discussion over tea to avoid generating derogatory gossip! We discussed and agreed my departure terms, the wording of the company notice to go on the noticeboard. A nicely worded notice was put out. I invited colleagues to a farewell drink at the local pub. Some colleagues attended. There was no 'farewell party' for me. That was that!

David Drennan did one positive thing for me, however. The Confederation of British Industry (CBI) was inviting companies to nominate people with a personnel management/industrial relations background to sit as members of industrial tribunals (employers' panel). Drennan nominated me to the CBI who then put forward my name to the Secretary of State for

Employment and I was duly accepted to sit as a member of the Employers Panel on Industrial Tribunals for England and Wales. The tribunals consisted of three members: one independent chairman with legal experience, usually a judge, one employers' representative and one trade union representative. This nomination meant that I continued as a member for many years, later to be included as a member of the race relations panel to sit on race cases.

After a period of four years, 1974 to 1978, I left Pedigree Petfoods. I would like to thank them, as well as the Civil Service and the Royal Air Force, for their help in granting me time off and help with the fees and purchase of books to pursue my studies for the Diploma in Management Studies (DMS), BSc(Econ)(London) and MSc(Econ)(London). Their willing co-operation was extremely important to me in getting ahead in Britain.

As I have mentioned elsewhere, I began to be noticed by the Labour Government. I got appointed to cabinet ministers' ministerial councils on race relations and immigration and other matters. My work at the CRE was relatively short-lived. It was an organisation with innumerable problems. My only significant achievement at the CRE was following Bill Reddin's book *Managerial Effectiveness*. I wanted to bring about some order and effectiveness, and indeed some efficiency at the CRE – which truly was chaotic! I got Bob Busvine, a senior management consultant in organisation development, a fellow of the Institute of Management Consultant (IMC) whom I knew as an IMC member, where I was also a fellow. Bob had the franchise for Bill Reddin (of Canada)'s Managerial Effectiveness Seminars (MES) which he was using in a large number of UK organisations, public and private, to bring about organisational development. With support from David Lane, the chairman, Clifton Robinson, the deputy chairman, and Peter Tucker, CRE's chief executive, I took the senior managers for an overnight workshop to a good hotel in Eastbourne, Sussex. The seminar went well. I was sure that the workshop input did some good at the top layer of management. But improvement down the line depended on leadership, performance and commitment of the attendees at the seminar. Bob heard some derogatory comments about me; I knew there was an extreme level of jealousy against me. Indians thought, *How come a Bangladeshi got the job?* Pakistani staff thought similarly: *Why not one of them?*

The internal problems of the CRE gave rise to the 'Review of CRE's

Efficiency and Effectiveness' by the Home Affairs Select Sub-Committee, culminating in a report recommending action by the commission.

David Lane and his colleagues got into a panic. They appointed a working party. The chief executive, Peter Tucker, wrote damning reports on four officers, but exonerating himself. The working party's recommendation was that two directors – me, an Asian, and a white, Charles Boxer, should go, together with two principals: Sydney Roper, white and Crispin Cross, black. This 'balancing act', hotch potch of a solution was short-lived. Once it reached the Home Office, the senior civil servants in the industrial relations department ruled that all four officers should be reinstated because the CRE had not followed the 'procedure'. Basically, none of the four officers had been given a chance to reply. My wife took a call from a Bangladeshi commissioner, Mrs Lulu Bilkis Bano, asking if I would call her back. I did not bother to reply. Likewise Charles Boxer had already resigned having been tipped off; Crispin Cross declined to go back. Only Sydney Roper went back but assigned to Edinburgh office. *The Times* reporter Lucy Hodges wrote a piece in May 1981 calling it, 'A fiasco over a working party'!

After leaving the CRE in 1981, I undertook a trip to Africa. I went to Salisbury, Rhodesia (now Harare, Zimbabwe) to assist my brother, Tabib Ibne Aziz, to explore business opportunities in jute manufactured goods exports from Bangladesh to Zimbabwe and one or two other countries in Africa – the Sudan and South Africa – also Iraq (a peaceful country then), and jute traders in Glasgow. I made good progress in finding one or two buyers. But the role of my brother as 'middleman' was a problem, that is to say, despite the goodwill I achieved with some potential buyers, after applying a margin for us, our price quotes were found to be uncompetitive. So I drew a blank with my brother's venture in trading in jute goods in Africa. I could not join him. This was not a viable route for me to enter business.

After leaving the CRE, two developments occurred. I was still feeling a pull towards Bangladesh. If I got a suitable job there I might return. So, I made an approach to the British American Tobacco (BAT) industries. They interviewed me after making enquiries from the Bangladesh High Commission. I met Mr Robin Keast, BAT man in Dhaka. A very attractive job offer was made. But after careful consideration by both of us, and as I was already making headway in England, I declined.

Similarly ICI was advertising for their chairman in Bangladesh. I applied, was interviewed at their London headquarters on Millbank, London, and was a finalist in their shortlist. After a few months, they came back to say, 'Mr Aziz, you would be an outstanding candidate except for one issue and that is that you have been outside Bangladesh for some considerable time, things have changed, especially in labour relations, therefore we have decided not to offer you the chairmanship of ICI Bangladesh.' I understood their wise decision.

Thus, altogether I had three top-level job offers inviting me for return to Bangladesh: Burma Oil Company (BOC), British American Tobacco (BAT) and Imperial Chemical Industries (ICI). I declined because Anna and I felt that we were making progress and were happy remaining in England.

After CRE I joined PA and worked on assignments in the Sudan. After about three years they ended. I was again looking for an appropriate opening. I saw in the Guardian an advertisement by the London Borough of Lewisham for the head of their employment and economic development division. I applied and was selected. I recall the vice-chairman of the Employment and Industry Committee saying, 'Today we hired the future Chief Executive of Lewisham Council.'

There was a flourishing organisation in the country, the brainchild of a man called Stephen O'Brien. It was called Business in the Community (BitC). Its mission was to engage with local communities, using its influence to bring large private sector organisations such as banks, City corporations, charitable arms of companies and others in public and private sectors into partnership for regeneration of deprived areas of inner-city London boroughs. My first port of call was BitC. Through them, and through my own contacts and connections in the Government and industry, I was successful in obtaining the support of organisations such as the Home Office, Lloyds and TSB, and the Wellcome Foundation. The Deptford Enterprise Agency was set up with the participation of these organisations under the chairmanship of the Employment and Industry Committee of the council. The word went round. With the Department of Trade and Industry (the old DTI under Michael (now Lord) Heseltine) we had a very successful conference at the council with full participation of neighbouring boroughs – Greenwich, Southwark, Lambeth. We all recognised that employment and regeneration efforts were linked; nothing was to be achieved in isolation. But my chief executive had made it clear to me that all the money had to be new money, not diverting funds from the council's numerous other activities ('the additionality test').

As in economic cycles of ups and downs, in a way there are cyclical ups and downs in human relations in any organisation. Old, successful people depart; new people come in; new agendas are set; new organisational cultures replace the old; thus organisational lives continue. General success continues but disasters, too, happen! The departure of my vice-chairman, Dave Harker, was significant. The Labour-controlled council had a strong group of women councillors earnestly committed to empowerment of women. One evening in 1988, there was a 'coup' at a Labour councillors' meeting. A group of women councillors, hitherto serving on various council committees at member level, not in lead positions like chair or vice-chair, succeeded in toppling all the male chairs and vice-chairs of every single committee of the council. My committee, the Employment and Industry Committee, was no exception. My chair and vice-chair, Cllrs Ron Stockbridge and Dave Harker, were respectively replaced by Cllr Mary Edmund and one other woman councillor.

I had been hopeful that, having single-handedly succeeded in the establishment of the Deptford Enterprise Agency, I would have the participation of Cllrs Stockbridge and Harker to lead DEA's Public-Private-Partnership (PPP) efforts. But that was not to be. Soon afterwards, Dave Harker departed for his London Business Sschool top management course. Ron Stockbridge, disheartened, persevered for a while. Having established the DEA, I was looking forward to being its first officer-director and giving effect to the dreams of bringing back Deptford into economic life. That hope too was dashed to the ground by the coup. The two councillors who had recruited me were gone. The writing was on the wall. Soon after, I left to enter management consulting in some of the third world countries. The two women councillors, as the new chair and vice-chair of the Employment and Industry Committee, took the chair and deputy chair positions at the DEA. They recruited a new manager to head up DEA. My satisfaction is that the DEA continued and proved to be the engine for growth. Today Deptford is a thriving area, full of economic activities, new shops, enterprises, new housing and community life.

Chapter Six

Race relations

It was 1956, my first year at the Britannia Royal Naval College Dartmouth. I was in the midshipmen's gunroom reading papers. I recall reading a piece in *The Daily Telegraph* about 'immigration'. Looking back I think that was the first time I had read anything about how race and colour were beginning to become a political issue and how it was to become people's major concern in Britain. I have mentioned the occasion when at the cadets' monthly dinner night at PNS *Himalaya*, our cadet training officer, Lt Cdr Anwar Sayeed, said something about problems facing coloured people in Britain. How the subject came up was thus: most of the cadets in our batch were from West Pakistan, they were mostly fair-skinned, contrasting with Bengalis from East Pakistan who were, like me, of a darker shade. One cadet made a comment that 'colour would not be a problem for them' implying that they (from West Pakistan) were generally fair-skinned. I was the only one out of the whole batch of eight cadets from the east wing of Pakistan present at the dinner but the cadet in question displayed no tact or sensitivity. I thought Lt Cdr Sayeed batted brilliantly to quash the 'skin colour superiority' of the cadet. He said various shades of skin colour did not matter in England, because all shades of skin colour are grouped as 'coloured'! Sayeed had been to England before for staff training, procuring ships from the Royal Navy for the Pakistan Navy, and he had served as a naval adviser at the Pakistan High Commission in London. So he knew what he was talking about. I, of course, did not have any understanding of the issues surrounding skin colour or how important it would become in the race and community relations scenes of Great Britain. Looking back, I was a bit naive.

In that piece in *The Daily Telegraph*, I read that Mr R. A. (Rab) Butler was Home Secretary in the Tory Government of Mr Harold Macmillan. I recall comments by liberal-minded politicians that immigration must not become a 'political football', that all citizens of the Commonwealth had an inherent right to come and go freely as they wished from Britain – the mother of the Commonwealth.

Ten years later when I came to England in 1966, I began to see how emotions were rising in some parts of the country against large-scale coloured immigration. The Government had to act to calm those fears, so it was planning to bring in restrictions on coloured immigration from the new Commonwealth for the first time. There was, of course, opposition to the Government's proposal but Mr Butler, as Mr Macmillan's Home Secretary, tried to calm fears and concerns from both sides – the host community and the immigrant communities from the West Indies, Indian subcontinent, parts of East Africa and so on. Faced with serious opposition Rab Butler was quoted as saying Government would 'apply the new rules benignly'. One has to ask: where are we now in 2020? Not just with coloured immigration, which has long since been drastically controlled, but Britain has become hostile to Europeans from Eastern and Central Europe. Numbers became a grave issue of concern, so much so that the majority of British people voted for Brexit! We wait to see how far that debate about Brexit takes us.

Coloured immigration is severely and almost inhumanely restricted. Deportation is frequent. The treatment of black and Asian people at Britain's detention centres is of concern to human rights groups. The Joint Council for Welfare of Immigrants (JCWI) files are full of horror stories about the treatment meted out to these immigrants. Mr Butler would be turning in his grave if he knew how 'benignly' (sic) the immigration rules of which he was the architect are being applied by the British authorities! People are refused entry, kept in detention cells like criminals, entry visas are ingeniously denied. The law is not 'benignly' applied. Colour of the skin and where one comes from in the new Commonwealth is generally an issue in today's Britain.

As I have described, Britannia Royal Naval College Dartmouth would arrange through the Victoria League and the Royal Overseas League for cadets/midshipmen to go and stay with British families during the college's Easter, summer or Christmas breaks. To this day friendships made in those days are amongst my happy memories.

Never in those associations with British families was I made to feel that I was coloured. But as the late Alex Lyon MP used to say: 'It was not racism as such. It was a feeling of "strangeness and foreignness".' He believed that familiarity, social interaction, working together and getting to know people overcame prejudices. I think this has already happened in Britain. I never had the feeling that I was somehow inferior because of the colour of my skin, although upon analysis of my later years in England I would conclude that my race or colour or my foreign name must have played an important part in the treatment I received in particular situations.

The class-conscious British society (as seen in the TV series *Upstairs Downstairs* or *Downton Abbey*) discriminates even against its own blue-collar white working class. There is discrimination regionally; one only has to ask someone from the North East, the North West, or someone from Ireland, Scotland or Wales. There is no doubt that society as a whole regards black and Asian people as inferior. The law cannot be expected to eradicate all prejudices; it can't get into people's minds. But, to quote Lord Bonham Carter again: 'Legal sanction in the background is a vital persuader.' In my view the law has largely worked in Britain in combatting various forms of overt or covert discrimination. We are not there yet, there is still some way to go. But undoubtedly enormous strides have been made.

I have served on several bodies which were set up by governments to improve relations between a diverse range of people who have chosen Britain as their home. The positive endeavours have largely come from Labour governments. Service on these bodies has given me some experience, impressions and insights. My service has been on a voluntary basis.

Over the years, I have been very fortunate to come into contact with people, such as the late Lord Mark Bonham Carter, Mr John Little, Sir Geoffrey Bindman QC, Sir Geoffrey Wilson, Mr Tom Connelly, Mr Richard Mills at the Gulbenkian Foundation, and many other leading figures in government and in black and Asian communities. Working with them in so many forums has, of course, been an honour, but more importantly it has given me a better understanding of race relations in Britain over the recent past.

My service on race bodies

Happily, during the early 1970s I felt I began to get noticed by government ministers. Even though I was unsuccessful for a job as an assistant conciliation officer, Mark Bonham Carter and John Little, chairman and chief officer of the Race Relations Board respectively, selected me to serve on the North Metropolitan Conciliation Committee of the Race Relations Board set up under the 1968 Race Relations Act. I also served on the community relations councils (CRCs) in Tower Hamlets and Nottingham. At Tower Hamlets I was instrumental in the preparation and submission of their views on the Home Affairs Select Sub-Committee's Report, 'Bangladeshis in Britain'. This report recommended action in the areas of housing, health, education, employment and community centres. I led the examination of these issues and assisted in the drawing up of an implementation plan.

At the Nottingham CRC, with a strong recommendation from Sir Geoffrey Wilson, chairman of the Race Relations Board, I was appointed chairman of the Employment Sub-Committee. Nottingham's employers were mostly white and employees were also generally white. Immigrant workers – Pakistanis, West Indians mainly – were employed in lower-grade manual jobs. The attitude of employers, even of some trade unions was: 'no problems here!' Thus it was felt that all was well. But deeper race problems were there; the difference was that those difficulties were not aired or were brushed under the carpet. When one saw the absence of black or Asian supervisors, not to mention managers, in a semi-skilled workforce in a factory, one has to ask, why? That sometimes ruffled feathers! A defence mechanism came into play. The nature of prejudice and its expression in behaviour is a very complex phenomenon. Unless all parties are committed to doing something to eradicate the underlying currents of discrimination, very little will change. 'Resistance to change' in any organisation in any aspect of its life is profound to start with. In my experience this gets more difficult if the 'change process' means that people keep their prejudices inside them, but take no steps to modify their expression in behaviour in relation to recruitment, training, promotion, discipline, participation in trade union activities. I was fortunate to have the total support of my employment sub-committee in Nottingham in aiming to bring about changes to employment practices by Nottingham and District employers. Happily my sub-committee had some excellent committed members on it. The lead given by David Purdy, the community relations officer (CRO) of Nottingham CRC, was worthy of note. He was relaxed, always approachable, including at his home for meetings – totally committed to race equality and justice.

The Rt Hon. Roy Jenkins (later Sir and Lord) and Merlyn Rees (later Lord) as home secretaries in the last Wilson governments selected me with a few others from black and Asian communities, to serve on the Home Secretary's Standing Advisory Council on Race Relations and Immigration. Our names were deliberately 'leaked' to the press (I saw my name with a few others in *The Daily Telegraph* at the time) before the Home Secretary issued his letters of invitation to us before making the appointments. This was the age-old practice of government to 'test the water', to suss out if there were hidden matters, 'skeletons in the cupboard', which needed to come out through objections from any member of the public or the black or Asian community before public appointments, such as the membership of the Home Secretary's Advisory Council, were made. This process allowed rare mistakes to be rectified in time. Minority community members had been found to be 'cooking up' or 'doctoring' their CVs to make them stronger, quoting academic qualifications they did not possess. False claims were very damaging to our image as black or Asian people. It took a very long time to recover from this kind of reputational damage.

About the same time, in the late 1970s, another body was set up: the Department of Employment Race Relations Employment Advisory Group, chaired by the Secretary of State for Employment, Mr John Grant MP. I felt honoured to have been selected as a member on this council; membership included, amongst others: the chairman of the Manpower Services Commission; David Lane, chairman of the Commission for Racial Equality; government departmental representatives; weighty representatives from national employers and trade unions; and minority groups and voluntary organisations.

I served about two years on these two councils before I resigned to avoid 'conflict of interest' upon joining the Commission for Racial Equality (CRE) in 1978, a government body under the Home Office. As a director and member of the top management team, my chairman, Mr David Lane, and I, could not, in my view, serve on the ministerial advisory councils at the same time. Issues were bound to come up, probably impacting on the work of the CRE itself, which would generate a conflict of interest. There was no suggestion from anyone that I should step down. It was completely my decision. However, I ought to say that I resigned from the councils with some regret. I believe that I could have continued to make a valuable contribution even when I became a senior official of the CRE. So I resigned from the Home Secretary's Standing Advisory Council on Race Relations and Immigration and the Department of Employment Race Relations Employment Advisory Group (DE-RREAG). Accolades not to be easily won but there you are!

I will now comment on the working of the Home Secretary's Standing Advisory Council on Race Relations and Immigration, as I saw it. The commentary below largely applies to the DE-RREAG as well, so I won't repeat.

The working of the Home Secretary's Advisory Council was largely, in my view, ineffective. The body was too large, some 20–25 members, I think, plus a number of senior civil servants from departments in attendance for relevant agenda items. It would be chaired by the Home Secretary himself. Mr Merlyn Rees MP was the chairman during my time. He allowed free and open discussions and controlled the meetings well. Membership from the Asian communities – Indian, Pakistani, Bangladeshi, Sri Lankan – made up a cohesive body. Jealousy and resentment amongst us Asians was not apparent. Proceedings were civilised. But in the 1970s, Bangladesh having just been born in 1971 after a bloody campaign and a war, there was an undercurrent of jealousy, even mild hatred, between Pakistanis and Bangladeshis in the wider world, and this was reflected in the council.

Civil servants would be taking note at the meetings and giving the official lines on issues. But one got the feeling that no matter what was discussed and what contributions were made by members of the council, whether action would ensue was uncertain. When the minutes of the meetings came out, one could see the skill and ingenuity of the civil servants in polishing them up, whilst at times losing the impact of the discussions. So it was safe to conclude that, no matter what, the die would already be cast on all the issues, thus ministerial councils lost their value and became, in due course, no more than 'talking shops'. One senior civil servant (a PhD) told me over a drink at a pub outside the Home Office: 'I would not recommend any of my friends to become a member of the Home Secretary's Advisory Council.' Plainly he was implying that the council's deliberations were not worth the paper they were written on!

It would perhaps be agreed by many within the black and Asian communities that the Government frequently used the ploy of setting up a body and appointing minority members – but those bodies achieved very little. There was, therefore, an element of dishonesty in setting them up. These bodies were not renowned for glowing success, though some were better than others.

Some of us would feel honoured to be invited by the Home Secretary or other ministers to serve on these advisory bodies. As the deliberations proceeded, members would be keen to make a contribution. They were not equally gifted as effective speakers. So when they wished to say something important, the body language of the chair and officials could be off-putting. Their contributions would not be given due weight – at least that would be the perception, rightly or wrongly, of the contributors. As a result such members would eventually withdraw, to the detriment of the bodies concerned.

There was another off-putting feature: some members' attempts to speak would simply be ignored. Sometimes they would keep trying to catch the eye of the chairman, but they would not be called. Such little things slowly build up as a big problem in the minds of such members, so they cool off; slowly they would begin to feel demotivated and absent themselves from meetings. They would finally withdraw – resign – or feel they had had enough humiliation. So the enthusiasm with which one joined waned or dissipated.

There was a more serious consequence of these withdrawal symptoms from these councils or forums or advisory bodies. There was no doubt that government wished to hear what the ethnic minority groups wanted, what their hopes and aspirations were; what they would want from the agencies set up to generate employment, build houses, provide education, NHS services. Governments always say that disadvantaged groups must be provided for, to assist the process of integration and social cohesion.

Enormous funds are allocated and spent. So these provisions must be taken up. The Government, local authorities and their agencies would genuinely want to hear minority views. For this reason governments set up advisory bodies. The contradiction was that once members of minority groups joined with high expectations, their interest was not allowed to flourish; they were largely ignored for the reasons alluded to above; their interest was not sustained – not fitting into the 'accepted demeanours' – so demotivation set in. Time and again I have seen how an English chairman – man or woman – lacked the skill and ability to make such members feel at ease and valued. If people are not made to feel welcome, or if they get an impression that they are simply tolerated, then the value of these forums is lost. And sadly, the supply of members of high quality from the ethnic minority communities slowly dries up; they withdraw because they do not see any point in wasting their time or exposing themselves to humiliation.

This is a policy question. Unless the authorities recognise this aspect of the problem, we are not going to make much progress in obtaining whole-hearted participation of high-calibre people from ethnic minority groups. The responsibility rests with both sides. The host white authorities need to be more aware and sensitive to the feelings of minority members on various bodies; and the minority ethnic people need to be more assertive in ensuring that their views are heard and not to give up because of a single negative experience. They should not be sitting quietly to be ignored. Training should be given to both sides: how to be sensitive, how to be assertive. The beneficial effect would be felt by white, black and Asian communities to the benefit of society as a whole.

There was an event of strategic importance organised by the Gulbenkian Foundation in the late 1970s. The event was titled 'Black People in Britain – the Way Forward'. I was fortunate to be associated with Gulbenkian initiatives at the time; under the forceful and sensitive leadership of Richard Mills, the foundation's assistant director, things of import were happening. Black meant black and Asians. The conference was held over two days at a major hotel's conference centre in central London. Worthy speakers – white, Asian and black – from government and voluntary organisations, well informed on issues facing us, addressed the conference. The steering committee for the conference came from a diverse background. Its membership included

Jocelyn Barrow (later Dame), Phil Sealey, Professor Stewart, Dr Sayeed, myself and one or two other ethnic minority members, plus of course Richard Mills – and the foundation's director on occasion. The energy level at the above conference was electric! We all felt very hopeful. In a very big way I believe it gave confidence to ethnic minority leadership that indeed we could push ahead in Britain. Black participation everywhere improved. We felt we could be more assertive. A conference report was produced and distributed widely, including to relevant government departments.

Following this conference, an advisory committee of the foundation was set up. I was invited to be a member of that body to advise on matters which impacted on minority peoples in Britain. I served on it for some years. That was the time when I was a personnel officer at Pedigree Petfoods, and later to become a director of the CRE. I felt I was assertive enough to make a contribution to discussions of the advisory committee without being ignored. I felt valued, which helped my motivation to continue on the committee.

We have seen the setting up of 'inquiries' under High Court judges to look into the causes of particular disturbances, e.g. the Brixton riots, the Lewisham riots, the Broadwater Farm disturbance, the Macpherson inquiry, the Croydon riots. Government would set up inquiries to determine causes and make recommendations for implementation. Reports would be written with recommendations for action. Over the years we have seen such reports gathering dust instead of the well-intentioned recommendations being implemented. The Lawrence Inquiry Report by Sir William Macpherson found racism in the Metropolitan Police. The judge made a large number of evidence-based recommendations for the Met Police to implement. After all these years we still have the same sort of view amongst black communities: 'The Met Police is racist.' Inquiries have been used as 'shock absorbers' to defuse situations – a process frequently referred to as 'kicking it into the long grass'! The deaths of young black people in police custody have aroused anger, suspicion and agitation among minority groups such as the West Indian community. The Independent Police Complaints Commission (IPCC) would promise to investigate but their reports were frequently seen as no more than 'whitewash', with no teeth to bring the offenders to book or victims to get justice.

However, personally I think I could claim some success during my membership of the Home Secretary's Advisory Council. When the 1976 Race Relations Bill was going through Parliament, I wrote to Mr Roy Jenkins, Home Secretary at the time, proposing that a strongly worded clause should be included in the Act to stop 'victimisation' by employers against employees for raising a complaint at industrial (later called 'employment') tribunals, for generating a grievance by an employee at the workplace or for trade union activities. I was pleased to see a strong 'victimisation' clause in the Act.

Commission for Racial Equality (CRE)

Statutory bodies were established by government under the Race Relations Act but how did they work? The Commission for Racial Equality (CRE) was a body established under the 1976 Race Relations Act. Was it successful, and if not, why not? How did black and minority ethnic people view these statutory bodies? How did the majority white society view them? Did they accept their mission and work? What about these bodies' efficiency and effectiveness, their fitness for purpose? I consider these issues here from my personal experience.

A name for the new commission!

I, as a member of the Home Secretary's Advisory Council, and a few others from the West Indian and Asian communities met David Lane, chairman-designate of the new commission to be set up under the 1976 Act, at the offices of the late Courtney Laws, chairman of the Brixton Neighbourhood Community Association (BNCA) and a member-designate of the commission. The sole agenda item was what should be the name of this new body.

David had given up his Cambridge seat as an MP after he saw there was no chance of a front-bench post for a politician like him. He had been a junior Home Office minister during the Thatcher period, but I think that after John Major became Prime Minister, he felt his chances of another ministerial post were much diminished. So when he was called upon to take on the role as chairman-designate, he took up the offer. He was an extremely bright person, serious and a fine gentleman. He had a fair knowledge of Indian subcontinent politics. His brother was in India. David frequently visited India to keep in touch with him. I guess David used his brother's advice in handling some of the commissioners from the subcontinent, like Pranlal Sheth (Indian), Cllr Bashir Maan (Pakistani), Mrs Anowara Jahan (Bangladeshi)! He knew their co-operation and advice would be needed for the success of the commission.

First, what was to be the name of the commission? The Government wanted a 'soft' name, such as Race Relations Commission or Community Relations Commission. They had to be careful not to antagonise the white majority in society. The body must not be seen to be aggressive or antagonistic or provocative by extreme right-wingers. Co-operation, acceptance, understanding and support of the white society for the new commission was rightly seen as very important.

However, I saw this as an opportunity to try to obtain the maximum benefit from the new 1976 Act. So I felt that the name of the commission should reflect what we wanted most from its operations. Our main concern was how to achieve 'race equality'. Equality and justice were the main objectives in our minds. In housing, education, employment, health and social services we wanted equal opportunities, fair treatment, free from discrimination or prejudice because of the colour of our skin. We wanted talent amongst us to be recognised without bias. I realised these objectives and wishes would be seen as ambitious and hard to achieve. I felt that we had to be realistic. I knew that basically British society was fair-minded and that there was a way to obtain things from the white people in power, without making them antagonistic. We wanted to play a full and fulfilling role in British society. In politics, for example, we wanted our people to get equal opportunities to become councillors and Members of Parliament. So a strong and powerful commission, armed with strong powers for 'formal investigations', would be necessary to bring about changes in practices of business, industry, local and educational authorities, and in the provision of goods and services.

But I felt we were naive in one respect: the subtlety with which 'power' was exercised in British society had to be understood. Good race relations, equality and justice would have to be granted by the white majority society exercising power. They would be the people in authority, in local councils, in government departments, institutions, business and industry. Unless they were willing to meet our aspirations and demands, freely and willingly, there was no hope, no way of getting these peacefully. Riots and racial disturbance were counterproductive. Those methods did not achieve a great deal for the minorities. This approach would only be alienating white society; they would become quietly hostile. They would stigmatise Blacks and Asians as 'troublemakers'. So a sensible approach would be needed.

These issues were not considered by our meeting to choose the name of the new commission. The fact that the British had the historic experience of administering and governing the colonies of black and Asian people must not be forgotten – 'the sun never set on the British empire'! They knew how to play along until we were exhausted and gave up.

Anyway, that afternoon we were scratching our heads to find and agree a name. David Lane was in a hurry. He was pressing us hard to decide on a name acceptable to us and to the Home Secretary and his top civil service advisers. After a lot of thought and soul-searching we came up with the name: the Commission for Racial Equality (CRE). We wanted race equality to be powerfully promoted through the name.

David Lane left us with this name, CRE. We felt we had achieved something of historical significance. But little did we recognise that the new commission and the new legislation would succeed or fail depending on whether they got the acceptance and support of the white majority society. If there was not that acceptance and support, all the efforts would flounder, as indeed happened! Over the course of the following years the Home Office switched chairmanship of the CRE from David Lane to Peter Newsam (white), Michael Day (white), Herman Ousley (black), Gurbux Singh (Asian) and Trevor Phillips (black). But the performance, efficiency and effectiveness of the CRE spiralled steadily downwards until it became a lame duck.

The essence of the problem was that the CRE and the legislation underpinning it did not enjoy the acceptance, co-operation and support of the white majority society. The Confederation of British Industry (CBI) did not show great enthusiasm; their attitude was mainly 'no problems here'.

The Trades Union Congress (TUC) was generally supportive but to no great effect. And of course the champions such as the late Lord Bonham Carter, John Little, Geoffrey Bindman, Lord Anthony Lester, Lord Pitt, Frank Cousins and a few others were no longer around to champion equality and justice for the black and brown minority groups in Britain.

Sadly, in my view, the CRE failed to deliver strong formal investigations (FIs) to bring about change in the practices of employers and institutions. For example, race discrimination cases would be brought to industrial tribunals against major employers. Complainants mostly lost their cases in the face of highly skilled and professional legal representation lined up by the employers, supported by the CBI. The union representative(s) or a representative from the Citizens Advice Bureau (name since changed to Citizens Advice) or from the local Law Society could not win cases in the face of such formidable opposition. Often formal investigations launched by the CRE against large employers or institutions in order to bring about change in their practices would fail because of lack of co-operation by the CBI and other trade associations. So the CRE's efforts would be frustrated. The trade unions were not seen to be much better! Although they were supposed to represent their members (all members – black and Asian) at tribunals and elsewhere, more often than not, such support would be ineffectual and half-hearted, so the aggrieved complainant remained unhappy and disgruntled. To him or her, the law failed to give them justice. This frustration would not stop there. The news would spread like wildfire amongst the Blacks and Asians, who in turn lost their faith and any confidence in the working of the legislation or its implementing agencies such as the CRE, the network of local community relations councils (CRCs), employment tribunals and so on. Confidence in the workings of the system would be diminished.

The CRE came about through the merger of two previous bodies: the Race Relations Board (RRB) with its network of conciliation committees, and the Community Relations Commission (CRC) with its wide network of the local community relations councils (CRCs) up and down the country. Mr Mark Bonham Carter, John Little, Tom Connelly, the dedicated members of the board with a high-quality 'handpicked' staff, led the RRB's work. The work was legalistic and intellectually demanding, and RRB was a success, even to a degree winning acceptance from the majority society. In bringing about race legislation in the country, the work of Mark Bonham Carter, John Little, Geoffrey Bindman, Anthony Lester and some others must be recorded. They were stalwarts leading the campaign for fairness, equality and justice for all ethnic minorities in the country. I believe a lot happened because of the courage, influence and style of the work of Bonham Carter and his ability to penetrate the 'system'. A descendant of the Liberal Party establishment of Lord Asquith, he was a man who understood what was needed by way of leadership to bring about attitudinal changes amongst white society.

The other body in the merger, the Community Relations Commission (CRC), was a 'softer' body, quite ineffective in fact. Its history, however, is significant. The Archbishop of Canterbury and Frank Cousins, general secretary of the Transport and General Workers' Union (TGWU), had been its chairmen. Their objective was to bring about good relations between people of various backgrounds: relations between the white majority society and the new wave of coloured immigrants into Britain. No doubt the CRC achieved a lot and broke new ground. The local community relations councils (CRCs) mostly succeeded in bringing white and black and Asian people into contact with one another. In a lot of cases, however, their work was not much better than 'motherhood and apple pie', having cups of tea together in an English garden or a local church. Black and Asian activists frequently ignored these local efforts.

The problem was that, although the CRC spent a lot of taxpayers' money, its work lacked teeth. It was largely seen as an interracial 'talking shop'. It had little impact in terms of bringing about real change in black people's lives – for instance in getting a job or a promotion or dealing with a person's grievance at the workplace. But some well-intentioned white people recognised that at least efforts were being made in the locality to bring about good race relations.

As I have mentioned earlier, I was appointed a director of the CRE to lead one of the three divisions. The divisions were: (i) the Equal Opportunities Division led by a very able Peter Saunders – Peter and his entire team were from the old Race Relations Board; (ii) the Community Relations Division led by Charles Boxer, a former priest and experienced in local charities – Charles' team was largely inherited from the old Community Relations

Commission; and (iii) the General Services Division led by me. The last division was new. My staff were a 'mixed bag', some from the old RRB and some from the old CRC, some like myself newly recruited from outside 'the race relations industry'. Obviously this entire new team would take time to gel together to deliver its diverse range of tasks.

My appointment came about from an advertisement in *The Sunday Times*. I was in Nottingham in those days working at Pedigree Petfoods as a personnel officer. Even though I knew of developments in the race field I did not know this job advertisement was coming up. I let some of my friends know that I was applying. I got shortlisted and was invited to an interview. I travelled by train from Nottingham to London (not driving, as I felt I had to be clear-headed and not tired). I found that I knew some of the people on the panel. The chairman was David Lane. Other members were deputy chairman Clifton Robinson (a Jamaican), chief executive Peter Tucker (a former top civil servant from Sierra Leone), Pranlal Sheth (a distinguished Indian businessman from Gujarat and a personal friend from my conciliation committee days at the Race Relations Board), Cllr Bashir Maan (a Pakistani councillor on Glasgow City Council) and a Home Office official present as an observer. Everyone took their turn in asking me questions. I felt I had done reasonably well at the interview with no apparent slip-ups or mistakes. After a few days, one early evening the telephone rang at my home in Nottingham. It was David Lane. He said, 'Suhail, I am calling to say that the commission has decided to offer you the position as director of the General Services Division. Would you accept it?' Without hesitation I said, 'Yes, David, of course I accept, I am delighted, thank you.' Then he went on to say something puzzling! He said news about the appointment had already appeared in the press, did I know anything about it? I said I had no knowledge of this, in fact I didn't know what he was talking about! He sounded a note of warning that 'things must not be leaked to the press'. Of course I readily agreed.

After the telephone call, I ran and embraced Anna and said, 'I got it, I got it!' She was delighted. I was pleased to get the CRE job because after about three years I was becoming unhappy at Pedigree Petfoods. I was making no progress in my career.

At Pedigree Petfoods my personnel director was David Drennan, a professional personnel man, a likeable man. He had selected me for the personnel job. He was rather proud of having got me into Pedigree Petfoods. As an aside I might mention that one fine morning he had a visitor in his office. I popped in to ask him something. He took the opportunity to introduce me to his visitor rather glowingly: 'Meet Suhail Aziz. I got him recently. Background in Dartmouth, Unilever, Ford – not bad!' I shook hands with his visitor, asked David my question, got his answer and left his office.

At the CRE I encountered problems. I had had experience of working with ministers and civil servants on ministerial bodies and on the RRB conciliation committee. But I had no induction programme at the CRE. I was thrown in at the deep end, and didn't know what was expected of me. The internal politics and workings of the CRE were not easy to fathom. People of different races and cultures pulled the CRE in different directions. When I left the CRE in early 1981, after about three years, *The Daily Mail* published a cartoon about the CRE showing people of different colours and cultures going round and round in circles – precisely the perception of the right-wing media as well as of the white majority society! There was some truth in the cartoon. With weak management at the top, the CRE was bound to be a weak organisation.

The General Services Division had seven units, each headed by a principal-grade officer, and employed people of different races, different backgrounds, different nationalities: African, West Indian, British, Indian, Pakistani, a Bangladeshi (myself). The units were: (i) Personnel (ii) Training, (iii) Aid to Complainants, (iv) Information and PR, (v) Research, (vi) Legal and (vii) Accounts. When appointing me, there was an expectation that the focus would be on personnel management and organisational effectiveness.

But there were constraints to overcome:

Organisational politics: David Lane was a politician, not an organisation or business man. He was impetuous, wanting things to be implemented at speed. More often than not he would be frustrated by the slow speed at which things were done.

His deputy, Clifton Robinson, was a teacher by background, a fine West Indian gentleman, softly softly in his approach but not ruthless enough to tackle the organisational politics and malaise of the CRE. Once I remember talking about the weaknesses of the commission as I saw it. I said to him, 'Clifton, I think we need strong external input from an organisational development (OD) consultant. Two organisations have merged [RRB and CRC] to form the CRE but not enough thought has been given to how to make the new organisation become effective. I would like some money to be allocated from the division's budget to be spent on the CRE's organisational development.' Obviously I was lobbying Clifton for his support before I opened a discussion at the monthly meeting of the top team. His reply was lukewarm. Eventually he said, 'I thought we brought you in to do all this.' I was surprised by this comment. I decided to broach this with Peter Tucker. To my surprise he said, 'Yes, I think we should do it. You raise it at the next meeting and I will support your proposal.' At the following meeting of the top team I raised the matter again. Peter said, 'Yes, if Suhail wants to do it, I think we should support him to bring in an OD consultant. We should allow the money from his divisional budget.' This got carried. Robinson quietly acquiesced. I invited Bob Busvine, an OD consultant I knew from my own institute, the Institute of Management Consultants. I took the senior managers on an away day to Eastbourne. The Managerial Effectiveness Seminar (MES) had an important input into the CRE's organisational development over time; even though resentment of my initiative from certain long-term 'race relations industrialists' was to be expected.

The Home Office: The Home Office was in fact the CRE's real 'boss'. Any matter of significance, such as budget, premises or initiatives which might need the Home Secretary's prior approval, had to be vetted. For example, if the CRE wanted to launch a formal investigation into a major issue such as racial discrimination by public and private sector major employers, the Home Office's approval would have to be sought. Sometimes approval might not be forthcoming. For example, we felt that the CRE needed more accommodation, as Elliot House in Victoria was proving inadequate with the expansion of activities under the new 1976 Act. After a brief discussion at the management committee meeting, I, accompanied by a senior executive officer colleague from the personnel unit, went along to see accommodation at Centre Point, situated centrally, with good bus and Tube connections, at the junction of Tottenham Court Road and Oxford Street. We were shown round the available space over two or three floors. But the Home Office had already heard through its grapevine that I was taking this initiative to ease the congestion at the CRE. Before I could report back to Tucker, the Home Office has been on the phone to David Lane to tell him that they would not wear such 'posh' accommodation for the CRE: there would be a public outcry! Presumably, as a black people's outfit our office accommodation had to look 'poor'. So that was that! Staff were dismayed at the Home Office intervention. We stayed put at Elliot House. Such was the sensitivity of the Home Office about public reactions!

Organisational strengthening: I mentioned above that it was agreed by the top management that I should take steps to strengthen the new organisation. I contacted Bob Busvine, who I knew from my association with the Institute of Management Consultants and who agreed to take on the job. We agreed that we had to address issues at the senior level of management at the commission, i.e. directors and all principals and heads of units down to senior executive officer (SEO) level. Essentially he was to carry out an organisation review, with an away day programme over two days. I asked Sylvia Carr, my principal in charge of organisational and personnel section, to find a good hotel for the away day. Bob decided that he would use Bill Reddin (the Canadian organisational psychologist)'s Managerial Effectiveness Seminar (MES) methodology to assess the CRE's organisational needs. The two-day workshop took place at the Midland Hotel (I hope my memory is serving me right as to the name), one of the best in Eastbourne. Everyone got a chance to give a frank and open opinion and views about the functioning, constraints, organisational politics and racial tensions between the staff coming together from different cultures and backgrounds, and so on. At one point, Bob suggested that he and I went for walk along the promenade. He gave me some personal feedback: 'Suhail, you have got a very difficult job here. There is hostility and resentment personally against you, some of it arising from you being seen as an "outsider". I could only note what Bob said. Anyway, overall, there were signs that the CRE was becoming a more effective organisation.

I knew I would be undermined whenever the disaffected staff got a chance. There was a feeling of sour grapes, especially from the Pakistanis and Indians: 'How come a Bangladeshi could be brought in on top of us?' I knew that unsuccessful candidates should not be appointed to positions in the same organisation, where their disaffection could be vented and management undermined. They should either be made to leave, as indeed Tom Connelly had tried to do, or offered 'out of sight out of mind' type of appointments. This had happened, but the staff concerned were regularly coming to the head office, which gave them a chance to make mischief.

I recall an occasion when there was a small party taking place on the second floor, with the old CRC crowd present. My secretary, Antoinette Fernandes (an excellent, trustworthy secretary of Portuguese-Goanese Christian ancestry), told me about it. I was not invited. So I decided to gatecrash! I joined the party being attended by senior staff. I think Tucker was there too because he had his 'hotline' to certain officers who provided him with support from the black staff and the (mainly black) union officials over his problems with the chairman, David Lane, who reportedly never wanted Tucker as chief executive after Tom Connelly left. The directors, chairman and deputy chairman were not invited, nor were members of the Equal Opportunities Division – mostly white staff. As I entered, one officer, an Indian, drifted across the floor towards me and with a grin on his face, asked, 'Are you sure you are invited here?' I said, 'I know I am not invited but why do you, being a fellow Asian, make a point of not inviting me?' Soon after, I left the party, where I had not socialised or bothered to speak to senior staff members or Peter Tucker. I realised that the Asian staff member must have been relishing the thought that I was not invited. Doing things behind one's back or manufacturing rumours was a chronic disease at the CRE.

Community relations councils (CRCs): The pre-merger Community Relations Commission (CRC) had established a network of local community relations councils (CRCs) up and down the country. As I said before, their main function was to bring together local community leaders with a view to improving relations between people of various races and backgrounds. They were sometimes viewed as 'talking shops', achieving very little. A benefit was that local people saw that efforts were being made. Local councils would be composed of representatives of leading people from large businesses, trade unions, churchmen, women from local women's organisations. A CRC committee might consist of fifteen or so members, one of whom would be elected chairman. In my experience there were good CRCs and poor, disfunctioning ones. They received funding from the CRE. A principal officer in charge of administering the CRCs. Their funding and monitoring of performance was done by CRE officials under the supervision of the director. Frequently there would be public outcry and media attacks about funding cuts or poor performance. The negative publicity would be debated at top management meetings but very little came out of them. As I said, I sat as chairman of the Employment Sub-Committee of Nottingham CRC. I believe some good came out of these local bodies. But they did not really have any meaningful impact in improving relations between people of various races.

Industrial tribunals (later renamed employment tribunals): Recourse to law was made possible by the 1968 and 1976 Acts. Employment cases went to industrial tribunals (ITs); complaints relating to goods and services, including housing, went to the courts.

My own experience related to three employment cases. After leaving the CRE, there was an occasion when I wanted to take London Borough of Tower Hamlets to an industrial tribunal for denying me one of the chief executive positions when, under Liberal control, the borough was divided up into five districts with their own administrations. I sought CRE assistance to pursue my complaint. Geoffrey Bindman had a small legal practice at King's Cross. He was asked by the commission to act as my lawyer. Cllr Sadiq (a fellow Sylheti) was the chair of the Isle of Dogs Council. Geoffrey decided that he and I should meet Cllr Sadiq. I made an appointment. A community friend of mine, Mr Ramiz Uddin, had spoken to Cllr Sadiq about my case. So Ramiz Uddin and I thought that Cllr Sadiq would be a good witness to stand by me in my case of racial discrimination by the council, which he headed up as the leader of the local Labour group. When we met, Geoffrey asked him bluntly, 'Do you think the council has racially discriminated against Mr Aziz in not offering him the Isle of Dogs chief executive post?' I was astounded when Sadiq replied, 'No'! That was that. Geoffrey, being a man of few words, called off the meeting. He reported this to the legal section of the CRE. Afterwards

Geoffrey followed up with the chief executive of the council, as a result of which he obtained a written assurance from the council's lawyer that 'the council regretted Mr Aziz did not get the job on this occasion but they would encourage him to apply for future opportunities when his application would be most favourably considered'. I gave up, as these were only meaningless words. I was disappointed by Cllr Sadiq's reply to Bindman; frankly I felt Sadiq was worried about his Tower Hamlets Council colleagues who he had to live with! I knew the council top officials were all white, in a place like Tower Hamlets where large sections of the community were coloured immigrants, mostly Bangladeshi (Sylheti) origin. The council was seen as a 'lily-white' body in the middle of multicultural Tower Hamlets.

My second experience of the law was when I had applied for the chief executive position of the Tower Hamlets City Challenge, a new scheme of the Government to bring about economic development in deprived areas where, of course, a large number of ethnic minorities lived. Again, I got CRE assistance for representation at the industrial tribunal. They appointed an excellent Sikh barrister to represent me. I was disappointed when I heard witnesses lined up by the City Challenge, for whom I had high regard, but who did not hesitate to speak untruths. They were all English, white witnesses. When giving the tribunal decision, the chairman said, 'Mr Aziz, you have big shoulders, we are sure you can take it in your stride.' The race Acts may be there, but when there is a confrontation between the law and white citizens' or institutions' interests, more often than not the indigenous side wins.

My third experience was when I had applied for the chairman post of the St George's Hospital NHS Foundation Trust. I had been shortlisted and interviewed for two chairmanship posts – (i) Bromley Group of Hospitals, including Bromley, Queen Elizabeth, Greenwich and Queen Mary's, Sidcup NHS Hospital Trusts and (ii) West London NHS Mental Health Hospital Trust, including Broadmoor High Security Hospital – but did not get either job.

I decided to complain to the employment tribunal for not even shortlisting me for the post at St George's. I didn't have the resources to finance the case, so I went to Citizens Advice. A black solicitor was assigned to the case on a no-win-no-fee basis, but I had to pay up front £500 for his administrative costs. I prepared the papers for the tribunal. When the response came from the government lawyers, the Citizens Advice lawyer got cold feet. He pulled out from my case saying it was too complex, as it was connected to my earlier case against Ian Mills (described elsewhere in these pages). I had, of course, told him the whole background but he got cold feet nevertheless! I asked for my £500 back. He declined. I complained to the financial ombudsman. Initially it was refused, but upon appeal I got my £500 back. However, my application for the St George's Hospital chair could go no further.

Ethnic minorities press: There were several ethnic minority owned newspapers in circulation – weeklies, fortnightly and monthly. The CRE would try to maintain good relationship with this section of the British press. Most of the papers were published in English but others were in Hindi, Urdu, Gujarati, Bengali. The interest of these papers in the working of the Commission for Racial Equality was intense. Sometime the top management of the CRE would wait in apprehension for the next issue of some of these newspapers to see any criticism of particular aspects of its work. Mostly this was because of a general level of criticism of the new Commission, some justified and well informed, others not. The CRE's Information section would deal with press and public relations which fell into the area of responsibility of the general services division of which I was the director. Maintaining good relations with the editors of these papers was important. I personally knew several of the editors like Mr Arif Ali of 'The Caribbean Times' and 'The Asian Times'; Mr Ramniklal Solanki of 'The Garavi Gujarat'; Mr C B Patel of 'The Gujarat Samachar'/ 'The Asian Voice'; Mr Talukdar of Bangladeshi weekly 'Jagoron' amongst others. The CRE would put job and other adverts in the e.m. press; also when the Commission needed to engage with a particular e.m. group, focusing on specific issues such as aid to complainants, immigration, discrimination at the workplace etc. the value of the e.m. press was generally recognised not only at the CRE, but also at the Home Office and many other organisations and institutions.

Chapter Seven

Management consulting

It was early 1982. I had just left the CRE. PA International Management Consultants was advertising for management consultants for their work with World Bank-funded projects in the Sudan and for other 'third world' country projects generally. Having prepared myself over some years, I felt I had obtained sufficient qualifications and experience to be a credible candidate for management consultancy work. I applied to PA. I was duly invited for an interview at their new offices in Slough, near Heathrow Airport – to facilitate international travel for their consultants. This was the new arm of PA focused on projects in the developing world. I was met by Mr Andrew Baldwin, a charming man – warm, smiling, welcoming. I achieved a good rapport with him at once and felt relaxed. At the end of my interview he was gracious enough to give me a copy of the book *Management Consulting* by Milan Kubr, published by the UN International Labour Office (ILO), Geneva; the book is truly the 'bible', a brilliant textbook on management consulting. As he handed it to me he said, 'Suhail, this is for you. This book will tell you all you need to know about management consulting.' We finished our discussion with his favourable comment: 'I like the way you come over. You will hear from us.' That was reassuring because I have always lacked confidence in people's impressions of me.

The Sudan: my first real consulting assignment in Imam Mehdi and Gordon Pasha's Khartoum!

I was appointed as an associate consultant of PA International Management Consultants. My first assignment was at the Mechanised Farming

Corporation (MFC), Khartoum, as an organisational development (OD) consultant, to review management structure, processes, practices and how the organisation could be made more efficient and effective in what they did. There was an unspoken reason for sending me to the Sudan: because I was a Sunni Muslim. It was important that I had that affinity with the Sudanese people. Most of the people in management spoke English, so even though it was an Arabic-speaking Muslim country mission, I felt comfortable and I did not need an interpreter.

MFC had its headquarters in Khartoum, with satellite organisations in Damazin, Gaderif, Kosti, Rahad and New Halfa – all in the important rain-fed agriculture sector of the Sudan. I carried out organisational and management reviews at headquarters and at the above places.

I got on fine with the chairman of MFC, Syed Tawfiq, and the senior management team. I would report for my work to the chairman of MFC, and, for the professional consultancy side of the job, to my supervising consultant, Brian Shaw, the team leader for our Sudan mission. I would be invited to dinner at the Sudanese officials' homes where I would meet their extremely kind and courteous Sudanese families. It was all very cordial. I carried out fact-finding by interviewing people at senior and middle management levels, did fact analysis as I saw the situation, produced draft reports for my boss, and discussed and mostly got acceptance of my organisational reviews and analyses, recommendations and implementation plans.

There was one particular episode with the personnel director of MFC. He did not agree with what I said about his own leadership in the key administration areas of MFC. So he and I engaged in a discussion about how far my recommendations impacted on how he did his own work. I tried to veer him away from thinking that it was anything personal and that what I was recommending was for the good of the organisation and he should not take it personally. I do not know how far I succeeded in persuading him that it was not all his fault, and pointed out good things about his department's work in the running of MFC, how much confidence he enjoyed from the chairman, Syed Tawfiq, and so on. I think I must have succeeded in winning him back, as soon afterwards I was invited to his home for dinner with his family.

Brian Shaw and I would present my findings and recommendations to the chairman, Syed Tawfiq, first at a confidential session, and obtain his acceptance before presenting to the entire senior management team and board of the rain-fed agriculture sector. Brian Shaw would just say, 'Chairman, Suhail has done the necessary work over the past few weeks. This is his report. He will present it as he saw things. Over to you, Suhail.' After these opening introductory words Brian would sit back while I did all the talking. Occasionally Brian made supportive noises to keep my presentation going. Of particular importance were the training programmes I developed based on my findings.

From Khartoum I returned to PA's Sundridge Park Management Centre, in Beckenham, Bromley, South East London, and with an introduction by my director, the late Derek Wynne-Jones, to John Chadwick, director at SPMC, I developed the training programmes, went back to Khartoum and delivered them in the presence of a World Bank official there. The training seminars were delivered at the huge and prestigious building built for the Sudanese Government by the Chinese on the other side of the Nile. I was pleased to receive positive feedback from the WB representative about the quality, content and delivery of the training programme to the Sudanese. As a person entering management consultancy for the first time I did all this single-handedly, with very little input from my supervising consultant. I couldn't believe that I enjoyed so much confidence. It showed that with a supportive organisational culture such as I experienced at PA, people could achieve results and flourish. In all my future work as chairman of organisations in the NHS and National Probation Service, I always applied what I learnt at PA by providing encouragement and support to top management teams to achieve high performance.

While on the Sudan missions, I worked with an interesting colleague, Peter Shepherd. Peter was a Canadian, a financial expert on our team. We both worked to Brian Shaw as our team leader. Peter and I shared many hours together. We worked from the same office, followed MFC office working hours – early start at 8am and early finish at 1.30pm because by then the heat was intense. We would go to the Sudan Club in Khartoum (we had both become members) for a very welcome drink of cool lager in the midday heat, followed by lunch; then to the hotel for a rest until early evening. We would go to eat at various restaurants in the city, which were cool by then. The evenings were pleasant, sitting out in the open. Fried fish from the catch of the day was delicious. We did not have much else to do. At the Sudan Club we would meet some interesting people: British expatriates, people working on oil company projects like Total Oil's oil exploration near Port Sudan, consultants and technical experts working on World Bank, International Fund for Agricultural Development (IFAD) and African Development Bank projects. One would not see many Sudanese at the club except on special occasions; they would not be seen drinking in public and mostly would be spending time with their families. They would be present only when high-level people – ministers, MPs, politicians, landed gentry – were at the club for events or functions. The Sudanese we met were extremely nice, always smiling and very courteous; their ladies were very smart, elegant and always happy and smiling.

Once our team was there working during the month of Ramadan. The working time of MFC staff was from 7am to 1pm. There was no lunchbreak because a Muslim wouldn't eat or drink from the time of 'Sehri' (last meal before dawn) and 'Iftar' (breaking of fast at sunset). Not that everyone kept to the fast. But this was the culture. One aspect of working at MFC during Ramadan was fascinating. Those staff members who were fasting would arrive after a lot of struggle travelling from far afield with poor transport communications. As soon as they arrived, they would clock in, enter their office areas and straight dive down on the office floor to sleep, because they needed to catch up on sleep lost after Sehri. No work was expected of them; they had clocked in, that was it! Peter and I would smile at what was happening but equally we had sympathy with their struggle and predicament. But it seemed that it was the 'culture' of the place during Ramadan; no one in the management hierarchy seemed to mind; turning a blind eye was the norm. There was no strong presence of trade unions in MFC or in the Sudan generally. People were happy to have a job. The sight of scores of Toyota pick-ups lined up to take people to and from their homes was striking. There was no hope that this situation would ever change. People would be struggling for ever! 'Development, what development?' they would ask!

It was not possible for me to fast during Ramadan as I was staying at a hotel in Khartoum – Taka House. I think I must have kept a few of the fasts, but I begged Allah's forgiveness and tried to give something to the poor for my omission.

Brian Shaw was PA team leader at MFC, the team being myself and Peter. As I mentioned, Brian was a PA man through and through. He generally left Peter and me to get on with our work with very little supervision or interference. He would keep a general oversight of our work, applying 'a gentle touch on the tiller' when needed. He was a quietly spoken, composed, smartly dressed chap, befitting the heat of the place. He was very supportive.

When I had produced the first draft of my report following the organisational and management review, Brian asked me for an advance copy for him to have a look at. Then he and I sat down to discuss it. He was generous with his comments and very helpful, not critical at all. He wanted to ensure that what I had to say was clear, not vague, not to be misunderstood or misconstrued; this was because we were dealing with clients who came from a completely different culture. Apart from a few senior managers, the understanding of written and spoken English was not very strong amongst senior MFC staff. So, my presentation would frequently be interrupted in Arabic by managers to ensure that their other colleagues were on board and following the proceedings as far as possible. We were dealing with three cultures: me the consultant whose mother tongue was Bengali, not English; my boss Brian Shaw who was an Englishman and whose mother tongue was English; while the Sudanese were of Arabic mother tongue with reasonable ability in understanding and speaking English. In carrying out our consultancy assignments in different cultures, we were heavily dependent on interpreters, not just to translate accurately but to interpret as well, so that the real sense and underlying meanings were not lost.

Brian was accompanied by his wife, Anne. They lived at a very nice fixed caravan site at the other end of the city, heavily tree shaded, green with plants and shrubberies. It was difficult to imagine such lovely places existing in Khartoum. Once Brian and Anne invited me to afternoon tea, which was very nice of them.

Suddenly there was an exciting development in the desert! While on assignment in Khartoum, I received a call from Anna to tell me that there was a telegram from the World Bank in Washington DC inviting me to go to its HQ as soon as possible for interview. I got it faxed over to me. My current assignment in Khartoum was coming to an end, so I was returning to London anyway. Upon return, I got in touch with the officer in their human resources (HR) department. I still remember his name: Mr Hevsep Melkonian. I agreed my travel schedule with him. He arranged for my ticket, *per diem* allowance and hotel in DC. He got a ticket issued in London in no time. I said to myself, this was the kind of organisation I should be working for. I really was very excited and interested, though I did not know the role or nature of the post they had in mind. It was enough for me to be called for an interview by the World Bank.

I wondered how this invitation from the World Bank had come about. Some years previous to 1981, I had read in *The Economist* that Robert McNamara had joined the WB from Ford Motor Company where he was an executive vice-president. He was joining the World Bank as the president. By that time I had worked at Ford of Britain, at their Warley headquarters, in central labour relations. So I had already got a flavour of the kind of efficient, effective, no-nonsense type of company Ford was. I had applied to the World Bank, I think, after leaving the Commission for Racial Equality (CRE) in early 1981 and was entering business with my brother, Tabib Ibne Aziz (Molik), in Jute Good Trading in Africa. After CRE, I was also planning seriously to enter management consulting. Soon after, I was to join PA International Management Consulting, as discussed above.

The World Bank

I had forgotten about my approach to the World Bank, writing personally to a vice-president, no less, seeking a job! Things of course moved very slowly but this invitation was the result. A scribbled note by the vice-president on my letter most probably did the trick. I was flying out to the WB, Washington DC, in business class, with accommodation arranged at a hotel in the Pennsylvania Avenue, near the WB. I found it all very exciting! Of course I could not go to an interview straight after arrival at JFK Airport, New York, then connecting to a Washington flight – quite tiring. Their travel department must have thought that all international travel people needed rest before any engagement.

The following morning I reported to Mr Hevsep Melkonian. I think he was Turkish or Lebanese. He was a very thorough professional, a through and through WB character. He told me what was to happen throughout the day. One interview in the morning, followed by lunch with him and introductions to some important people relevant to my proposed job. Then, after lunch, a couple more interviews before the end of play that day. I was to report back for a couple more interviews next morning, also to hear about what was to happen next. Of course, throughout the time preceding my visit to Washington for the interviews, I was receiving information about family accommodation in a condominium ('condo' for short) in Washington, terms and conditions for employees at the WB, administrative matters like domicile, passport, family details etc. This was so that while at interviews I did not have to waste time on mundane matters. Hevsep had told me that one main purpose of the visit was to ensure 'that you like us, and we like you'! Hence the selection process had to be thorough. My final chat with him was friendly and warm. He said that before the final stage, a WB official, another PA man as it turned out, would see me in London to conclude the formalities of interviews. He said he would get in touch with me again while I was still in London to arrange this final stage, before I needed to return to Khartoum. He did not tell me if there was any other candidate competing. Disappointingly I was to learn that the PA man 'spiked' my chances by appointing one of his mates to the post, despite Melkonian sending a telegram asking him 'to keep the interests of the WB in mind'! After hearing the story, Mrs Pauline Hyde, at 40+ Consultancy who was helping me find a suitable job after I had left the CRE, said to me, 'Suhail, you had better forget about the World Bank!'

Institute of Management Consultants (IMC)

The IMC is the recognised professional body for individual (sole practice) management consultants – people enter consulting work after a career in management, or after gaining professional qualifications in their main field of work, or from academia or business. Grades of membership are AIMC (associate), MIMC (full member) and FIMC (fellow). I am an FIMC, also a Fellow – Certified Management Consultant (FCMC). Policies of the institute are developed and determined by the IMC Council. Accreditation to various grades of membership is given by the council. (With the recent name change to Institute of Consulting (IC), my present grades are FIC, FCMC.)

The IMC has been through good times and bad. Depleting membership numbers, financial pressures, turnover of key members have all affected the life of the IMC. Benefits from IMC memberships have always been critically questioned. Many members joined the institute thinking membership would bring concrete benefits such as consultancy work – either as an individual or for firms they belonged to. It is alleged that whatever work came to the notice of the IMC would invariably be taken by influential members on the IMC Council who came from large consultancy practices, either for themselves or for their firms, while a vast majority of members would not get a bite of the cherry. I for one fall into the latter category. In all my years as a member and fellow of the IMC since the early 1980s, I did not get one single assignment for myself or for my company. It was not just me, it was a general phenomenon. Cream was sliced off by the key people at the 'kitchen cabinet' of the IMC, who invariably belonged to the larger practices.

I served two terms of three years each as a member of the IMC Council. It was a large body, some 30–40 members, supposedly individual members, but in reality these individual members came from the larger practices, thus tilting debates and discussions on policies and practices towards their self-interests. Anyway, I learnt a lot about the world of management consulting, the institutions which dominated the business of consultancy: the government departments in the UK and overseas governments in the developing world, the institutions which funded development, such as the World Bank, various UN agencies such as the UNDP, IFAD, Inter-American Development Bank (IDB), the Asian Development Bank (ADB), the African Development Bank (AfDB), the Caribbean Development Bank (CDB). Then the specific country bilateral and multilateral aid programmes of some countries in the West and their commitment to economic development of the third world: British, Danish, Swedish, Japanese, German and Canadian. The consulting business generated by all these activities is vast, running into billions of dollars annually.

When I joined the IMC, one thing that hit me was that a large number of British consultants, either individually or through associateship with larger consultancy practices, were working in developing countries with very little to show as evidence of development or outcomes. As a man from one of those countries, Bangladesh, at the receiving end of aid, I knew that consultants from the western world would go out on assignments, stay at the best hotels, 5-star generally, waiting for an assignment to start or waiting for a meeting with a minister or top civil servant. After a week or more of waiting, they would return home having earned fat fees but nothing else to show – and the countries' development remained where it was at the start. The wastage of well-intentioned international aid money was alarming.

Mike Jeans, a senior partner at KPMG, was the president of the IMC and I, as a fellow, was a council member. I approached Mike and told him about the above phenomenon in third world aid. To his credit Mike responded positively. IMC had several activities groups focused on relevant consulting areas, such as change, ICT, governance, SMEs. I proposed that we set up a group focused on third world development. Mike and the council agreed to the setting up of the Third World Specialist Group (TWSG) and I became its founder chairman. The idea caught on with general IMC membership who were engaged in third world assignments or had knowledge and experience of doing consulting work in developing countries in Asia, Africa and Latin America. I set up a small committee to steer the work of the group. After a couple of years, the number of IMC members interested in the group grew to some 400. The council gave us a small regular budget to finance the activities of the group – for hosting a speaker, cost of hiring venues, out-of-pocket expenses etc.

The activities of the TWSG included regular bi-monthly meetings when we would invite speakers from aid institutions such as the World Bank, UNDP and ADB, and government ministers, major charities active in the third world, visiting aid officials passing through London, academics and so on. The TWSG met at prestigious venues in central London: the Royal Air Force Club, Institute of Directors, Institution of Civil Engineers and Caledonian Club. I made regular reports to the IMC Council. The interest generated was infectious. I was very grateful to Mike Jeans for giving me support in setting up the TWSG. This process also meant that I was elected to the council for two consecutive terms while I began to be noticed by the top hierarchy of the IMC, resulting in my being invited to join the City Livery in Consulting. My other preoccupations prevented me from pursuing my interest in that direction.

As one of the group's founders I remained its chairman for almost ten years, when I handed over to another person named Abbas Baba. But soon afterwards interest in the group's work waned. Abbas emigrated to Morocco. I also felt that after years of being a full member and a fellow of the IMC, it had brought no business benefits to me whatsoever, whereas I knew large practices were siphoning off business enquiries for their own benefit. This was not for me; I had heard these complaints from many individual members of the IMC. After years of membership I could ask myself, 'What was all that for?'

Some negatives about the IMC

I have sat on many committees and forums. A common feature experienced by many ethnic minority people in Britain is that, however much one tried to participate, one tended to be ignored when participating in discussions. This gave rise to disappointment. Worse, it meant that slowly but surely, disappointed and disgruntled ethnic minority members would withdraw from such bodies. However much these committees made public pronouncements that they wanted minority participation, the lack of understanding of good race relations on the part of the lead members gave rise to antipathy.

I recall upon being elected for the second term to the IMC Council, during a break in the meeting, I went to the loo. I had just been re-elected for another term. Next to me was standing a PA colleague, also a council member. He said something which stuck in my mind: 'Suhail, you must like punishing yourself!' No congratulations but this sad observation. I thought, *One can never win!* One tries hard for recognition and to make headway but time after time efforts get thwarted. Quite often I felt depressed but always I remember what Lord Young, a secretary of state for trade and industy in the Thatcher Government, said to me: 'You keep pushing!' He knew, he was a Jewish person, and he had made it in England despite the obstacles of prejudice, discrimination, spite and ignorance about his community.

On another occasion, while I was chairman of the Third World Specialist Group I recall being invited by a colleague, who had worked at PricewaterhouseCoopers consultants, to lunch at a Moroccan restaurant near St Martin-in-the-Fields at Trafalgar Square. I don't know why he invited me to lunch; perhaps in expectation of some consultancy business coming my way as chairman of the TWSG which could be shared. I talked to him about my thoughts on minority participation in society – in government, politics, charities, voluntary organisations, forums such as the IMC. I told him about some of my disappointing experiences and asked him why he thought it was like this. Trevor was frank: 'You are not accepted, you are tolerated.' That has stuck in my mind. No matter what, we will never be 'accepted' in this society, we will be 'tolerated'. We won't be thrown out or forcefully repatriated with incentives, as Enoch Powell wanted to do in the 1960s. It couldn't be done because Britain also wanted to belong to world forums and it could not withstand the backlash from such negative acts in today's world. So, we may be 'swamping' England; but we won't become 'one of us'; we will always be 'them' in 'us and them' situations. Tolerated but never accepted. This feeling of rejection thus generated becomes a negative force inside of ethnic minority people, resulting in their withdrawal. This may not be apparent or visible but it is always there.

But I profoundly believe in good race relations in Britain. See my entry in any copy of *Who's Who from 1978*. I have worked hard in this field – see elsewhere in these pages. I fully understand one cannot rid oneself of prejudices – that includes me. We can never fathom the feelings and prejudices in one's mind. All we should be working on, and hope for, is that prejudices should not get translated into overt behaviour detrimental to others – whatever their race, colour, creed, gender or nationality. Overt racial or sex discrimination is illegal. As the late Lord Bonham Carter said at the time of enacting race discrimination laws in this country: 'Legal sanction is a vital persuader.' Britain basically being a law-abiding country, it was possible for the law generally to play a positive part in working towards eliminating overt racial or sex or disability or other types of discrimination, direct or indirect, conscious or unconscious.

The Brettonwood Partnership Ltd ('Brettonwood') –
international management consultants

It was a cold winter evening when our company, Brettonwood, was conceived as an idea at the Caledonian Club, London. I, with a small group of our regular Third World Specialist Group (TWSG), were meeting at the Caledonian Club near Victoria. After a lot of co-ordination and liaison with the United Nations Development Programme (UNDP)'s New York office, I had secured our next speaker from UNDP. He was the director of UNDP in New York. It was a stimulating speech and his talk certainly whetted our appetite at the thought of limitless consulting opportunities with the UNDP and numerous other UN agencies around the developing world in Asia, Africa and Latin America. As chairman of the group I established contact with the director for future follow-up. The meeting was well attended by some thirty consultants, all senior members of the IMC, with an interest in third world work.

That evening, after the meeting, some of us stayed back for a drink and chat, reflecting on what we had heard from our speaker. One of us, it could have been Brian Smith, said, 'Suhail, we hear all these speakers from important institutions at the TWSG's regular meetings. They give us many ideas and leads about consultancy business. We seem to be letting these opportunities pass us by. Why not pursue some business from all these things we hear?' To cut a long story short, a few of us stayed back to discuss the idea. We were really keen to set up a company. It fell on our most creative and imaginative colleague, Brian Smith, to think up a name for the proposed company. After considering many suggestions, he hit on the idea that our company name must reflect the connection between the developed world in the West, and the 'third world countries' – the developing world: the 'haves' (richer countries) of the world helping the 'have-nots' (the poorer countries of the world struggling for a livelihood).

Brian led our search eventually to come up with the name 'Brettonwood', formed from Bretton Woods, New Hampshire, USA. 'Join the two words, drop the s!' It maintained a connection with the original UN conference in New Hampshire in 1944 that launched the World Bank and the IMF, and the focus on delivering management consulting in the third world. We decided on the name of the company: The Brettonwood Partnership Ltd – partnership between the 'haves' and the 'have-nots'. From that meeting at the Caledonian Club, we found that seven members were deeply committed to the concept behind the company. So they joined the board of the new company as its founding members/directors. I got the company duly registered with Companies House in 1985. I was honoured to be elected its first chairman – and remain its chairman and principal consultant to this day (See Annexe C).

Summary statement of capability: I feel it might be of interest if I set out here something about our company, The Brettonwood Partnership Ltd, which I have successfully run for some years:

'The Brettonwood Partnership Ltd (Brettonwood) was formed in 1985 to support the aims of the United Nations Conference (Bretton Woods, New Hampshire, USA, 1944), which brought about the IMF and the World Bank. This set the scene for the developed countries to help less developed nations of the world towards true economic growth. The broad objective of the company is to provide consulting services that assist developing nations and nations in transition to strengthen their economic growth through technical assistance and transfer of knowhow, thus leading to knowledge being brought to bear on critical development issues.

Brettonwood's principals are professionally qualified, multidisciplinary experts who have extensive consulting experience in over sixty countries, working in multicultural environments. All are professional members of the Institute of Management Consultancy (IMC), UK, and are bound by the institute's Code of Professional Conduct. They provide the skills needed to analyse problems, provide solutions, manage large-scale projects, implement cost-effective improvements in public sector reforms, health, education, equal opportunities and access, communications etc.

Brettonwood encourages the use of local consultants, working in partnership, and is committed to a policy of transferring technology and knowhow to client staff and counterparts. This policy reduces client costs through effective use of local skills and means that Brettonwood provides only the consultancy services that are clearly not available to the client from indigenous sources. This approach to working closely with local experts has given them experience of different cultures, which makes them more effective in achieving minimum lead-in times to projects.

Brettonwood is dedicated to bringing to bear leading-edge knowledge to issues in development to achieve sustainable improvement. It specialises in the area of 'project cycle' consultancy, institution building, civil service reform, organisational and management reviews and improvement, assessment of training needs, development of training programmes and their delivery, SMEs, equal opportunities and access programmes for minority groups, urban regeneration, local economic development through employment creation, training, economic strategy, and infrastructure development, marketing, MIS, economic and industrial planning, economies in transition, privatisation and institutional reforms.

Brettonwood is particularly strong in assisting minority groups, and has delivered major programmes for these groups through equal opportunities and access initiatives in education, employment, training, enterprise development and social housing. Its UK clients include government, major public and private sector organisations, training and enterprise councils (TECs) and Business Links, urban development corporations, housing corporations, housing associations and co-operatives dedicated to assisting minority and disadvantaged groups in the UK. Brettonwood's principal, Mr Suhail Aziz, has sat on ministerial advisory councils advising ministers at Cabinet level on immigration, race and community relations and employment discrimination issues. He has been a member of several organisations with the mission to assist minority groups and their wider social integration. He has done an internship in the USA to study initiatives to help minority groups through training and support.

Brettonwood is widely registered as consultants within the international DACON System of the World Bank and UN System, with the European Commission (DG1-Tacis/Phare and DGVIII), with EBRD, with the British Know How Fund, DFID, Asian Development Bank, Inter-American Bank and so on. The company has an associate consultants register of over 200 multidisciplinary consultants with multi-sector experience.'

At the start, our team of seven directors of Brettonwood were assigned some duties – who would do what etc. Initially, although each of the directors had experience of working as individual consultants, sole practice consultants, or working in larger practices under supervision on projects, none of us from the seven had the experience of preparing detailed 'expressions of interest' for bidding on major projects. One of us was assigned the responsibility to keep sending Expressions of Interest to aid institutions such as the UNDP, World Bank, Asian Development Bank and bilateral aid agencies. Although we put out 'a lot of fishing lines', we did not hook any fishes! So we had to learn fast, with steep learning curves. Soon we began to get invitations to make presentations, for example to the British MoD procurement department for major projects. Because of lack of experience of running a consultancy company business on international projects, we were not successful. But because of the accumulated experience in our team and a large number of hugely experienced associate consultants, we began to win contracts. Brettonwood soon was gaining confidence and credibility in the international consulting market.

In the UK, Brettonwood worked with government departments and various government agencies, training and enterprise councils (TECs), local authorities, housing and housing co-operatives led by Bangladeshis living in deprived parts of East London, Newham, Birmingham, Rochdale, small and medium-sized enterprises (SMEs), and many public and private sector organisations and companies. Brettonwood's jewel in the crown was its Nationwide Asian Business Symposia Programme, which delivered fourteen events up and down the country, which brought Asian SMEs into contact with agencies on the ground providing assistance to businesses. This conference programme was a great success and enjoyed support from the public, private sector organisations and agencies, and raised awareness of the Asian SMEs about what was on offer, and, more importantly, how to go about getting what was on offer – 'getting a bite of the cherry'!

In developing countries, Brettonwood has successfully delivered public administration reforms, public finance management (PFM) and economic development projects; some examples are given below:

Bangladesh – Brettonwood, in association with experts from the UK

Civil Service Commission Recruitment and Assessment Service (RAS), delivered the Institutional Strengthening of the Bangladesh Public Service Commission Project. World Bank funded.

Afghanistan – Brettonwood, on its own, and in partnership with the British Council, delivered Public Administration Reforms projects. Asian Development Bank (ADB) funded.

The Maldives – Capacity Building of the Public Administration Commission. ADB funded.

Azerbaijan – Capacity Building at the Ministry of Economy. ADB funded.

Tajikistan – In partnership with Cranfield University School of Management, Brettonwood delivered the Strengthening of the Khujand Centre for Entrepreneurial Development. TACIS programme of the European Commission (EC) funded.

Ukraine – In association with the University of East Anglia, Review of Effectiveness of UN-Funded Aid Programmes in Ukraine. UN/DFID funded.

India: EU-India Partenariat – With the British Chamber of Commerce, Brettonwood assisted in a partnership development between 300+ EU SMEs and a similar number of SMEs from various states of India. They met at the Progoti Maidan, New Delhi, over a two-day period. It was acclaimed a great success story. EC funded.

The Sudan – as described above, I worked as an associate consultant with PA International Management Consultants as an organisational development (OD) consultant at the Mechanised Farming Corporation and its satellite agencies, in the rain-fed agriculture sector of the Sudan. World Bank funded.

As years have gone by, the number of Brettonwood directors has shrunk. Sadly, some colleagues have passed away; others have moved or emigrated to faraway lands – Australia, New Zealand; and some have started charitable activities. For a while now I continue as the chairman, managing director and, as they say, the 'bottle-washer' of The Brettonwood Partnership. The company continues to be in business albeit low key.

Brettonwood is a small consultancy with a strong base of associate consultants on its associates register. The company always successfully punched above its weight. As the managing director, I have always tried to bid for major projects funded by the international aid agencies, with full realisation that it could not be done by my company on its own. We must team up. For example, in the case of the Tajikistan Small and Medium-Sized Enterprise (SME) Project, which was a large project, I decided to team up with Cranfield University because the university's School of Management was the contractor for the UK Government's major programme of support for the SME sector. I didn't know anyone at Cranfield University directly. But I was on the board of governors of London Guildhall University. I decided to have a word with Professor Sir Roderick Floud, vice-chancellor, to ask him to introduce me to the vice-chancellor at Cranfield. This quickly resulted in my gaining access to the top management of the School of Management and their SME support unit. I travelled with a colleague to Brussels to meet the officials handling the Tajikistan project under the commission's TACIS (Technical Assistance to the Commonwealth of Independent States – that is the former Soviet Republics) to do a presentation of our technical proposal. Together we bid for, and won, the tender for the SME support programme in Tajikistan funded by the TACIS programme of the European Commission. The Brettonwood/Cranfield partnership managed the successful delivery of that project. Not only was the Tajik Centre for Entrepreneurship and Management institutionally strengthened but the centre was able to become the hub of an SME support network in North Tajikistan. At a human level, I and my colleagues on this project became great friends with the director Kasim Islamov and his senior colleagues Rashid and Yussouf; we enjoyed warmth and hospitality, Tajik style, in their homes and families. It reflected the value of achieving sustainable development at a human and practical level.

Likewise, I decided that Afghanistan offered new opportunities for reforms, to strengthen the country's new civil service. From my own research I knew that the Asian Development Bank (ADB) was funding a large-scale civil and public administrative reforms programme for Afghanistan. Again, Brettonwood was a small company to aspire to engage in such a large civil and public administration reform programme on its own. I spoke to my team leader Tol Bedford, a distinguished occupational psychologist of the British

Civil Service Commission Recruitment and Assessment Service (RAS). He was team leader for Brettonwood's Institutional Strengthening of the Bangladesh Public Service Commission, a civil service reform programme in Bangladesh. Tol introduced me to the British Council. We teamed up, with the council in the lead and Brettonwood supplying experts. Together, the British Council and Brettonwood were able successfully to deliver civil and public administration reforms in a new country like Afghanistan.

I believe I had the skills and approach to bring about these business tie-ups. It wasn't easy. My race, my 'strangeness and foreignness', my English, my accent – prejudice had to be overcome. Credibility had to be established at the very first meetings. At times, I had found resistance was too much. By sheer perseverance and determination, more often than not I managed to overcome these obstacles to deliver Brettonwood's projects internationally. Racism was not overt; it was there underneath, covert. Being an Asian in a totally white management consultancy field, I had to fight, win and progress. There was never a question of giving up. I always remembered Lord Young's advice: 'You keep pushing.'

Chapter Eight

Public appointments

Home Secretary's Standing Advisory Council on Immigration and Race Relations (1977-1978)

This body was created by The Rt Hon. Roy Jenkins MP for Glasgow (later Lord Jenkins), as the Home Secretary in the Wilson Government, as part of his reforms of race relations legislation in the UK. This council was established with very good intentions. It was meant to give policy advice to government in relation to all aspects of immigration and racial discrimination: housing, employment, education, health, youth, arts. The 1976 Race Relations Act was enacted in the UK by Roy Jenkins following the American concepts of 'direct' and 'indirect' discrimination. The work in the background by people such as Lord Mark Bonham Carter, John Little, Lord Anthony Lester, Sir Geoffrey Bindman, Dipak Nandy and many other distinguished thinkers must be gratefully acknowledged.

The way my membership of this exciting new venture in race relations was announced, along with some of my black and Asian colleagues in the field, was interesting. It showed how the government 'systems' operated in such matters. As mentioned earlier, the list of members was leaked to *The Daily Telegraph*. No doubt it was meant to attract objections from any black or Asian organisations or individuals or groups about any of the proposed members of the advisory body, their suitability for such appointments, etc. If any objections came, then it gave the Home Office room to delete the name(s) concerned and wriggle out of the press leak; also stopping sending out the specific invitation(s) from the Home Secretary only to be retracted if the objections became fierce! On occasion, advance leaking is how the civil servants protected the name of ministers from any controversy. I was not told in advance that I was being invited to join the council, which of course I felt was a great honour for me. Someone telephoned me to give me the news – 'Have you seen *The Daily Telegraph*? Your name is in it!' I suppose the civil servants in charge thought that it would be OK to leak the list in the press in advance to test the water. The invitees would not object as they would be 'eternally grateful and honoured' to receive such personal invitations from no less than the Home Secretary of HM Government. I must say the officials were not far off in their calculation! As far as I know, no one objected about the 'Home Office leak' in *The Daily Telegraph*! So I got the personal letter of invitation from Mr Roy Jenkins, the Home Secretary, to join his council.

We began working as a council of advisers. Soon, however, I began to feel that the council was too large for effectiveness. Too many views, quite diverging at times, would be presented for discussion. A meeting would not last more than one and a half hours. It was difficult to manage a large agenda within the time available. A lot of the time agenda items were carried forward to the next meeting, maybe in another two months' time, since matters got aired but not discussed. As elsewhere mentioned, I believe I was beginning to be noticed by the Labour Government. Mr Merlyn Rees became Home Secretary after Roy Jenkins. So he assumed chairmanship of the advisory council. Mostly it would be continuation of the previous agenda items, not with any visible impact. As already mentioned, I recall one civil servant, an official with a PhD, who was servicing the council, once telling me over a lunchtime drink in the pub outside the Home Office Queen Anne's Gate building: 'I would not recommend any of my friends to join the council' – because he regarded its deliberations as a complete waste of time! I did not agree. But for a senior official of the Home Office to have that kind of view or attitude showed what policymakers like him thought of the ethnic minorities' needs and aspirations! Anyway, I felt he was being a bit pompous. As far as I was concerned I believe that I influenced the development of the 'victimisation clause' into the Race Relations Act 1976. For effective deliberation in, and positive outcomes at, bodies such as this council, they should always be kept small, although one has to recognise that the Home Office has a difficult job satisfying many vocal minority groups in Britain.

Department of Employment – Race Relations Employment Advisory Group (1977-1978)

The Rt Hon. John Grant MP, who was also my local MP, Member of Parliament for West Norwood, formed this ministerial advisory group with membership at the highest level from employers, trade unions, statutory bodies like the Manpower Services Commission, the Commission for Racial Equality, and from the voluntary and charities sectors. Again, it was a large body. I was glad to be invited to join the group to participate in its advisory role to influence policy formulation and implementation. There were ethnic minority members on the group. I developed a good relationship with them. But we did not feel that we were any more than what came to be known as 'statutory Blacks' on the group, able to participate in deliberations but with little evidence of impact on policies or practices. We did not feel we were achieving much. It was a good thing to include in one's CV that I was a member of this ministerial group, not much else! It was a disappointment to be a member of the group although, in case a race relations problem erupted at a workplace, the group's work had a calming influence on the situation.

Commonwealth Scholarship Commission (1996-2002)

I don't know how exactly my invitation to join this august body came about, most probably via the Cabinet Office who handled public appointments generally. But I was deeply honoured to receive the letter from the Foreign and Commonwealth Office (FCO) asking me if I would be interested to join this relatively new body, the Commonwealth Scholarship Commission (CSC). Of course I accepted. This commission brought students and scholars from across the whole of the British Commonwealth to pursue their studies in UK universities and institutions for one or more years, depending on their chosen fields of study. I felt honoured to have been identified and appointed a commissioner at the CSC by the Secretary of State for Foreign and Commonwealth Affairs, and by the Secretary of State for International Development. It was a joint appointment. Altogether I served on the commission for two three-year terms from 1996 to 2002. The membership consisted of university professors, research scientists, scholars from the world of high-level academia, economists and sociologists. Although I had degrees in economics and business, I felt that I was probably the only 'layman' in the commission's membership. Of course, being a Commonwealth body, the membership represented all communities: white, black and Asian. It was a well thought-out, pleasant mix.

Our job was to sift applications for studies and research mainly at British universities. The applications came already sifted from Commonwealth universities and institutions. So we were reviewing applications from mature students with First Class passes in their fields of study and research. On top of this, sifting would have taken place at the CSC itself by its own staff and consultants. The chairman of the CSC led the discussion. We were more or less rubber-stamping the recommendations and gave our support or otherwise to marginal cases.

Apart from participating in this process of selection and referrals to individual universities to confirm the students' choices I had very little else to do! However, I was called upon to do an important thing. A large number of the annual intake of scholars would be from Africa and Asia. I felt very proud when the chairman suggested I go on the stage after him to say a word. The aim was to make the young scholars feel welcome, what to expect at British universities, including racial prejudice and behaviours, how to tackle them and how to take advantage of the universities' support mechanisms to make them feel at home. Some friendships developed. I kept in contact with one particular Bengali scholar from Calcutta (now renamed Kolkata) for some years – but, as I said before, things do fall by the wayside. People move on. Contacts fade. Life goes on.

Industrial tribunals (1978-1996)

I was nominated to the industrial tribunals (later employment tribunals – ETs) for England and Wales when I was a personnel officer at Pedigree Petfoods, a division of the Mars Group. The nomination came about when the Confederation of British Industry (CBI) was asked by the Department of Employment to put forward names of possible candidates to be invited by the Secretary of State for Employment to sit on the industrial tribunals (employers' panel). My personnel director, Mr David Drennan, put forward my name with glowing words of recommendation. Accordingly I was invited. First I sat in the East Midlands Region, then when I moved to London, I was assigned to London South Region at the tribunals offices in Croydon. Altogether I served as a member for some twenty years on employers' panels. Later I was also assigned to the race relations panel as a special adviser on cases of alleged racial discrimination in employment. It was a very satisfying experience over a number of years when I took part in hearing, debating and deciding on cases, as it were, working at the 'coal face', listening to grievances, complaints and responses, sometimes assisted by lawyers, but individuals also presented and argued their cases themselves. I felt I had developed the skill of cutting through the 'jungle' of evidence, separating the 'wood from the trees' and, once the crunch issues had been identified, then deliberating amongst the three of us – two members, one each from the employers' and employees' sides (usually a trade union representative), with a legally qualified judge – deciding on and delivering the tribunal's decision.

Member, London Electricity Consumers Committee (LECC), (1992–1995)

This appointment came about in a strange way but I was happy to receive the invitation. Out of the blue I got a letter of invitation from the chairman, asking me if I would be interested in joining the London Electricity Consumers Committee as a member. Before anything I asked the chairman how he came to get my name for the invitation. He said it was from the Public Appointments Office at the Cabinet Office. Of course I felt honoured and so I responded positively. The chairman saw me for an hour or so to find out a bit more about me and to reconfirm if I was still interested.

I was duly appointed to the LECC. Initially I found the work of the committee not very exciting or important because the systems in place seemed to work well. However, as I learned more about the issues, it was clear that electricity consumers, especially from the ethnic minorities who had poor understanding of English or the issues involved, needed assistance over electricity charges, how to pay their bills, defaulting etc. The official attitude was 'no problem here', but in fact there was a lot of unhappiness, and grievances did exist. Awareness of the problems being faced by the ethnic minority consumers had to be communicated through training and open discussions with the officials. I was pleased to serve with the chairwoman of the LECC whom I had suggested should offer herself for the vacant chair position. I remember her telling me, 'Look where your suggestion has got me!' She was a very energetic, positive person to lead the committee's work.

I was pleased to have been able to raise awareness of the LECC to the problems being faced by ethnic minority disadvantaged groups. I believe that London Electricity became aware of the problem and 'sensitised' the 'system'.

Department for International Development (DFID) – Steering Committee, International Development Forum (1997–1999)

I was invited to join this forum which was doing some important work in getting DFID to consider its aid programme's sensitivity to the needs of the poor in the third world. The participation by the TUC in this forum was important. I provided input into development of certain programmes for third world countries receiving British overseas aid. I learnt DFID's methodology in considering projects for funding, both in its bilateral and multilateral aid programmes with the World Bank, UN and others, including their framework programmes which came in useful in my consultancy business through my own company, The Brettonwood Partnership Ltd.

During my business trips to Bangladesh and some other developing countries where my company, Brettonwood, would seek business and deliver projects, I felt that somehow ethnic minority-owned consultancy businesses were not getting a fair share of contract awards from DFID-funded programmes. I made a complaint to express this concern. I am glad that, due largely to my expressed concerns, the National Audit Office launched an investigation into DFID's working methods in developing countries. After a lengthy investigation into DFID's contracts awards procedures, the NAO found some areas of DFID's work which needed improvement, transparency and openness. I met senior NAO officials to hear from them about their findings, which went a long way to allay my concerns. It was reassuring that the NAO inquiries did not find any reason to believe that DFID was racially discriminating against any ethnic minority-owned consultancy but their inquiry improved a lot of DFID systems and procedures for contract awards.

Opening of Brettonwood Partnership's offices on the South Quay, opposite Canary Wharf, London Docklands. Here Lisa Aziz, a director of the company, addressing the Reception

As chairman and managing director of the Brettonwood Partnership Ltd. I am seen standing near our offices on the South Quay

Above: At a Reception organised by Brettonwood Partnership in the Houses of Parliament to celebrate the company's work with the DTI Enterprise Initiative, here I am seen welcoming The Rt Hon Michael Heseltine MP, President of the Board of Trade. Others on the platform are: The Rt Hon Robin Cook MP, Keith Vaz MP, and friend Sarosh Zaiwalla

Below: Here Lisa Aziz, hosting the Reception, is seen garlanding Robin Cook MP. Amongst other guests were: Michael Vigor, director of Enterprise at the Cranfield University School of Business, and other friends and well-wishers of my company

Above: In discussion with His Royal Highness Prince Charles at a Commission for Racial Equality (CRE) function at the Commonwealth Institute, London. Seen here with another guest sharing our conversation

Below: At a reception held in honour meeting an Indian dignitary, from left: Mr Praful Patel, chairman Uganda Resettlement Board, Suhail Aziz, Mr Crispin Cross, head of research, CRE, Indian guests, and Mohammad Anwar, senior research officer, CRE

Above: Ms Eithne Wallis, director-general of the National Probation Service for England and Wales, seen here visiting me at my office as chairman of the London Probation Board. Eithne had recruited me through a nation-wide competition for the role

Below: Farewell to Probation – I am seen here with my Board member colleagues at the London Probation Board, March 2007. Seated from Left: David Scott, chief officer; Suhail Aziz, chairman; Board members: Derek Sawyer; Mark Blake; standing from right:Lincoln Beswick; Judge Kennedy; Carole Markham; Maureen Salmon; Ken Ashken; Emma Mandley; Max Telling; and Hon. Judge from Crown Court.

Above: Hundred years of Rotary Celebrations, Chicago 2005. Rotarians from the world over representing 31,000 clubs worldwide with some 1.2 million membership, attended the centenary celebrations in the spirit of Rotary fellowship

Below: At a Rotary District 1130 London annual conference dinner-dance, Eastbourne. Seated at the dinner table from (L to R): Rotarians and spouses/friends: Lona, Nick, Stan, Chan, Maureen, Raj, Anna, Suhail, and Lona's friend

Anna and me with fellow Rotarians from the Rotary Club of Streatham, on a boat ride to Lake Michigan during 100-years of Rotary celebrations in Chicago 2005

I am seen here Exchanging Rotary greetings with club banners between President of Rotary Club of Streatham with President of the Rotary of Manila Bay, Philippines, while I was on a visit to the Asian Development Bank, Mandaluyong City, Manila, on consultancy business

I initiated two Rotary Foundation grants to the Jalalabad Disabled Rehab Centre and Hospital (JDRCH) from Rotary Clubs of Streatham and Tooting, along with other fund raising efforts to assist them establish their Surgical operations theatre. We worked in partnership with the Rotary Club of Jalalabad, Sylhet

Above: Some of my Sylheti friends living in London formed a group – "The 1952 Batch" – named after the year in which we passed our matriculation examination in 1952. Here we are with wives and few relatives at a lunch in one of our homes. Lunches would be held in rotation at our homes

Below: Vidya Anand, an Indian scholar and author, was a great cricket fan. Here I am with Vidya on my right and Pakistani international cricketer Alim Uddin on my left, at the members' enclosure at the Lords, as Vidya's guests

Lisa's Wedding

Above: Lisa on her wedding day, June 9, 1990: Lisa's younger sister Rebecca , mum Anna, most important person of the day Lisa, and me, dad Suhail, Chelsea Registrar's Office, London

Below: Some of our relatives at the steps of Chelsea Registrar's Office. It was a memorable day. Lisa being already a TV star got extensive coverage in the British media. Here some of Lisa's and Frank's close relations at the wedding. I was particularly pleased that my aunty Lucy (left, in Sari) and her family was able to join us from Bangladesh

Rebecca's Wedding

Above: Rebecca's wedding day, 27th June, 1998: Here Rebecca and Rickard with close family members at the Ritz, London. From left: Rickard's friend and 'Best Man', me, Anna, with little Leah (Lisa's daughter), the bride and the groom, Rickard's mum Greta, his niece, and Lisa and Frank

Below: A very happy couple Rebecca and Rickard after their marriage ceremony, off on their honeymoon

Above: Lisa Aziz receiving "Asian Who's Who" and "Asian of the Year award 1989-90. Here the Rt Hon Douglas Hurd MP (back to the camera) is seen with Lisa as he was about to give his speech; behind Lisa our very dear friend Dr Akram Sayeed. Douglas Hurd had arrived at the ceremony as Home Secretary and left as Foreign Secretary in the Thatcher government

Below: Prime Minister The Rt Hon Tony Blair MP with Lisa and her co-presenter during the PM's visit to ITV West studios in Bristol

Above: Lisa with her children Leah and Jacob at the Selsdon Park Hotel, DeVere Estates, Selsdon, during a coffee morning

Right: Rebecca, Rickard, Eleanor and Konrad on a family outing

Left: During our holiday in Rajasthan, India, our trip ended with a visit to the Tajmahal. Here Anna is seated on the famous Bench. We had a very memorable two weeks in India. The serenity of the Tajmahal with its history behind it is enthralling

Below: We managed to go on an elephant ride in Jaipur. Anna needed to gather some courage to climb on to the elephant but once on top she was relaxed

Above: On holiday in Europe: Anna, Lisa and me at a spot probably in Greece - photo taken by Rebeca. Our holidays covered most of Western Europe. I was driving my Volkswagen beetle which had clocked up 400,000 miles!

Below: Same holiday, Rebecca and Anna protecting from hot sun – photo taken by Lisa. I became extra tan in that holiday!

Above: Going for a walk after breakfast. Sometime we walked miles. Anna's interest was always buying curios from road side stalls for our home. She filled up the dresser with items of curios, ornaments and potteries

Below left: During my consultancy assignment on a World Bank funded project in the Sudan, I was staying in Khartoum. Anna and children joined me. Here we are about to go on a launch to cross the Nile near Khartoum

Below right: Our launch driver (Coxswain), a thoughtful Sudanese gentleman

Above: "Last cornet in Teignmouth" – that was our last holiday in Devon. We are seen with (l to R) Lynda - Anna's sister, Gary - Lynda's husband, and Gary's parents, summer 2013

Left: Anna's portrait which hangs on a wall in the sitting room of our bungalow enthrals her life's serenity

Anna and I at a Ball, Officers' Mess, RAF Swinderby, 1969

This was Anna's last painting of two flower pots, one pink, the other blue, made at the St Christopher's Hospice during the time of her palliative care at the Hospice

I believe that my own and my company's international consultancy experiences enabled me to be an effective member of this DFID forum.

National Health Service (NHS) (1997-2000)

I held two public appointments at the NHS: first, as chairman of the Lambeth Community and Mental Health NHS Trust, based within the Borough of Lambeth (1997–99) succeeding Lt Gen. Sir John Rae, and second, as chairman of the newly created Community Health South London NHS Trust (1999–2000).

During 2000, mergers and reorganisation of the NHS in South London were in progress. The NHS was again being reorganised south of the Thames. Community health and mental health were being separated, covering the three boroughs of Lambeth, Southwark and Lewisham. Upon their separation, community health became Community Health South London NHS Trust (CHSL) whilst mental health went over to Maudsley and Bethlem to form South London and Maudsley Mental Health NHS Trust (SLAM).

My appointments were through open competitive processes. At Lambeth it was from following press advertisements of the job in *The Sunday Times*, *The Guardian*, health journals etc. The CHSL appointment was via internal NHS reorganisation.

For the Lambeth appointment, I was interviewed by a panel of three from a shortlist of eight candidates – all except me white. I prepared for the interview by reviewing the information sent to me in the candidates' pack. I was selected. But a strange thing happened. Despite a strong CV – Dartmouth, Unilever, Ford, Mars, Royal Air Force, British Civil Service, Lewisham Council and high-level management consulting – I was offered an appointment for only one year to start with – 'on probation' as it were – with a provision that, after a year, I would be reviewed for satisfactory service, and if all was well I would be confirmed. I accepted this condition because I was confident I would pass this probationary period.

After a year of service, when I was about to end my one-year service, I got a call from the regional chairman of the South Thames NHS Region, Sir William Wells, to go and see him at NHS offices in Eastbourne Terrace,

Paddington. Sir William said to me, 'Suhail, before the Secretary of State (The Rt Hon. Frank Dobson MP) confirms you in your position, there is a step to go through. Would you write a couple of pages for me telling us why we should confirm you in your position?' I happily accepted the challenge. I wrote the piece describing how I approached the job, how I established rapport and relationships with my peer group chairmen in the area, other key players and stakeholders. How I took things in a positive way. Not long after I submitted my paper and before the end of my one year, I was pleased to be confirmed in my position as chairman of the Lambeth Community and Mental Health NHS Trust by the Secretary of State for Health.

I was glad to be appointed as a chairman of an NHS trust. My life-long ambition was coming to fruition and my belief in myself that I could do jobs at the top in Britain. So the chances came about through the public appointments: as chairman of two NHS trusts; and as chairman of the London Probation Board, National Probation Service (NPS), for the Home Office.

I enjoyed my job at Lambeth Community and Mental Health NHS Trust very much. This was a fulfilling appointment. I had a board of five non-executive and five executive directors. All very fine people. The chief officer, Erville Miller, an Irishman, a mental health professional to the bone, expressed his delight with my appointment to his trust and promised me his support and co-operation. At our first meeting he said to me, 'We are delighted to have you here,' a statement I felt was very sincere and never contradicted by him or his team's attitude or behaviour towards me in the following years. I enjoyed similar support from his top team, as indeed I did from Lt. Gen. Sir John Rae, my predecessor chairman, whenever I came into contact with him. Sir John served the Lambeth trust well. He was affectionately held in high esteem; one of the new trust buildings was named Rae House in recognition of his service in the creation and transformation of the Lambeth trust, following the sale of the Tooting mental hospital site. I knew it was a difficult act to follow at the Lambeth trust after Sir John Rae. In the months that followed, whenever I came into contact with him he treated me with respect and empathy. At my request I met him for coffee, when I knew I had been shortlisted for the post, to obtain some tips about the job. He was glad to give me some tips but made it clear that he was not in any way connected to the recruitment process, which of course I acknowledged. I had no intention of seeking any unfair advantage over the other seven candidates on the shortlist. That wouldn't be me.

As mentioned above, CHSL Trust came into being after the merger and separation of the community and mental health functions in inner city South London boroughs: the mental health side of the Lambeth trust merged with the existing very large mental health trusts, Maudsley and Bethlem, to form South London and Maudsley (SLAM); and community health in Lambeth merged with community health in the Southwark and Lewisham boroughs. This latter process included transfers, terminations, allegations of bias, recrimination, etc. I was chairman of CHSL Trust till the middle of 2000 when I resigned, along with the other non-executive directors of the board following a judge-led review initiated by the chairman of the regional health authority. The following describes what happened:

"-----Original Message-----
From: Gareth Hadley [mailto:gareth.hadley@appointments.org.uk]
Sent: 06 November 2009 17:32
To: Suhail Aziz
Cc: Andrea Sutcliffe
Subject: RE: Interview note

Suhail
My note is attached.
Have a good weekend.
Regards
Gareth
Gareth Hadley
Commissioner
Tels: 020-8789 2601 and 07824 372177

PA – Donna Ogunbiyi
Tel: 0113 394 6741

Note for file

WEST LONDON MENTAL HEALTH TRUST

On 8 December 2009, along with Lord Norman Warner and Virginia Crowe, I interviewed candidates shortlisted for appointment as chair of the West London Mental Health Trust. One of the candidates interviewed was Suhail Aziz.

Beforehand, Suhail Aziz had been advised that, during the course of the interview, he would be asked to offer insights into the circumstances surrounding his resignation as chair of the Community Health South London NHS Trust (CHSL). I asked that question. In response, Suhail stated:

- That he was appointed chair of CHSL following the reorganisation of health trusts in South London , having been formerly the chair of Lambeth Community and Mental Health Trust. The chair of the Regional Health Authority (RHA), Sir Ian Mills, had been against his appointment from the start, wishing the position to have been given to someone else. Moreover, the Board of CHSL included two other aspirants to the chair position, one of whom had been the person who had been favoured by Sir Ian as candidate for chair. Given this, there were potential difficulties within the CHSL Board from the outset.
- That CHSL was late off the mark in appointing a chief executive (due to factors external to the Trust). The person appointed was not the best candidate within the competition: she was one foisted on the Trust by the then chief executive of the RHA, Nigel Crisp. In doing this, Nigel Crisp had the support of his chair, Sir Ian Mills. This led to further difficulties within the Board.
- That, during Suhail's absence on leave, Sir Ian Mills initiated a review of CHSL. Following the review, all of the non-executive

directors including Suhail resigned. They did this in the interests of the NHS. All of the resigned NEDs remained eligible for public appointments: Suhail went on to be appointed chair of the London Probation Board.

- That this all happened almost ten years ago. Suhail had moved on, subsequently holding another major public appointment. He felt that there were lessons to be learned in terms of future NHS reorganisations: it was important that the redeployment of people should be handled more sensitively than was the case in South London and better planned so that there was not the impression given of there having been a takeover. Also, it was important that selection was based on merit.

GARETH HADLEY"

I received a written apology from the NHS appointments commission; a letter from the regional chairman with words of appreciation for my statesmanlike demeanour; and a letter from the minister of health, the Rt Hon John Denham MP, for my services to the NHS. I moved on to another major public appointment as chairman of the London Probation Board.

I was pleased to have been called upon to assist the process of mergers and amalgamation, separating community health from mental health, and thereby creating the two much larger trusts, to serve the communities of inner city London in Lambeth, Southwark and Lewisham.

During my time at NHS trusts I met some very pleasant people who I regarded as good friends. First among those was Patricia Moberly, chair of Guy's and St Thomas' NHS Foundation Trust. This was a very large, mega NHS trust. She led the transformation of these two trusts by extensive additions, refurbishment, renovation and external and internal thematic painting and decoration, making the ambience very cheerful, liked by patients and visitors alike, with staff contentment at its peak. During my time as chairman of NHS trusts, Patricia was always asking me to let her know if she could do anything to help. When I was going for heart surgery, she visited me and met my wife in a ward. When I became chairman of

CHSL Trust, Patricia came to know about some 'little local difficulties'. I received a note from her offering help if needed.

The Adelina Children's Hospital next to St Thomas' Hospital, and the addition of the brand new cancer centre with its own new building at Guy's Hospital must be the 'jewels in Patricia's crown'. After she stepped down following a successful chairmanship spanning over eleven years, Patricia was appointed by Prime Minister David Cameron to be a member of the Committee on Standards in Public Life. Alas not long after, Patricia passed away, taken by the dreaded disease. Her husband, Richard Moberly, and I served as governors of Lambeth College. It was Richard who gave me the sad news that Patricia had died from cancer.

Some others from my peer group of chairmen I want to mention. It is almost twenty years since I ended my association with the NHS but I still have fond memories. Because I was entering the NHS direct as a chairman from a business background, it was felt necessary by my regional chairman at the time, Sir William Wells, a distinguished businessman himself, for whom I had great regard, to appoint a 'mentor' to me, to act as my guide and as a sounding board for me in my new role in the NHS. Brian Otley, chairman of Invicta Trust, was to become my mentor. I used to meet Brian every month for a drink or lunch in his patch and chat about almost everything under the sun. I found Brian very amenable, immensely helpful; time spent with him was valuable.

Another person was Mr Bernard Williams, chairman of Maudsley and Bethlem Mental Health Hospital Trust before the creation of South London and Maudsley NHS Trust (SLAM). Bernard was a man of distinction, very keen on the NHS and seemed to be a first class chairman of a very large mental health hospital trust. He organised my visit to the Maudsley and Bethlem, and was kind enough to show me round himself, starting at the hospital's Denmark Hill site and covering the entire Bethlem Hospital site. The stories he told me about these hospitals and some mental health patients were fascinating. I was most impressed by his mastery of the history of the hospitals and how patients were looked after by very capable clinical staff.

There were many others I felt honoured to have come into contact with; some became my friends. They were my board members in Lambeth, CHSL, my peer group chairmen and of course the senior managers and nurses. I was particularly happy to have met Mrs Linda Smith, chair of Lambeth, Southwark and Lewisham Strategic Health Authority. She was always very supportive and gave me advice whenever I needed it. I express my deep gratitude to all of the people I met in the NHS.

National Probation Service for England and Wales (2000-2007)

I was appointed chairman, by the Home Secretary following the Nolan Committee procedure, with full responsibility as board chairman for Greater London Probation Service. My duties included corporate responsibility, governance, 'change' and organisational excellence, strategic direction, accountability and control; external/internal relations; ambassadorial duties at high level; organisational effectiveness, performance and monitoring; staff – 3,000+; budget of some £140 million, multi-site operations; caseload 30,000 offenders at any point in time (60,000 pa); leading, directing, advising in the London Probation Area.

I was recruited by Ms Eithne Wallis, director-general of the National Probation Service for England and Wales, through a competitive process, advertised in the national press following 'Nolan Committee rules' for public appointments. But changes were afoot.

Steve Murphy was a former chief officer of the North-East Probation Committee, based in Newcastle. He succeeded Eithne Wallis as the director-general (D-G) of the National Probation Service (NPS) for England and Wales when Eithne became a joint director, with Mr (now Sir) Martin Nairey, of the newly created National Offender Management Service (NOMS) of the Home Office, which was established by an Act of Parliament. It was the brainchild of Mr John (later Lord) Birt, a former director-general of the BBC. Mr John Gieves was the Permanent Secretary at the Home Office, with Jack Straw as the Home Secretary and Paul Boateng, a Home Office minister. Eithne was chosen as the D-G of the newly created National Probation Service (NPS) by Jack Straw and John Gieves. Through her unique style and originality of thinking, Eithne achieved a meteoric rise from a senior probation officer. I felt I got on fine with her.

But not long afterwards Eithne left NOMS to join industry. Steve Murphy became the new director-general of the National Probation Service.

As D-G, Steve Murphy supervised the headquarters in London with various national directors in his team. He also had oversight of the thirty-two county-based probation boards in England and Wales. All chairs and chief officers reported to the D-G separately on a parallel line-management relationship, while at the same time the chief officers also reported to chairs and their boards in a dotted-line relationship (an organisational arrangement of Eithne's creation, what she called the 'new choreography' for the NPS!). In practice this parallel reporting arrangement gave rise to some problems in governance, accountability and management.

These boards had overall responsibility for providing probation services for ex-offenders coming out of jail at the end of their sentences, to assist in their rehabilitation. The boards were uniform in their responsibilities, although their areas varied in size depending on their population. Each board had a chairperson and fourteen lay board members drawn from former probation committees, crown court judges, local communities and agencies.

Of all the probation boards in the NPS, my board, the London Probation Board (LPB), was largest – in fact the largest in the world outside Los Angeles. It was created by the merger of five probation committees of Greater London: Inner London, North East, South East, South West, North West. LPA had 30,000 ex-offenders on its books at any one time, a throughput of 60,000 every year, and a multi-million pounds budget at the time. My selection as chairman of LPB was through a nationwide competition, the job having been advertised in national newspapers such as *The Sunday Times* and *The Guardian*, under the Nolan Committee rules for public appointments. I had responsibility for running my board, for governance and accountability of the London Probation Area (LPA) through the chief officer (John Powls)'s, team. My board comprised the above-mentioned five former London probation committees' chairs, leaders of local authority councils, crown court judges, former senior civil servants, economists and local community leaders. The Home Office, LPB HQ and my London board offices were within close proximity of each other – a mere stone's throw!

I, being an appointee of the Home Secretary, reported to him via the Probation Service D-G. But in practice, both the chairman of the board and its chief officer had direct but parallel reporting lines to the D-G. In theory LPB chief officer Mr John Powls (JP) was responsible to the board for day-to-day running of the LPA, attending board meetings with the LPB top team. The arrangement meant that the LPB chief officer could go straight to the D-G without the board's knowledge. But if anything went wrong the board would be called upon, along with the chief officer, to account. This anomaly of parallel reporting lines to a single boss became serious when financial irregularities were discovered. Eventually it was decided that the chief officer had to go. The D-G had decided that the 'chair and chief must go'. So after the chief, it was the chair's turn!

But after the departure of the chief officer, I and my board pressed the D-G to urgently fill the vacant post of chief officer in London. Following the advertisement, a good number of candidates applied for the vacant chief officer job at the LPB. A long list of fifteen candidates was carefully considered by the selection panel (Steve as the D-G, myself as the LPB chairman, and the chief executive of NOMS, formerly chief officer of North-West Probation Service based in Manchester, but new in her NOMS role – from the Home Office). The long list of candidates was whittled down to three candidates in the final shortlist: (i) Steve Murphy's ex-wife, a fact unbeknown to me up to this point in time, but Steve was aware of the conflict of interest that could arise if she was successful; (ii) David Scott, currently chief officer of the Hampshire Probation Service; and (iii) a third candidate (male) who was internal from the NPS HQ. The panel agreed on the interview schedule. Interviews were duly held at the HQ with D-G Murphy in the chair. He seemed to have been very impressed by my skills and abilities in the drawing up of the shortlist, in my asking crisp incisive questions. After deliberation, the panel settled on David Scott. He was chosen for the London Probation Board chief officer post. My clear choice was David Scott. As chair of the LPB, the D-G recognised that I should have the final say because I and my board and the London Probation Area (LPA) itself had to live with the decision. At the end of the deliberation, Steve Murphy took me to one side of the room and told me something about David Scott's performance at the Hampshire Probation Board, then he asked me, 'Suhail, are you sure about David?' He got an unequivocal answer from me: 'Yes.' Steve duly authorised David's appointment. Steve knew I organised a warm welcome for David in LPA's work.

After a few days Steve invited me to his office for a cup of tea. Steve started: 'Suhail, I and the independent panel member found your contribution to the selection process of the chief officer for the London Probation Board extremely helpful. Therefore I will arrange for a "note" to be placed in your personal file to record the panel's appreciation, and I will let others in NOMS and the Home Office know.' I was most grateful to Steve for his kind appreciation.

There remained the outstanding matter, the D-G Murphy's mission: 'Chair and chief must go.' The chief had gone, it was the chair's turn! Attempts were made to oust me. I was going nowhere. Happily for me, it all came to nothing.

I would like to add that when my first three-year term of office was coming to an end, Steve Murphy had just become D-G, succeeding Eithne Wallis. It was Steve who, after receiving official advice, had recommended to the Home Secretary, Jack Straw, that I be reappointed for a second term of three years as chairman of the London Probation Board. I was most grateful to Steve for his confidence in me.

So what are my experience, impressions and insights from my time at the London Probation Board?

First: the resentment and jealousy I experienced – 'What is this coloured immigrant, a Bangladeshi guy, on top of us, doing here at the top of LPB?' Racism was at play. Chapters could be written under these headings! I often remember what I read from a famous columnist in *The Guardian*: 'British society is dripping in racism.' No matter what, I experienced racism or racial prejudice at every turn. I recall a saying I picked up from the Thatcher era: 'Not one of us!'

Second: no matter what, it was a 'no-win' situation. I was selected through an open competition for the position of chair of the London Probation Board from a nationwide shortlist of eight. The job was advertised in *The Sunday Times*, *The Guardian* and a few other national papers and public journals. The Home Office was directly recruiting without any recruitment consultants. My success in getting the chair job was not by any back door. I didn't know anyone to pull strings or anything like that. I believed that I had a lot to offer. It was a public appointment, following the Nolan procedure governing recruitment into public bodies, overseen by the Commissioner for Public Appointments. The appointing authority was the Home Secretary himself assisted by his officials. But I was to hear later that my appointment was for 'political correctness'. Apparently the Home Office minister Paul Boateng had instructed Eithne to 'find a black person for chairman of the London Probation Board'. So it's a no-win situation: if I didn't get the job – 'Oh, but he was not good enough'; if I got the job – 'Oh, it was for political correctness'. One could never win!

The Inner London Probation Committee (chief officer John Harding and his top team) was assisting in the setting up of the new London Probation Board and London Probation Area, for the whole of Greater London. Harding and some of his senior officers were co-ordinating the chairs' meetings of the five former London committees, leading to their merger into the London Probation Board.

One of the preparatory meetings for all the senior probation service staff was organised at the Commonwealth Institute, at High Street Kensington. The main attraction was going to be an afternoon tea and address by the new chairman – me – and the new chief officer for the London Probation Area, John Powls. When I finished my talk, John Harding, seated at the top table with me, passed me a little note which read, 'Wise words – John.' I turned to him and whispered, 'Thank you, John.' I felt encouraged, as I was told that John was a seasoned long-serving probation service man of high reputation, and the high-level gathering at the Commonwealth Institute was very much in my early days as chairman-designate of the LPB.

Probation Service 'not fit for purpose'

This is a tale about where responsibility lay – as I saw it:

An ex-offender, James (not his name), was coming towards the end of his jail term for murder. He was intelligent, well read and was well behaved in jail, for which he had only to serve half of his custodial sentence. Whatever duty was assigned to him by the responsible warden, James carried it out responsibly and diligently – be it in the kitchen, library, sweeping, cleaning his cell and so on. He was regular in attending classes for education and vocational training such as in the use of computers. He spent time in the library where he was seen to be very keen on using the computers. Overall he was viewed as a prisoner of good conduct and character by the jail governors and other authorities.

Under the rules, he was considered to be a good prisoner candidate to be recommended for parole to the Parole Board. The prison-based probation officer was happy to agree with the warden's opinion of the prisoner. However, it was thought to be reasonable not to take too much risk with this prisoner's early release lest he went back to committing crimes again. The authorities – namely the prison governor, the prison-based probation officer, assistant probation officer concerned, the chief officer – were all accountable to the Home Office for their decisions and actions. There was the chance that the prisoner, being very clever and intelligent, was covering up his real character to commit serious crimes.

After due diligence and thorough review of all aspects of his case, it was agreed by all concerned that the prisoner should be recommended to the Parole Board for early release. It was agreed that he would spend a period under the supervision of the probation officer and the hostel manager. The hostel was based in the Brixton area.

The probation hostel regime was firm and fair. The aim and purpose of a period in a probation hostel was to prepare prisoners to return to the world of work, become ready to engage with the life in the local community and prepare them to rejoin their families or be housed on their own by the local authority concerned or by a housing association. There were facilities, indoor games, learning new skills and so on at the hostel. He was seen spending time in the hostel library, reading newspapers and magazines. Frequently he would not go out, remaining instead in the hostel spending time on the library computers.

The probation hostel life was good if one behaved oneself. The inmates at the hostel enjoyed quite a lot of freedom. They were made aware that with that freedom came responsibilities. The probation officer would be fully engaged with James on a one-to-one basis, helping, training, educating and supervising the prisoner on parole. He/she in turn would report to their superiors about the conduct of the resident concerned. Prisoners on parole were allowed to go out after breakfast as long as they returned to the hostel by suppertime, at 8pm. Of course the hostel residents were tagged and monitored. They had to report to a police station during the day while out. During that time they were completely free to visit their families and friends, go to shops, see movies etc. as long as they acted responsibly. They knew that any reoffending might be met with a harsher prison life.

Being keen on computers, and reading newspapers and magazines, the ex-offender became very good at researching. When out of the hostel, he would spend time with his old school friend. Both had criminal records. They decided to study *The Sunday Times Rich List*. They began to research the life of a Chelsea banker. He worked at an international bank in the City. They knew that the wife of the target would take their child to the nursery school, return home, get herself ready to go out shopping or for coffee mornings with friends from about 11am to 1pm. Then she would pick up the little one from the nursery and go home for lunch. The husband would return from work in the evening.

One day, while the husband was at work and the wife was out shopping in King's Road, the pair broke into the Chelsea flat, having cut the alarm lead. They took jewellery, money, valuables and ornaments. As they were leaving, they bumped into the banker who was returning early from work. To stop him calling the police, they wrestled with him and put a knife in his heart. He died on the spot. The robbers ran off with their loot. The ex-offender on parole was back at the hostel on time for his supper. No one suspected anything. He had tucked away his share of the loot in his room.

The wife returned home after collecting her child from a friend's house only to find her husband lying in a pool of blood in the hallway. Completely traumatised, she managed to dial 999, the police came and the rest is history. It was not long before the police arrested the two for committing the murder and for robbery. Before the prisoner could go to the Parole Board for confirmation of his complete release, he was back inside for a life term.

So what about the Probation Service's performance? An inquiry was carried out, led by a High Court judge. His report placed the responsibility and accountability at the area chief officer's door. The press learnt of the report and suggested that a number of other officials were to be blamed, too. Because of the adverse publicity, the Home Secretary declared at a press conference that the entire Probation Service was 'not fit for purpose' – a phrase that really caught on, gained currency and has been repeated in different contexts. In accordance with the weaknesses identified by the High Court judge, the

Home Secretary decided to call for the chief officer of the London Probation Committee to go and see him. At the audience, the Home Secretary was furious. The press was demanding the Home Secretary's resignation.

According to press reports there was a chain of failure: the prisoner was clever, deceived everyone concerned – the warder, the prison governor, the prison probation officer, the probation committee and its chief officer, the Home Secretary – and ultimately the Government, all bore some share of responsibility. Were lessons learned? Not really! As far as I know no one was forced to resign.

Rates of reoffending never go down; the phenomenon of the 'prison revolving door' goes on and on. A service is stigmatised wrongly. Heads roll. Someone is scapegoated; someone else loses his or her job – and livelihood. But the cause is never dealt with. Effects and symptoms are immediate priorities. Lessons are claimed to have been learnt but are these tenable? Wait for the next time round? Meanwhile cuts in the number of probation officers, coupled with a failure to recognise the value of education and rehabilitation, continue to contribute to replicate the 'revolving doors' phenomenon. As well as undoing the cuts there are other ways of reducing the rate of reoffending: more emphasis on prisoners' education and training to prepare them for life outside in the community.

It happened again in the London Probation Area. A couple of years after I left I heard that another murder incident had taken place from the same hostel. A prisoner under probation committed a very similar offence. I was sorry to learn that David Scott (my favourite chief officer whom I had recruited with Steve Murphy when he was the director-general of the Probation Service) was called into the Home Office to see the Home Secretary, Jack Straw MP, and was dismissed on the spot for failing to prevent a repetition. He was to lose his job without regard to where precisely the fault lay or to the impact on supervision of ex-offenders of the severe cutback in probation officer numbers.

Farewell to probation

My six years at the London Probation Board were ending at the end of March 2007. It was quite a sad feeling that it would soon be over. My secretary and a staff member were tidying things up, official files were being checked and sent down for archiving, personal and confidential ones being separated carefully. My own private files I was taking home.

My chief officer, David Scott, would come in to talk about arranging the board farewell party, as my whole board was standing down after having served with me two terms of three years – preparation of the invitation list, speeches etc. During the last few days in office when these arrangements were being made, I was thinking about the people I should talk to and say goodbye to.

One morning David came into my office without any notice. After a bit of small talk, he came to the point of his visit: 'Suhail, is there anything you would like me to do?' I was taken by surprise. I didn't expect such a question as he and I had had an open, amicable 'chair-chief relationship'. I didn't quite understand the question. So I made light of it: 'Do what you would have liked to do for your previous chairman at the Hampshire Probation Board!' With hindsight it was an off-the-cuff reply. David's question was serious and now, after all this time, I realise his question had perhaps more to it, it had more behind it. My reply must have baffled David! I think he was asking me about an 'external recognition' that Steve Murphy had MENTIONED. Otherwise I could not find an answer to the serious question of my chief officer. Maybe now that Scott is retired I could ask him one day just out of curiosity!

At the farewell party I addressed the well-attended meeting. In attendance were my board members, senior managers, high officials, judges, officials from the new National Offender Management Service (NOMS), my personal invitees from other neighbouring probation boards. There must have been close to a hundred people. Food and wine was served. I gave my ten-minute speech, thanking everyone for their help and co-operation during my time at the London Probation Board. I also took the opportunity of stating that a retiring chairman of LPB disagreed with the view that the Probation Service was 'not fit for purpose'.

My talk was followed by my chief officer, David Scott, who gave a magnificent talk in his inimitable style, covering the work of the London Probation Board.

The format of the occasion did not include Q&As. Mixing and mingling among the guests continued for a while after.

Chapter Nine

Voluntary work

My family were committed to, flourished in and enjoyed voluntary work. They had great voluntary spirit. My father, both my grandfathers – maternal and paternal – uncles, aunts and cousins were all active in voluntary work. My father stood out in high-level cultural, voluntary and community work – more so in politics. At a very early age in his education my father participated in community wellbeing meetings. He would be gone to day-long meetings; sometimes even for a few days at a time. My mother would not know his movements; when asked where he was, she would say, 'Don't know where he is, I haven't seen him for some time'! He was very committed and selfless. He had a band of like-minded friends and compatriots, Hindus and Muslims, all working away together. He was deeply involved in politics. With the end of the Second World War, the independence movement in India against British rule was gaining momentum. My father responded to those calls for the *Khilafat Andolon* (the Caliphate movement) by religious leaders and the independence movement led by Mahatma Gandhi under the banner of the All India Congress.

I was only about eight or nine years old. In 1943–44, the war was in its final years. The Japanese had already taken Burma and were bombing parts of Assam (Dibrugarh, Manipur), getting close to Shillong and down the hills to Sylhet, my hometown. As described elsewhere I was experiencing the war-charged atmosphere – the blaring sirens, getting into trenches and staying there for hours at a stretch, getting caught up with calls from Air Raid Precautions (ARP) to take shelter. With the ending of the war in 1945, it was time for distribution of sweets and processions to celebrate British

India's victory against the Germans and the Japanese – young and old in processions chanting, 'Left right left right... German Bhagaya' ('We have driven out the Germans')! I was taking part in this excitement, for days on end, without regard to food or my parents wondering where I was. Time did not matter. Schools were closed anyway because of these events. I and my friends in the neighbourhood were all in it together – fun but serious too! It was all voluntary.

Of course my life was to take a huge turn. After finishing my school and halfway through a science degree course, I joined the navy as a pre-cadet in 1954. During my training and commissioned service in the navy, from 1954 to 1961 (Dartmouth, Pakistan Navy), I could not take part in any community, voluntary or political activities. There then followed jobs: East Pakistan Inland Water Transport Authority (EPIWTA), Lever Brothers Pakistan Ltd (Unilever), from 1961 to 1966, during which there was no time to engage in any voluntary or political activities. Back in England in 1966, for the first couple of years I was finding my feet and settling in with my young family. Anna and I were desperately trying to keep our heads above water, with little Lisa only four.

During 1968, when I came into contact with Mr (later Lord) Mark Bonham Carter, John Little *et al.*, my eyes began to open to the areas of race and community relations. I tried for jobs which would give me a deeper understanding of those fields. My feelings and a growing interest in this kind of work were taking shape while I was still in commissioned service in the Royal Air Force. For instance, I would write to the editor of *The Economist* on current issues with a *nom de plume* and they would refuse to publish, as they did not publish under noms de plume!

My involvement in voluntary work in England was to commence in earnest from the time I had left the Mars Group in 1978, to join the Commission for Racial Equality (CRE) as a director. This was to give me a diverse and varied range of experience and insights, some good, others not so good. I was, of course, very fortunate to have been exposed to such an extensive range of community and voluntary work, and I express my deep gratitude to all the good people who gave me the chance to serve. It was my great honour and privilege to have worked with some distinguished charities and voluntary organisations right across the spectrum: Christian,

Jewish, Muslim, Hindu, Sikh, Buddhist and others. I worked easily with black and Asian communities and made many friends and acquaintances.

I have been involved with many black and Asian organisations, taking leading roles, serving on their executive committees, representing them to authorities, lobbying, advocating or pleading for them on specific issues; fundraising, campaigning and so on. I have served as elected chairman and other official positions in numerous voluntary organisations. I believe that I have been effective in what I did, for which I am kindly remembered by many with whom I have had the honour and privilege to serve communities locally, nationally and internationally.

I mention below some of the voluntary and community-based organisations on which I have served:

Race Relations Board – Member, North Metropolitan Conciliation Committee (1971-1974)

I was recruited by Mr Mark Bonham Carter, chairman of the Race Relations Board (RRB), and John Little, chief officer, RRB, into this committee, one of several committees set up nationwide under the new Race Relations Act 1968. My chairman on the committee was a distinguished professor, Dr Fred Bayliss. Other members were from academia, business and trade unions. I was very interested in the concept of 'conciliation' in resolving race (human) relations problems arising in industry, commerce, education, employment, housing, health, community relations. It was to be achieved through mutual acceptance of a decision by parties in dispute, through conciliation committees up and down the country. The Race Relations Act 1976 was based on concepts and ideas imported from the United States by the then Home Secretary in the Harold Wilson Government, The Rt Hon. Roy Jenkins MP, the grounds having been prepared by stalwarts like Mark Bonham Carter, Frank Cousins, a former general secretary of the Transport and General Workers Union (TGWU) *et al*. This Act brought in the more sophisticated concepts of tackling discrimination by introducing direct and indirect discrimination, which, as the Act's provisions got more and more refined over time, was also to tackle conscious and unconscious discrimination. Today's Britain is a much better place to live in, with opportunities for ethnic minorities opening up in most walks of British life. But that is not to deny that an undercurrent of subtle and at times brutal racism remains ingrained in British society.

A couple of points worth mentioning from my time at the North Metropolitan Conciliation Committee:

1. As a member of a committee, I felt I was ignored during discussions and that I was not valued. On the other hand, white members got a respectful attentive hearing. I was to learn later in life that this indicated something fundamental. Other black and Asian members of such committees had the same or similar experience. As a consequence, ethnic minority members lost interest and 'withdrew'. Not only did those members lose out on participation in committees' work but Britain lost out, too – not hearing what they had to offer from their experience. In the long term, racial integration in Britain would suffer, probably for a long while.

2. Dr Fred Bayliss had to leave the chairmanship of the NMCC for personal reasons. The RRB decided that the chairmanship would go to Mr Ron Keating, a senior trade union official of very personable qualities and with employment relations experience in the workplace. My anecdotal understanding of how an important change in a committee was made was that the chairman of the RRB, Mark Bonham Carter, or at least the chief officer, John Little, would call the white members of the committee over the phone to let them know and advise them that, in the case of the NMCC, Dr Fred Bayliss was moving on and Ron Keating was taking over. But intriguingly, it would be an assistant conciliation officer serving the NMCC who would call me to tell me of the change. I recall when such an officer, an ACO, white, called me, I made a light off-the-cuff comment saying something congratulatory for Ron. The officer said something like, 'You have got a funny way of saying things, Suhail!' Somehow it stuck in my mind, confirming the suspicion that the culture amongst white members of staff, even on a race relations body, was to accord less importance or respect to ethnic minority people.

3. I recall attending a race relations annual conference of the RRB at the University of Warwick. Professor Hugh Clegg, from LSE, was one of the guest speakers. He made a comment which to me was profound: 'Do not scrutinise the inscrutable!' People would hold on to their private views (their personal or private prejudices) but scrutinising these would be futile, one would not get to the bottom of them! Such deeply held prejudices come out in behaviour, consciously or unconsciously, but are not revealed openly. To quote *The Guardian* columnist again: 'British society is dripping in racism.'

Calouste Gulbenkian Foundation (1976-1982)

Calouste Gulbenkian Foundation is an international charitable organisation founded in Lisbon, Portugal. Its UK branch was established in 1956. In Britain the foundation is mainly focused on arts and culture, social welfare and education. Its project-related help was targeted at bringing about profound and long-lasting effects in Britain and beyond.

In line with Gulbenkian's philosophy to engage on social welfare programmes to bring about profound and long-lasting effects, the foundation embarked on a major project in the race relations field – Black People in Britain: the Way Forward. In those days (1976) I was working as a personnel officer at the Pedigree Petfoods division of Mars Group, in Melton Mowbray, Rutland, Leicestershire. I was already quite involved in voluntary activities. I was very pleased to receive a personal invitation from Richard Mills, deputy director of the Gulbenkian Foundation, giving me some details about their proposed national conference, '*Black People in Britain: the Way Forward*', and asking me if I would like to join the steering committee tasked with bringing about the conference. I was of course delighted and felt honoured to accept.

The steering committee brought together a small number of leading community leaders from ethnic minority communities, black and Asian. It had to take into careful account the complicated diversity and sensitivities of the black and Asian communities in Britain at the time. It was a major initiative, completely untried before in Britain. There was a lot of nervousness about how it might go. As usual there was serious opposition to such an initiative from community groups who felt they had been left out, or who suspected it was an initiative by 'whites', not truly sensitive to black people's needs. So, the steering group had to proceed carefully, keeping the Gulbenkian Foundation in Lisbon in the picture. It was not an easy job to steer towards Gulbenkian's social welfare objective. All the expenses involved for steering committee members were to be borne entirely by the foundation.

To cut a very long story short, the conference was successfully delivered on time. Some 500 delegates from ethnic minority organisations in Britain, plus some individual representatives from institutions concerned, came together at a hotel in central London, to spend two days in discussions. A hefty conference report (A5 size), ¾ inches thick, titled *'Black People in Britain: the Way Forward'* was produced by the steering committee immediately following the conference. The report brought together summaries of discussions on racial discrimination, racial prejudice and disadvantages suffered in housing, employment, education, community centres, etc. A series of practical recommendations were made. The report was distributed widely in Britain. Its recommendations were to impact on policies, procedures and practices in many institutions, organisations and community-based councils and bodies up and down the country. I felt humbled and proud of my little contribution to the success of the *'Black People in Britain: the Way Forward'* conference and the work of the steering committee.

An incident depicting inter-racial relationships while serving on the steering committee of *'Black People in Britain: the Way Forward'* is worth mentioning. As a rather enthusiastic member of the committee, once following our meeting at the foundation in Great Portland Street, I made a telephone call to a member of the Gulbenkian staff, assisting the steering committee, to request something. The young lady was very capable and efficient. But she must have reported this rather officious, business-like request to Richard Mills. At our subsequent steering committee meeting, the air felt rather thick and charged. I carried on contributing to the discussion completely unaware of what was 'cooking'. Towards the end of the meeting, everyone had departed, rather in a pre-planned way, and I was asked to stay behind. Another member of the committee, Mr Phil Sealey, a West Indian, also stayed behind. Phil was an extremely vocal West Indian; he had lived in Britain most of his life and was well known for his views. Unbeknown to me Sealey must have been briefed by Richard Mills about my 'officious' request to a member of his staff for some assistance in a committee-related matter. I didn't mean it to cause any offence. Suddenly, without any small talk, Phil went straight into insulting and challenging me in an aggressive way, shouting, 'Who do you think you are, giving orders to the staff of this office, etc. etc.?' I was shocked by this tirade. He wouldn't let me get a word in edgeways! I think I managed to say that I was sorry to have caused the offence. I left the building. Sealey must have gone back to Mills' office to report that he had done the job. I saw no more of Sealey after the end of the steering committee or ever again.

I thought that this episode must have finished my association with Gulbenkian. But no! My sincere, effective and relevant contribution must have received some recognition. And indeed Richard continued to be a close friend and a colleague. He was a big man with a big heart. Some months later I was to receive an invitation from the director, Richard's boss, asking me to join the Gulbenkian Foundation Advisory Committee on Social Affairs. I felt honoured. I accepted the foundation director's invitation to join that advisory committee of distinguished social scientists, professionals, academics, senior civil servants from the Home Office and eminent people from the four nations: England, Scotland, Wales and Northern Ireland. As Richard Mills was the only person working closely with me who knew me, it must have been without doubt Richard who got me invited to join a much more substantial body of the Gulbenkian Foundation's advisory committee in the UK. To give them input from my knowledge and experience in Britain was a humbling honour and privilege. I ended my association with Gulbenkian in 1982. Some years later I heard that Richard Mills passed away. Paul Curnow, who was being groomed for succeeding Richard, and who I had met during my time at the foundation, took to the helm as assistant director. He too was bright, a sociologist, very committed, handpicked to serve to continue the invaluable work of Gulbenkian in Britain.

Labour Party Race Relations Action Group (LPRRAG) (1975-1980)

It has always been the Labour Party which has been at the forefront in the race and community relations field in Britain. LPRRAG was a Labour Party initiative to influence government policies and work towards eradicating racism in the Labour Party. Those days I was working as a personnel officer at the Pedigree Petfoods division of the Mars Group, in Melton Mowbray. I knew this organisation had been formed. So I contacted Alex Lyon MP, its chairman, and the LPRRAG general secretary, a former general secretary of the Fabian Society. I was taken straight into the executive committee and invited to become its vice-chairman. Meetings were held in national locations. I was particularly pleased to work very closely with The Rt Hon. Alex Lyon MP, at policy level. He was a distinguished, radical Labour politician, and served as a Home Office minister in the Callaghan Government.

I organised a meeting of the association in West Bridgford, Rushcliffe borough council offices, Nottingham. At a dinner at my place in West Bridgford, I and my family were pleased to entertain Alex Lyon, Clare Short and the secretary, before proceeding to the meeting in Rushcliffe Borough Council hall. At that time I was to learn something new from Alex Lyon: that 'it might not always be racial discrimination. It could well be that people have a feeling towards ethnic minorities of "strangeness and foreignness", a feeling of the unfamiliar or different. Over time these feelings always give way to "acceptance", and thus discrimination would be diminished.' But this has to be weighed against the deeper racial prejudices of British society, generated by history, including the colonial past. To repeat, as a *Guardian* communist (a white man) once wrote: 'British society is dripping in racism.' Margaret Thatcher once said, 'Not one of us!' and 'We cannot be swamped by these people!' The fight against racial prejudice and discrimination would continue. 'Affirmative action' following American experience would take time, the ground had to be prepared. We have to make progress by 'chipping away'. Pragmatism will be the key.

Nottingham and District Community Relations Council (1975–1978)

I had moved to Nottingham upon joining Pedigree Petfoods as a personnel officer. So my RRB conciliation committee membership in the London NMCC ended but I remained interested in continuing my work in race and community relations. I was gaining experience and, with that, a greater and deeper understanding of the 'race' field. Sir Geoffrey Wilson, retired permanent secretary from the Overseas Development Administration (ODA, now the Department for International Development – DFID), had been appointed to take over from Mark Bonham Carter as chairman of the Race Relations Board. So I approached Sir Geoffrey to express my interest in continuing my work in this field. In due course I was invited to join the Nottingham Community Relations Council. I was appointed chair of its employment sub-committee.

One prominent race discrimination case was being handled by the employment sub-committee against Boots, a major employer in the East Midlands region, indeed in the country, with thousands of employees, a substantial number from black and Asian communities. The case was to prove a landmark in the fight against racial discrimination in employment.

BBC Asian Unit Advisory Committee (1977-1982)

This was a committee set up by the BBC Board of Governors for providing advice on ethnic minority broadcasting needs of the growing number of Asians in Britain. The communities were mainly from the South Asian communities – Indians, Pakistanis, Bangladeshis, also touching on the Nepali and Bhutanese communities, including, of course, those who lived elsewhere in the world: USA, Canada, Europe. The committee's work came under the BBC Charter: to inform, educate and entertain. Internationally, BBC World Service provided programmes in certain important languages of the world such as Arabic, Russian, Persian and so on.

The Asian Unit programme output was directed at Hindi- and Urdu-speaking Asians from the Indian subcontinent who had made their homes in Britain. Every Sunday morning two distinguished Asians, Mr Mahendra Kaul from India and Mr Saleem Shahed from Pakistan, would broadcast/present a one-hour programme called *Apna Hi Ghar Samajhye* ('Please Do Feel at Home'). The programme name was later changed to *Nai Zindagi Naya Jeevan* ('New Life [Urdu], New Life [Hindi]'). Lord Chitnis (a staunch Liberal Party man) was a member of the Board of Governors and also chairman of the Asian Unit Advisory Committee. The listening figures were encouraging to the BBC. My membership came about in an interesting way. I suppose my name was doing the circuit. I got an invitation to join the committee. I liked the aims and objectives of the committee. So I accepted. The committee meetings were held at the BBC in Birmingham where the above programmes were produced and broadcast.

The politics in Britain under Labour was to push for racial integration, not racial assimilation. The high-ups of the BBC thought, wrongly, that *Apna Hi Ghar Samajhiye* or *Naye Zindagi Naya Jeevan* had run their course, and were slowing down racial integration amongst the young Asians of subcontinental origin. That meant the programme was not getting strong support from the top management, or the finance needed. Cuts in funding led to the Asian programmes being wound up. Our advisory committee sank as well. But the BBC management was, in my view, right that the rising young Asians, who were mostly British born and English speaking, had aspirations similar to their peers from the white majority society. But it was also true that the Asian programmes assisted the racial integration of the first- and second-generation Asians. They helped to make the Asians feel at home – a major objective of the programme.

While living in Nottingham, an outdoor broadcasting team under the leadership of my friend at the Asian programmes, Mr Mahendra Kaul, a distinguished Indian community leader in Britain, organised an outdoor broadcast of a variety function from a community centre in Nottingham. Lisa Aziz, my elder daughter still at secondary school in Nottingham, was asked by Mahendra to host that community event. The event was broadcast on the following Sunday morning's Asian programme. My family was delighted to see Lisa in action on the programme. In a way that was the start of Lisa's interest in the media, culminating in a career in broadcasting, eventually making her an award winning TV/Radio personality in Britain. I acknowledge Mahendra Kaul's talent spotting of Lisa with deep gratitude.

Bangladeshi community

Following establishment of Bangladesh as an independent nation in 1971, my involvement with the Bangladeshi community in East London continued.

The following are examples where I mention some of my experience and achievements. Firstly, I got to know some Bangladeshi friends to whom I grew close – M/S Ramiz Uddin, Aziz Choudhury, Aklis Choudhury, Abdul Goni, Mustafa Ahmed, M. A. Talukdar, Mr Nipen ('Nipen da' – respected brother Nipen), Barrister Syed, to name but a few of the many. Some are no longer with us; others, with the passage of time, are no longer in touch with me or me with them, people having moved on. Together we worked in some of the initiatives listed below.

East London Bangladeshi Enterprise Agency (ELBEA), formed 1985

With my Bangladeshi friends and partners I was able to establish this agency focused on the economic disadvantages of the Bangladeshi community in East London as revealed by the House of Commons Select Committee report, 'Bangladeshis in Britain', referred to above. As its elected founder chairman I was able to mobilise support from some key players in enterprise and entrepreneurship, such as Business in the Community (BiTC), and through their network of contacts in the business community who wanted to engage with the East End's disadvantaged minority communities. I was instrumental in mobilising support to establish the only business support agency in East London focused mainly on the Bangladeshi and other minority communities' business efforts. I was saddened to discover a bit of racism from a Labour MP, the late Mr Ian Mikardo, a Jewish MP for Bow. Despite my best efforts and success in bringing about the successful establishment of the East London Business Enterprise Support Agency, Ian Mikardo, supported by one or two at Business in the Community (BiTC), blocked my being elected its first chairman, or even my inclusion on the executive committee of the agency; instead another Bangladeshi from my group was selected. I did not have an issue with that appointment. However, I learned something else: when it came to the inclusion of ethnic minority members to committees, the natural propensity of the majority in positions of power would be to select relatively docile and even ineffective members rather than consider the wider interests of the body in question by selecting people on merit.

London Boroughs Bangladesh Association (LBBA), formed 1980

Likewise, I was responsible for establishing another organisation: this was focused on 'education' of Bangladeshi men and women who could not speak, read or write English and yet their children were going to mainstream schools speaking good English. This too was following up on the major recommendation on education in the House of Commons Select Committee report, 'Bangladeshis in Britain'. Taking advantage of the Government's support for English as a Second Language programmes in Lambeth and Merton, I led the setting up of Saturday morning classes, negotiating funding for teaching staff, obtaining spaces for classes in local schools, getting them opened on Saturday mornings and other logistical support for strengthening language skills in Bangladeshi parents. We would provide transport, personally picking up parents for classes and dropping them back at the end during term time on Saturday mornings. The co-operation of Merton Borough Council education departments in their assistance is noteworthy. I record this with gratitude.

There were a few organisations in the mainstream where I must admit to having been selected to serve as 'the statutory Black'. Although I felt I was not able to contribute, or even encouraged to contribute, to the deliberations of these committees, I did not want to disengage from them for fear of being stigmatised as a 'leaver'. I suppose if one asked about my involvement, there would be some derogatory comments: 'He had nothing relevant to say,' or simply, 'He was out of his depth.' A feeling of 'one can never win'!

The Jalalabad Organisation in the UK (1983-2002)

I was also keen to form an association of likeminded Sylhetis to focus on the development of our home district, Sylhet, as well as remaining alert to the needs and campaign for Sylheti people's interests and wellbeing overseas. I was elected chairman of this organisation in addition to the ELBEA and the LBBA described above. We had a small number of committed community people as members. We campaigned on issues such as writing to ministers about Sylheti people's immigration problems and the restaurant industry's acute shortage of competent Sylhet chefs; this had become a perennial problem. The Home Office would not appreciate that home-grown Sylhetis, having been brought up and educated in Britain (some were even Oxbridge graduates), had higher aspirations than their parents and grandparents in the UK, and therefore they were not interested in entering the catering trade to serve as chefs, waiters, managers or even as proprietors. Furthermore, it was unrealistic to say that East European migrants could be recruited to be so-called 'Indian tandoori' restaurant staff. The culture and deep understanding of what constituted, for example, the 'chicken tikka masala' is sadly missed! I could not say that our organisation was successful in persuading the immigration authorities about the industry's needs. Our community's efforts with the Home Office in this regard remain unsuccessful to the present day!

In all the above Bangladeshi community-based activities of voluntary organisations I had to be careful. One could easily get tangled up in community politics, or financial scandals, or just plain politics of jealousy, resentments, innuendos, unfounded allegations, false accusations, defamation or cant. It had happened once or twice to me in my own experience that money meant for charitable funds had been pocketed by ill-intentioned people. Chasing them became a tough task. They got away with it by going into hiding, so I didn't see such people again. This was sad because until then they worked closely with me. Such people were tremendous talkers, a skill they used to deceive or cheat.

I would like to record my appreciation of one of my associates from the Bangladeshi community in Britain with whom I had worked in the above organisations. He was my most dear and respected friend, Mr Ramiz Uddin. He came from a respected family of Sylhet. He was deeply involved in the Bangladesh independance movement from London. Ramiz Uddin was our vice chairman in all of the three organisations listed above of which I was chairman. He was a man of calm disposition, deep knowledge and had wide experience in community politics. I knew I could always rely on him for his sound advice. When I worked as the head of employment and economic development at the Lewisham Council I had arranged for a business-cum-residential unit to be allocated to Mr Ramiz Uddin and his family. He successfully conducted his leather goods business in Deptford for some years. Then they moved on. I lost my contact with him. Much later on, there was a message on my telephone answer machine: "Aziz Saab, this is Ramiz, you please forgive me". I never heard from him again until I got the sad news from my friend Saleh Khan that my dear friend Ramiz Uddin had passed away.

Queen Mary College, University of London, Research Advisory Committee, Department of Political Studies, (1987–1996)

Initially, under a previous leadership with chairman The Rt Hon. Patrick Jenkin MP (later Lord Jenkin), I felt motivated to work with this committee. I contributed ideas to some of their research programmes focused on ethnic minorities' educational needs, especially the large Bangladeshi community in the catchment area of QMC in east London.

While working there I came across Sydney Roper. As discussed elsewhere, he was a principal officer at the CRE in the Community Affairs division. When following the 'fiasco over a working party', as *The Times* reported it in May 2001, four senior people departed; Sydney was one of the two whites, I and Crispin Cross were the black/Asian two, presumably used by the commission to balance for 'political correctness'. The Home Office overturned the CRE decision as, reportedly, 'procedures' were not followed. So all four were invited back. Sydney did go back, the other three didn't. Sydney was sent off to Edinburgh. After that tenure in Scotland he took up a research associate position at QMC. He was organising seminars for local authority personnel and others. I volunteered to take a slot in one of the seminars focusing on race relations, based on my own experience at the CRE and elsewhere. Sydney Roper gave me feedback, which was not very glowing. Clearly I had not hit the button with my narrative of insightful experience in race relations. Then Roper did not pay my agreed consultancy fee. I got paid but it was a sad episode with a former colleague of mine from the CRE.

Ethnic Minorities Business Development Unit, City of London Polytechnic, (1986–1994)

Member, Board of Governors, London Guildhall University,(1995–2002)

My involvement with London Guildhall University in East London spanned a period of sixteen years, which started with its precursor institution, the City of London Polytechnic, Ethnic Minorities Business Development Unit (EMBDU). At the start our work was with the local Bangladeshi community to get them setting up in business on their own, rather than working in the local garment and leather goods manufacturing industries. The imagination and entrepreneurial flair shown by the principal, Professor Sir Roderick Floud, later to become vice-chancellor of London Guildhall University, supported by his colleagues at the business department, namely Mrs Cynthia White, was phenomenal.

Penetration into the Bangladeshi community of East London was not easy. They had their own prejudices and belief that there was no point in working with the whites, who did not understand the community. So I mobilised what support I could through people I knew in Brick Lane and the adjoining conurbation to encourage the local Bangladeshi population that it was worthwhile engaging with the City Poly's EMBDU. I persuaded the polytechnic's senior staff – Roderick Floud, Cynthia White and some others – to appoint a local Bangladeshi at the unit to generate thrust into the enterprise. I identified Mr Badrul Ludi. Ludi had briefly met me once when he was working as a clerical assistant at the local branch of the Sonali Bank. I was not aware that Badrul Ludi had me in his sights to help him progress. Ludi's English was not up to the mark to communicate freely with staff at the poly. He came from the Biyani Bazar area of Sylhet. That population in Britain was overwhelmingly represented in the catering trade, in the so-called 'Indian tandoori' restaurants where they worked as owners, managers, chefs and waiters.

I was instrumental in getting Badrul Ludi appointed to lead the unit's work with the local Bangladeshis. He was very skilful. Eventually the unit's work progressed, engaging with Bangladeshi youths who had little or no experience in business, who had business acumen but poor English. But they did not have to speak fluent English to do business; that realisation helped the process. The unit recruited potential entrepreneurs. Ludi and some Sylheti tutors were recruited to give lessons in basic English as a Second Language (ESOL), arithmetic, accounting etc. The unit's work flourished. It was able to point the Bangladeshi entrepreneurs to potential business opportunities in thriving East London, including of course Canary Wharf.

About that time, in accordance with the Department of Education new policy, all the polytechnics in the country were to become universities. Accordingly, when the Polytechnic of East London became London Guildhall University, the EMBDU's work was absorbed into the new university's structure. I was interviewed by the chancellor of London Guildhall University, Lord Limmerick, the Earl of Limmerick, and the vice-chancellor, Sir Roderick Floud. I must have impressed them at the thirty-minute interview. I was duly appointed a governor on the board of London Guildhall University. My appointment was not just to remain focused on the Bangladeshis in East London at the basic level but to contribute to the work of the university more widely. So, gradually I was to see myself appointed a member of the university's audit committee, of the university's strategy committee, its consultative committee for policy formulation and implementation, and a member of the board of Metro-New Media Ltd, an adjunct subsidiary outfit under the able chairmanship of a colleague on the board, a retired NatWest bank senior executive as its chairman.

I saw to the recognition of Ludi's work. Slowly but surely he was promoted to senior lecturer grade. His work was mainly to assist recruitment of Bangladeshi businessmen and some women, their business education, assistance in setting up in business through signposting to support agencies in East London and the City. The leadership, faith and confidence in the whole enterprise of EMBDU by Roderick Floud, Cynthia White and their colleagues were commendable. Without their enthusiastic support we would not have achieved much through this groundbreaking initiative of London Guildhall University for local Bangladeshis. I stood down from the governorship when Guildhall was to merge with North London University to become London Metropolitan University. Slowly things fell by the wayside. Sadly, I lost contact with the good people I worked with, although on occasion I would see them at meetings at Toynbee Hall.

Tower Hamlets Education Business Partnership (THEBP), (1995–2010)

Engaging the major business organisations with local educational institutions to enable pupils to find employment in the City of London and elsewhere in mainstream business was the main objective of the Education Business Partnership (EBP) movement in local communities up and down the country. This successful nationwide initiative was the brainchild of Business in the Community (BiTC) under the leadership of its chief executive, Stephen O'Brien CBE. I was honoured to have been called upon to be a director on the board of the THEBP. My focus was on the educational and employment needs of the local Tower Hamlets Bangladeshi community: to advise business representatives on the board of the EBP how to encourage Bangladeshi boys and girls at Tower Hamlets schools and colleges to aspire for more by engaging with business mentoring through the EBP; and how to raise awareness of City institutions about the existence of minority groups such as Bangladeshis who were falling behind. The THEBP member support network of business organisations offered local students bridges to job opportunities. I served on this body for over ten years. My association with the EBP's chief executive, Mark Tyler OBE, was to last for many years, eventually becoming a friendship. He was a great man – honest, forthright and always cheerful. Mike always supported and encouraged me. It was most gratifying to me when, at one of the major events of the EBP, to which my elder daughter, Lisa, and I were invited, the chairman of the EBP, a BP person, acknowledged my contribution to the EBP's activities in glowing words. However, and it is a big however, my sadness was that for the duration of my board membership, I kept one item alive on the EBP agenda: how to get suitable representation of local Bangladeshis on the board of the EBP! Somehow, despite my best efforts, the local Bangladeshis could not be motivated to take up one or two memberships on offer from the EBP board. I was there on the board as an 'immigrant' from South London! It is not that qualified Bangladeshis were in short supply but they asked, 'What's in it for me?' Or as the American would say, 'Where is the beef?' It was a particular weakness of my Sylheti community in East London. It held them back.

South East London Community Foundation (SELCF), (1998–2005)

I was headhunted to become a trustee of this newly established charity in South East London. I was invited to meet the founder chairman, Mr Peter Jefferson-Smith, and one of his trustee colleagues over coffee at the Ritzy cinema building in Brixton to talk about the charity's aims and objectives, its sources of funding and the officers. I felt honoured to have been invited to join this community-based charity. I believe I contributed to the work of the charity in helping process applications for funds from small groups who could not apply for funds from larger bodies or organisations. I carried on with the trusteeship while Peter was still chairman of the board of trustees. After him the chairmanship changed to individuals whom I did not know much about. I tried to keep up my interest. A new director was chosen. I began to feel demotivated. Later on I learnt that disaster struck SELCF, as indeed happens to many organisations in the voluntary and charitable sectors. The new director turned out to be a fraudster. She was sacked for misusing the trust's American Express credit card, swindling funds etc. The losers were the small ethnic minority groups in South London. I don't know what became of SELCF. I lost track.

The board of the Corporation of Lambeth College, (2000–2009)

I was a resident of Lambeth borough from 1978 to 2011, over thirty-two years. During this time Dame Lorna Boreland-Kelly, a distinguished black lady, was the chair of the board of governors at Lambeth College. She also lived in Lambeth and was working locally in the health sector, I think somewhere in the Croydon area. I got to know Lorna through a mutual friend, Jennifer Beever, who lived near me. Both Jennifer and her husband, Colin Beever, were my close friends and neighbours. Colin was my boss, my mentor at the Commission on Industrial Relations (CIR) mentioned earlier. Jennifer was active in the Labour Party, in the Co-operative Party and in the Fabian Society. She was well connected in the Labour Party and knew a very large number of senior figures. Lorna was a member, too, of the Lambeth Co-op Party. I was a member of the Labour Party as well as Lambeth Co-op

Party. I met Lorna at one of Jennifer's parties at her house.

These introductions culminated in my being encouraged to apply for membership of the board of governors at Lambeth College where a vacancy for a governor had come up. Lorna was very thorough. Even though she knew me and something about my background to date, I had to apply with others for the vacant position at the Lambeth College board. Lorna chaired the selection panel, consisting of herself in the chair, the college principal and three other board members. The interview was thorough. Lorna had declared that she knew me, to keep things above board. The interview lasted about thirty minutes. I recall a question being asked by the principal, arising out of my written application: 'The board would supervise the college management committee comprising senior staff. In discharging that duty by the board, what would be your management style?' My answer was given in my written application: 'Gentle touch on the tiller.' I was asked to elaborate what I meant. I gave my answer. The body language and expressions on their faces indicated to me I had satisfied the panel. I was duly elected a governor. I was assigned to two sub-committees: finance and general purposes, and the search committee, and at a later date as chair of the audit committee.

But after finishing my six-year stint as chairman of the London Probation Board in 2007, I had to have heart surgery in August 2007, followed by replacement of both knees in 2008 and 2009. So my health forced me to resign from the governorship of Lambeth College. I also had to withdraw my application for membership of the Judicial Appointments Board. (Through my encouragement, Lorna had successfully applied to become a member under the chairmanship of a long-time acquaintance of mine from my Race Relations Board conciliation committee days: Ms Usha Prashar, a Kenya Asian, now Dame Usha Prashar. Lorna had been keen for me, also, to join the Judicial Appointments Board. But I could not pursue that opportunity for health reasons.)

All organisations go through human relations problems and Lambeth College was no exception. I understood Lorna was doing succession planning preparing another black female governor, Mrs Jennifer Powell, to take over from her as chair of governors when she stepped down in the near future. Jennifer Powell, an employee of renowned American HR firm, Towers Perrin, was an extremely able person. Her performance at board meetings was outstanding. As part of preparing Jennifer for the chairman role, it was decided to appoint her to become chair of the audit committee. I was not consulted. My health problems caused me to be absent on a few occasions but I believe I should have been consulted. Anyway, I had in mind that upon my resignation another able member of the audit committee, Richard Moberly, Lorna's vice-chair previously, would take the chair. So I queried the process adopted. I felt I should have been told what had happened. Unfortunately the clarifying was left to the clerk/secretary. The secretary, in my view, became very defensive, so much as to involve the college legal advisers. I made a complaint about the clerk's handling of the situation. It was not upheld. The local education authority decided that she had acted properly. In fact, I had no quarrel with the board secretary. She took it upon herself quite unnecessarily. In my view the process of appointment adopted lacked transparency and openness. The upshot was that I lost Lorna as a friend. I put it down to experience.

The Community Development Foundation (CDF) (Home Office/ DCLG) (1999-2008)

CDF is a major charity funded by the Home Office. Later it became accountable to the Department of Communities and Local Government (DCLG). I was spotted and selected as a trustee by the then chief executive and chairman, a very strong, committed Labour MP of Liverpool. I served for ten years as a trustee under two chairmen; the last one was also a former Labour MP from the Derbyshire Peak District, Mr Tom Levitt.

An official from the Home Office would regularly attend the board meetings of the charity to maintain government oversight. CDF's away weekend was a regular annual event. Most trustees would attend regular board meetings and the annual away meetings. The trustees were distinguished people, very experienced in their own fields and had a lot to give to the deliberations of CDF. It was active in research-based activities, advising and influencing government policy on its impact on communities and their development.

CDF networked with many voluntary organisations and charities with a view to giving them grants and support. This was a difficult job because the organisations had to agree to some monitoring and evaluation of their performance. This generated reactions from the recipients of aid. They, being voluntary bodies, were free to complain. Frequently they would complain to the Home Office Voluntary Services Unit (VSU). This would then filter down to the CDF board of trustees for action and/or advice. I was particularly struck at one or two of CDF's annual gatherings when the Home Office official would extremely tactfully point out that in the eyes of numerous voluntary organisations with whom CDF came into contact, it was seen as 'arrogant', 'bureaucratic' or 'unhelpful'! So, indicated the Home Office official, some 'humility' was called for. One got the impression CDF could never get it right. Of course, not all the CDF officers interfaced with their contacts in the respective voluntary bodies successfully. CDF did invest in training and development of its staff working with client organisations. But there remained the need for some humility within the CDF in its relationship with client organisations in the voluntary sector.

The Home Office was developing policies about fighting terrorism, stopping Muslim radicalisation and finding a long-term solution through community engagement. As the charitable arm of the Government, CDF was called upon to assist in bringing about 'community cohesion' mainly focused on the muslim community of Britain. The Home Office put a few million pounds at the disposal of CDF, which then launched into a programme of bringing together community organisations to start working towards the goal of community cohesion. Altogether it was a major multi-million-pound government initiative.

I, being a Bengali Muslim trustee of CDF, was assigned to its grant-giving programme. There was also a CDF officer assigned to work with a project evaluation committee and a consultant who did the actual work of coming up with grant-giving analyses and recommendations for particular Muslim organisations. Essentially the Muslim organisations would put up project proposals as to how they would work with mosques, madrassas and other Muslim community groups to bring about community cohesion in the Muslim community. Larger organisations got larger grants; smaller ones got smaller grants or pump-priming grants to enable them to get off the ground with their attractive ideas.

Although CDF disbursed a few million pounds of public money for the community cohesion programme, in my view this was a poorly conceived idea and a difficult programme to implement. In the case of the Muslim community, radicalisation of young Muslims could not be countered simply by giving away grants to organisations purporting to be credible representatives of the Muslim community. First, community engagement had to be done effectively. To do that, there was the question of gaining the trust of the young Muslims vulnerable to radicalisation. This is a complex process requiring serious honest engagement. Second, de-radicalisation comes after we have understood and acted on community issues such as deprivation, alienation, their causes, then the question of making people see the value of inclusion: inclusivity would show people that policymakers are serious about community engagement. Once policies are developed and put into effect to meet these challenges, we may aspire to success in community cohesion. I met many important figures in the community deeply committed to bringing about community cohesion. The last chairman I worked with was the Hon. Tom Levitt MP, a former under-secretary of state, with whom I still kept in touch. He continues his good work, writing books on corporations' responsibility in the community.

Standing Conference of Asian, Caribbean and African Organisations in the UK (1978-1980)

This was a very encouraging development following on from Gulbenkian's *'Black People in Britain: the Way Forward'* discussed above. That conference brought many of us from black and Asian communities to know one another right across Britain's ethnic minority communities. Coming from all over the country, some amongst us in leadership roles decided to form this association. We had a few monthly meetings trying to decide what we wanted to do. Slowly aims and objectives were identified. But then the realities of this world began to hit us. How were we going to finance the running of this organisation? It was always difficult to get funding for a newly born organisation. We did not get any government or statutory funding. Fares and out-of-pocket expenses of committee members were met by themselves but it could not be done to any sustainable level. Therefore the Standing Conference of Asian, Caribbean and African Organisations slowly met its inevitable end. It was a noble multiracial, multicultural experiment. I recalled what Mark Bonham Carter said: 'It is always easy to form an organisation, it is difficult to sustain them!'

Bangladeshis in Britain – British-Bangladeshis

With the passage of time the 'Bangladeshis in Britain' community have transformed themselves into 'British-Bangladeshis'. When we talk about Bangladeshis in Britain we mean predominantly the Sylheti community. Maybe 95% of the Bangladeshi community here originate from the district of Sylhet, the north-eastern part of Bangladesh. (For more please Google 'Sylhet'.) The number of British-Bangladeshis in Britain is just over 600,000 (2015); it is a young third-generation community, although the first generation of today's Bangladeshi community must have started here in large numbers from the 1950s.

The economic base of the community is the successful catering industry, which started building up from the 1960s and '70s. The so-called 'Indian tandoori' restaurants to be seen in almost every city, town and village of Britain are owned, run and managed by Bangladeshis (Sylhetis) in Britain. The word 'Indian' associated with the restaurants' name is mainly a brand name to signify connection of the cuisine with the Indian subcontinent. But technically it's a misnomer! The catering industry's growth has been phenomenal. The estimate of total home remittances is £15 billion annually supporting the Bangladesh economy and is the second highest export earner after the garment industry of Bangladesh.

The social and economic base of the community in Britain is continually being strengthened by the work of the following organisations:

Bangladeshi Women's Association: This association was formed before the Bangladesh independence movement in Britain. They had their office in Ledbury Road, London W11. I have personally known some of the leading members of this association: Mrs Zebunnessa Baksh, president (also chairman of Bangla Education and Cultural Centre) and Mrs Anowara Jahan (also a CRE commissioner). The association joined the Bangladesh movement in the UK and campaigned for recognition of Bangladesh. On occasion we have joined hands to campaign on issues of concern to the community as a whole. BWA was at the forefront of campaigning for Bangladeshi women's education and wellbeing in Britain. Sadly some of the leading figures are no longer with us. I felt very privileged to know and work with some of them.

The Bangladeshi Caterers Association: This association was formed by the energetic initiatives of some very successful restaurant owners in the UK but mainly from Greater London. This body represented most of the Bangladeshi (Sylheti) restaurants with staff numbering up to ten or more in each, including the hundreds of 'takeaways'. I have been involved with some of their work, writing up papers, advising etc. and have known some of the leading members of the association. I recall the campaign for getting more chefs from Sylhet, which was started by the staunch community relations officer from Sheffield in the 1960s, the late Aley Rasul, many years ago and the Home Office's repeated refusal to accept their case to this day.

The Annual Awards Ceremonies: The Bangladeshi catering industry is flourishing. Every year several awards events are held mainly in London but also in Birmingham and Manchester. Prominent amongst those is the annual award ceremony held in about November under the auspices of Mr Enam Ali MBE at Battersea Park, London. He has successfully enlisted the participation of British Cabinet ministers; Prime Minister David Cameron and his senior colleagues have been chief guests at Enam Ali's annual awards ceremony. These occasions are hosted by distinguished TV and radio personalities and addressed by ministers. The function is a black tie occasion attended by restaurant proprietors and their relevant staff who might be receiving an award for a particular skill in the trade. Enam Ali enjoys a particular accolade: he was once described by Mr Cameron as 'the formidable Enam Ali'.

There are other similar events on occasion to recognise talents in the restaurant industry. They are held in similar style to Enam Ali's events at Battersea Park. These are held in various banqueting halls in the above major city locations.

British-Bangladeshi Who's Who: I was invited to another special event with my daughter, Lisa Aziz. That was at the launch of the 2012 edition of the book, held at Alexandra Palace in Wood Green, London. The editor-in-chief of the publication is Mr Abdul Karim. This *Who's Who* follows the pattern of the *International Who's Who*. Under the leadership of Mr Abdul Karim the publication is already successful. Mr Karim's staff are dedicated to holding up with some pride the numerous achievements of many Bangladeshis in Britain through the annual events held at prestigious venues in London.

The British-Bangladeshi community has arrived at its third generation. The young generation is ambitious; they are achieving more. Their parents and grandparents must have worked extremely hard in running their restaurants, earning a living and bringing up their families. But their children, the present third generation, are forging ahead in education and employment, with high standards of living. Bangladeshi children are entering the Russell Group of universities. Their aspirations are high. This means that they do not want to go into their parents' restaurants to be managers, chefs or waiters. This fact is not understood by the Home Office immigration officials who are critically strangling the industry by insisting that the 'home-grown community members', that is, the third-generation children, should be available to enter the industry rather than meet the constant demand for more staff from Bangladesh. The immigration authorities, the border control authorities, use this argument to cut immigration from Bangladesh. As a result the Bangladeshi restaurant trade in Britain is facing a critical staff shortage, resulting in a large number of closures.

The work of the Bangladesh Catalyst Chamber of Commerce and Industries, Bangladesh-UK Chamber of Commerce and Industry, and other trade and professional societies of lawyers and accountants show some energy and foresight in strengthening the community. The large number of Bangladeshi newspapers – weekly and fortnightly – all continue to make a significant contribution to the economic and social wellbeing of Bangladeshis in Britain.

However, representation in the world of politics, media, culture and sports of the 600,000-strong Bangladeshi community in Britain remains proportionately high among Britain's ethnic minority population. There are four Bangladeshi MPs, a life peer, half a dozen or so mayors of various local authority councils, aspiring politicians of various parties, and leading members in various fields including the civil and diplomatic services, music, drama, sports, business and manufacturing – ICT, leather goods, bespoke tailoring etc. It can be rightly claimed that altogether it is a formidable representation. This community is no longer 'at the bottom of the pile' as it was once described!

The House of Commons Select Sub-Committee Report 'Bangladeshis in Britain' (1986-1989)

Following their major groundbreaking report on the West Indian Community in Britain, as an executive committee member of the Tower Hamlets Community Relations Council (TH-CRC) I led the preparation of the community response to the report and assisted organisations in the preparation of implementation plans. As the vice-chairman of the Labour Party Race Relations Action Group (LPRRAG) referred to elsewhere, I worked closely with The Rt Hon. Alex Lyon MP who was a Home Office minister and chairman of LPRRAG. He was also an influential member of the Home Affairs Select Sub-Committee on Immigration and Race Relations. As I said before, Mr Lyon gave me valuable insights into white people's thinking, both in private and public, on race relations issues. This understanding helped me in considering the report and its implications for the Bangladeshis in Britain. My community had to understand what was and was not possible or practicable to achieve.

It must be said that some so-called leaders in my Sylheti community did not like my involvement in the East End – Brick Lane, Aldgate, Spitalfields, Bethnal Green and other pockets of Tower Hamlets where Bangladeshis lived and worked in relatively large numbers. They saw me as an 'immigrant from South London' who had no business to be there. Thankfully this was not a major impediment for me. But no doubt there was some jealousy and resentment towards me. Some even saw me as a 'threat' lest I sought the parliamentary nomination for the safe seat of Bethnal Green and Bow! In those days of the 1970s and '80s when I was considered to be a good candidate, to be obstructed by the 'village politics of Brick Lane' was seen by many to be unfortunate and regrettable.

At the time when there was a vacancy as a result of the death of The Rt Hon. Peter Shore MP, a champion for the cause and creation of Bangladesh, the excitement and agitation amongst the Sylhetis in Brick Lane and Aldgate reached such fever pitch that they thought one of them would be selected as the prospective parliamentary candidate (PPC). Neil Kinnock was the leader of the Labour Party. According to press reports, the Labour Party HQ 'parachuted in' Ms Una King (now Baroness) who became MP for this Bangladeshi-populated constituency because the party did not consider any of the crop of local aspirants to be strong or serious contenders. I believe that if I had not had to encounter the jealousy and resentment of certain elements of East London Bangladeshis, I would have beaten Una King at selection meetings to win the constituency Labour Party (CLP) nomination. I understand that Una King worked as an assistant to Mrs Glenys Kinnock when the latter was an MEP in Brussels, which could explain why she was 'parachuted in'. Reportedly the sop to the Bangladeshis was that Mrs Paula Uddin, who was deputy leader of Tower Hamlets Council's ruling Labour group, was made a baroness!

However, against those odds, I admire the courage of my non-Sylheti Bangladeshi friend Mr Sayeed, a UK-qualified, but non-practising barrister, who was also the community relations officer (CRO) at the TH-CRC to get me co-opted on to the TH-CRC executive committee to assist with the implementation of the select committee's report and its recommendations. We had to work at all levels – with the Tower Hamlets local authority, MPs, ministers, select committee members, leading members of our own and other minority communities. These were intellectually demanding engagements.

Essentially the report made important recommendations to improve the plight of the Bangladeshis living in East London, Birmingham, Luton, Bradford, Cardiff and other UK-wide conurbations where the Bangladeshi community had settled in relatively large numbers. The Home Affairs Select Committee acknowledged that of all the immigrant communities in Britain, the Bangladeshis remained at the 'bottom of the pile'. The select committee report recommendations drew attention to some key areas on which government and other policymakers were urged to focus.

The key areas of the report were: housing, education, employment, community centres. Race issues impacted on all of these major areas. So strategies for fighting racial discrimination had to be developed in close consultation with councils and councillors, the Home Office, the Department of Education, the Housing Corporation, Department of Employment, the media, the Commission for Racial Equality and many others. We developed a community response to all the report's recommendations to sensitise authorities to the need for action to move this community out of extreme poverty.

So, has the world changed for our community? Yes, I think in many ways, it has. I saw the evidence of this when (early 1990s) I was at Fullemploy leading a major community development project as the managing consultant and team leader, advising the London Docklands Development Corporation (LDDC) on aspects of ethnic minorities' wellbeing in the Docklands boroughs of London. I personally prepared the detailed project proposal to win that high-value LDDC tender. We carried out a 'mapping' exercise of all the minority communities to determine where they lived. Then we carried out a community consultation exercise to determine the communities' aspirations and, more importantly, some of the constraints which were holding them back from fulfilling their aspirations. Then we considered what was on offer: what government and local authority agencies, and others – public and private – were on the ground to offer help and assistance. And finally, we examined whether what was on offer was reaching the communities and how to enable the communities to engage with authorities to take advantage of what was claimed to be on offer to them. These were complex issues. But with a positive attitude of mind a lot could be achieved.

There is no doubt that all ethnic minority communities have come a long way in respect of improved housing, better educational achievements, good jobs and employment prospects. Better economic growth in the economy has enabled communities to take advantage of what was on offer. A widespread network of community centres has enabled communities to come together to articulate their needs, to raise awareness and gain wider acceptance in society. In today's Britain a lot is visible: for example, the Bangladeshi community is living in good housing; entering education at all levels, gaining entry to universities in ever larger numbers; obtaining good degrees and entering better employment opportunities. They are in business, finance, legal practice and other professions. But complacency is to be avoided. A lot remains to be done to overcome persistent racial discrimination in every sector of the economy affecting this and other minorities.

Brixton Neighbourhood Community Association (BNCA) (1979-1982)

My friend and colleague Courtney Laws, a leading member of the West Indian community in Britain, was chairman of BNCA. He and his committee invited me to join the association as one of their trustees and executive committee members. I felt honoured to join this influential community-based organisation in Brixton. The youth of this community was in the news because of the Railton Road riots in Brixton in 1981 (resulting in the Lord Scarman Inquiry). Race relations were intensely sensitive.

Courtney was very influential. Quietly spoken, he was a distinguished West Indian. He and his wife were active in community work in Brixton. He was very capable, a man of few words who excelled in engaging with authorities with ease and achieving favourable outcomes. In obtaining funding for BNCA's work, Courtney's approach was to develop programmes and projects in a professional manner before seeking funding from the local council, the Home Office and charities and others with success.

As discussed before, BNCA was to play a major role in the naming of the Commission for Racial Equality. To repeat, we – Courtney Laws, Praful Patel, myself and one or two others – were to meet David Lane at Courtney Laws' BNCA office in Railton Road, Brixton, to come up with the new commission's name. BNCA and the late Courtney Laws, chairman of BNCA, would be very proud of this important milestone in Railton Road, Brixton. I was honoured to have served on the BNCA committee of trustees at an important moment in its life.

I was to remain a trustee of BNCA for some years. But life moved on for all of us. After leaving the CRE in 1981 I had entered international management consultancy. My company, The Brettonwood Partnership Ltd, was formed in 1985. It was undertaking projects in Britain and internationally. After some years I heard that Courtney Laws had passed away. Not long after, his wife died. I came to know that a financial scandal hit BNCA. But their work must remain rooted in the Brixton black community for years to come.

Sadly, it has to be said that time and again one heard of scandals, corruption, nepotism and favouritism enveloping many ethnic minority organisations and individuals. The downside is that it gave rise to suspicion amongst the authorities and funders, which made it difficult to obtain funding, no matter how justified the need for specific funding requests and questions.

Dr A. F. A. Sayeed OBE

A fellow Bangladeshi, Dr Sayeed, a very influential member of our community, a gentleman of quiet disposition, a practising GP, excelled in making high-level contacts with government ministers and community leaders. He was a good personal friend who encouraged me over many years. He had some affection for me and my daughter Lisa who was already an accomplished media personality.

After I had finished my two three-year stints at the London Probation Board in 2007, he wrote to me saying that now that I had finished with that important role, it was time to move on to other things in public life. He told me he was going to write to Lord Douglas Hurd, who he knew well, and to Lord Navnit Dholakia, a fellow Asian community leader from the Indian community in Britain, a one-time principal officer at the CRE during my time there, to sponsor me for a 'working peerage' in the House of Lords. Dr Sayeed was going on holiday to Bangladesh and was going to approach Lords Hurd and Dholakia upon his return. Sadly, Dr Sayeed, whose diabetes had already rendered him blind, never returned to England. He passed away in Dhaka, leaving his most dedicated wife and partner and his children to survive him. I think the family continue to live in Leicester where Dr Sayeed had served his local community as a general practitioner (GP) in distinction for many years. He also served the Government of Bangladesh in important advisory roles in the health sector.

It was Dr Sayeed who had recommended my inclusion in *Who's Who* when I had joined the CRE as a director in 1978, as a member of the CRE's top management team. I remember Dr Sayeed with a deep sense of respect and admiration. He was a member of the Race Relations Board and the Community Relations Commission, and was very active with Asian doctors. He served some years as chairman/president of the Overseas Doctors Association (ODA), secretary-general of the Standing Conference of Asian Organisations, and many other charities.

Apart from *Who's Who*, and leading on from that, I was mentioned in *Debrett's People of Today*, *Asian Who's Who* and *British-Bangladeshi Who's Who* for many years. I express my deepest gratitude to the late Dr Sayeed, a truly great man and a friend and a well-wisher.

Rotary clubs of Stepney, Streatham and Tooting (1992–)

The root of the Rotary movement was in local business communities. In 1905 Paul Harris, with two or three of his local business colleagues, founded Rotary International. It was to embrace virtually every country in the world, with over 1.2 million service-minded men and women belonging to more than 32,400 Rotary clubs. In line with its philosophy, 'Service Above Self', Rotary helps people and projects locally; nationally it participates in countries with projects and programmes in aid of the needy; internationally it leads with its multi-billion-dollar programmes of eradication of polio, HIV/Aids and malaria, and disaster relief – natural disasters like the tsunami of 2004 and humanitarian disasters.

Colin Bryant was a Rotarian at the Rotary Club of Stepney in East London, recently retired as a vice-principal from the Tower Hamlets College of Further Education. I also knew him as a neighbour and a friend. His wife, Zoe, and my wife, Anna, became quite close; one of my daughters, Rebecca, went to the Julian's Primary School where their son also went. Later on Colin was chair of the school governing body. So we became quite close socially.

I knew Colin was very active in Rotary District 1130 London. He persuaded me to join the Rotary because it would be good for my business but more importantly I could do some philanthropic work – Service Above Self – as I get a lot of approaches for help. Rotary provided the channel. Anna and I were enthusiastic about Rotary. We used to attend Rotary District conferences every October where we would make new friends, enjoy the mixing and mingling and the Saturday night ball at the Winter Garden in Eastbourne.

We used to see Colin and Zoe at their stall selling and promoting dictionaries for schools and colleges. Colin's Dictionaries for Schools project really caught on after his perseverance over some years. He became extremely successful distributing dictionaries across several countries in the world. It was a major programme of work single-handedly led by Colin.

I had heard about his work on other major projects in Bangladesh and elsewhere. My international management consultancy company, The Brettonwood Partnership Ltd, had set up its office in London Docklands, right across the water from Canary Wharf. Having established the office, I was thinking of connecting up with the local community and businesses in the Docklands and Aldgate areas. Colin persuaded me to join the Rotary Club of Stepney. We both lived south of the River Thames. He used to drive to the club meetings once a week. The meetings used to take place at Toynbee Hall on Commercial Street, E1. He offered to take me in his car to attend his club meetings. Through chatting during the long drive from South West to East London across the Thames, I began to understand the commitment required to become a Rotary club member which eventually led (or not!) to a member becoming a true Rotarian. I was excited by the prospect and opportunities.

My interest in Rotary was to undertake major project work – like Colin did for his dictionary and other international projects. I had had some approaches from people I knew in Sylhet. I wanted to help in raising funds to assist individual international humanitarian projects. I wanted to assist particular projects in Sylhet in the north-eastern corner of Bangladesh.

But bad luck struck! My company had to pull back from the Docklands in East London as prospects for projects in the short term disappeared. It was a great disappointment. My contacts at the London Docklands Development Corporation (LDDC), Elizabeth Finkley and David Powell, who I got to know well, tried to award me some work but in the competitive bidding process my company was priced out. So I persuaded my wife and two daughters that due to changed circumstances I had to run my consultancy business from home. Fortunately our house in West Norwood, South East London was very large. Their understanding and agreement also meant that sometimes we would put 'all hands on deck' to help out with some major project work.

Having moved my business to West Norwood there was the need to review my work with Rotary. I transferred my membership from the Rotary Club of Stepney to the Rotary Club of Streatham. Having done that, I was thinking about Rotary international projects. There had been a delegation from the Rotary Club of Jalalabad, in Sylhet, who did a presentation at the Rotary Club of Streatham. I listened to their presentation carefully. They were travelling in the UK to raise funds to establish a surgical operations theatre at the Jalalabad Disabled Rehab Centre and Hospital (JDRCH), which was to become a permanent major project of the Rotary Club of Jalalabad. Being from my hometown, I invited the delegation to dinner at my home. This was a further opportunity to discuss the project with them, to understand what they had in mind a little more in detail. Eventually I agreed that through our two clubs working jointly, we would raise funds and then seek match funding from the Rotary Foundation.

I was chairman of the international committee of the Rotary Club of Streatham. I was glad to persuade my club to support a gala fundraising dinner at my club in Mayfair, the Royal Air Force Club. I had used my club for socialising and holding business meetings ever since I left the Royal Air Force in 1970, almost fifty years ago! I led the fundraising campaign mainly directed at Rotary clubs in our Rotary District 1130, and also I approached other sources for donations. The funds raised through the gala dinner were then matched by the Rotary Foundation. Eventually I was able to hand over some US$6,000 to the Rotary Club of Jalalabad as a contribution from the Rotary Club of Streatham, London, towards the cost of setting up the surgical operations theatre. We had to be careful about handling funds internationally. Therefore we had to agree a monitoring mechanism and periodical reporting between our two clubs, so that things remained on track and above board. During my subsequent visit to Bangladesh, I saw suitable acknowledgement and recognition of Rotary Club of Streatham's contribution to the project at the hospital.

My business's move from Docklands meant that I lost contact with

Colin Bryant for a while. I saw Colin off and on at the Rotary District conference in Eastbourne. I knew he had bought a house there. Then I heard that Colin had also moved back to Streatham, his home territory. But for some reason he did not join his local club, the Rotary Club of Streatham; instead he decided to join the Rotary Club of Tooting, which was not too far away. As I have said, I was interested in doing some major projects together with Colin. So I decided to follow him and moved my membership to the Rotary Club of Tooting as well. By that time Colin had added an important feather to his cap: he became the district governor (DG) for our Rotary District 1130. At Tooting, and as a former DG, he wanted to bring about some reforms to the way in which the club was run. Unfortunately some members took offence at Colin's criticisms and resisted his attempts at reform. Eventually Colin left. He went on to join the neighbouring club – the Rotary Club of Brixton, Battersea and Clapham (BB&C– the '&' is important to avoid confusion with BBC in the world of TV and radio broadcasting!). I never got round to working with Colin on any international projects!

I persuaded my new club, R C Tooting, to support me to launch another fundraising event at the RAF Club – a gala fundraising dinner. This time we wanted to raise funds for two causes: (i) to support Mercy Ship UK in their work with children for cleft lip and palate repairs by doctors on board their ship, and (ii) to provide further support for meeting the needs of the surgical operations theatre of JDRCH, the project of the Rotary Club of Jalalabad. The ballroom at the RAF Club was full; we achieved capacity attendance at full ticket price. With funds raised from the gala dinner, contributions from our club and individual donations, and then Rotary Foundation match funding, we raised a total of some US$12,000. This was divided up half and half between Mercy Ship UK and the Rotary Club of Jalalabad for the JDRCH surgical operations theatre project. Once again the gala dinner was a huge success. Our guest of honour was The Rt Rev. Christopher Chessun, Bishop of Southwark. He provided the 'pulling power' to draw in a lot of people to fill up the RAF Club ballroom's 120-seat capacity, a huge success by any account. Later the Rotary Club of Tooting wrote to the bishop to express our deepest gratitude for his support.

To join in the centenary celebrations of a hundred years of Rotary, Anna and I went to the Rotary Convention held in Chicago, where Paul Harris and his handful of colleagues launched the Rotary movement in 1905. There were some 50,000 Rotarians attending the convention. We enjoyed it enormously. I learnt a lot about Rotary and the movement's evolution over time, the history and the institutional development, with a well-acknowledged need for some reforms. Socially, we met other Rotarians; we visited places of interest in Chicago, visited jazz clubs, ate in numerious restaurants; and looked up our relatives in Detroit and Ann Arbor. In all respects it was a fulfilling trip to Chicago.

The other convention Anna and I, with others from London clubs, attended was the Rotary International Convention in Copenhagen and Malmao. It was a Sweden and Denmark two-country joint convention of Rotary International. Once again there was a lot to learn; learning in Rotary never ends. In addition we thoroughly enjoyed visiting Copenhagen, learning about Danish history and the Vikings; and Malmao, appreciating how Sweden is such a positive-minded, liberal country. As always in new places on our travels, Anna was able to visit places of interest and do some shopping while I attended Rotary Convention meetings.

All organisations experience problems of human relations. Rotary clubs are no exception. When I attended Rotary International (RI) conventions in Chicago, Copenhagen and Malmao, at the more serious sessions of the proceedings there were quarrels and disagreements right at the top: about revision of legislation governing RI worldwide; about which country should get the RI presidency next; about accounting and finances. RI is a democratic body where debates and differences are to be expected. But it is important that acrimonies are kept within bounds so that the Rotary movement is not permanently damaged. I have learnt a lot by attending workshops on different subject matters at the conventions: about the Rotary Foundation's work globally; fair practice in allocation of funds for programmes and projects; how to run a Rotary club locally; how to resolve problems; custom and practice to be observed at the local level; what it takes to be a Rotarian from just being a member of a Rotary club; the enormous amount of information that is available to help Rotary clubs and individual Rotarians; how to get ideas from the conventions, bring them home and translate them into local projects and long-term programmes and action plans for the benefit of local communities;

participation in national programmes for disaster relief internationally.

My view is that one could keep attending the Rotary conventions every June at some expense. But we must ask the question: 'What benefits to our local clubs come from such frequent attendance?' If we bring back ideas but nothing can be done to implement them, then it's the age-old adage of: 'Flogging a dead horse'! One can think of some brilliant ideas about a project. A member introduces the subject, finds no great imagination or enthusiasm or support amongst the members attending a club regular lunch or dinner. The idea falls by the wayside; the member gets demotivated; he/she might even decide to leave the club for pastures new. The role of a club president is vital for the success and image of the club.

All voluntary associations face problems. We had our share at the Rotary Club of Tooting when, quite unwittingly, we allowed in a member, Mohammed Akbar. To cut a long story short, Akbar defrauded the club and the district of some thousands of pounds, for which he was convicted in a crown court, imprisoned and asked to reimburse the club. The aftermath is that trust is fractured and, in the current climate of feelings against Muslims, I as a Muslim member of the club sometimes feel the cold draught! But one has to weather such events with integrity, honesty and perseverance for the long run.

Meeting some members of the British Royal Family

I want to note here that during my time in Britain I have had the good fortune of certain notable encounters with the following members of the British royalty:

I have noted elsewhere how, during my Easter term, 1956, at the Britannia Royal Naval College Dartmouth, as an inpatient for a short time at the Royal Naval Hospital Devonport, **Princess Alexandra**, during a visit to the hospital, came into my cabin, with her QARNNS naval entourage, to say hello and have a brief chat. Many years later in 2014, I was to have another encounter with HRH, this time on a visit to the hospice. I was very pleased to see a large portrait at the entrance of St Christopher's Hospice, Sydenham, London, where my beloved wife, Elizabeth Ann Aziz, was to pass away. I hope to write to Princess reminding her of my meeting at the

RN Hospital Devonport over sixty years ago. I just feel the HRH might be pleased to hear from me.

When I was chairman of Lambeth Community and Mental Health NHS Trust in the late 1990s, I was invited to a dinner at King's College, Strand, London. I was honoured to be presented to **HRH the Princess Royal**. I sat at a table of eight dignitaries including Sir Hayden Phillips, permanent secretary at the Lord Chancellor's Department at the time. I remember at the end of the dinner Hayden Phillips handing me his business card saying, 'It was nice to meet you. Let me know if I could be of help in any way.' Then when I became chairman of the London Probation Board in 2001, one of my board members had a problem about sitting at his crown court and attending the LPB board meetings which he was very keen to do – as a very committed crown court judge in South London. I arranged an appointment with Hayden Phillips, and spent thirty minutes in a meeting which was useful. I felt Sir Hayden was very courteous, jolly and helpful.

I met **HRH Prince Charles** twice. When I was working as a director at the Commission for Racial Equality (1978–81), I was invited to an event organised at the Commonwealth Institute where Prince Charles was the guest of honour. I had a chance to engage in a serious conversation with the Prince, in the presence of a very pretty young black lady, on some current issue on race relations. He was a patient listener and very much to the point in what he said. A picture of me with Prince Charles and the young lady at the Commonwealth Institute adorns my study. On another occasion, when I was living in Nottingham, I was invited to one of Buckingham Palace's annual July Garden Parties when I saw Prince Charles again at close range and was able to exchange few light words with him.

During a royal visit to Pakistan by **Her Majesty the Queen and Prince Philip, Duke of Edinburgh**, I was a very young newly commissioned sub-lieutenant in the Pakistan Navy, just freshly returned from my training at the Royal Naval College Dartmouth in July 1958, and the Duke of Edinburgh was paying a visit to PNS *Babur* (formerly HMS *Leviathan*). During the visit Prince Philip briefly spoke to me about my Dartmouth training. More importantly, I was to read in the press reports that HM the Queen, then young Princess Elizabeth, had met Prince Philip during her visit to the college for a passing-out parade when he was passing out following his training at the Royal Naval College.

There have been other occasions when I got invitations to Buckingham Palace Garden Parties when I was working at the CRE and as a member of the Nottingham Community Relations Council. I was able to see Her Majesty and a some Royal Family members quite close up during their walkabout, meeting the guests and exchanging greetings. On one occasion I remember seeing The Rt Hon Denis Healey MP (later Lord) seated pretty close to me in a tent having a cup of tea! I always had a great admiration for Mr Healey as a distinguished, no-nonsense Labour politician. Anna and I were pleased to have this brief encounter too.

In July 1958 **Lord Mountbatten** took the passing-out parade at the Britannia Royal Naval College Dartmouth on behalf of HM the Queen when I was awarded the Queen's Commission, by the British Board of Admiralty, as an acting sub-lieutenant. I remember the invaluable advice he gave to all the newly commissioned officers on parade in the quarterdeck of the college: 'Keep in contact with your civilian friends, they will prove to be very useful and important.' I was deeply saddened to learn that, not long after, while on holiday in Ireland, he and his family members were killed as the boat they were in was blown up by an IRA bomb. Lord Mountbatten left behind a legacy of love and affection from the people of the Indian subcontinent for his contribution in the Second World War, earning him the accolade of 'Mountbatten of Burma' and as the last Viceroy of India steering India's independence and the creation of India and Pakistan in 1947.

Slapton Beach, Dartmouth: Anna enjoying an apple, resting on our first ever car, a Ford Anglia. She was full pregnant expecting Lisa. Shortly after Lisa was born at the Bromborough Hospital, Totnes, Devon

Above: Anna and little Lisa on the roof of our flat when I was working at Lever Brothers (Unilever), Chittagong

Left: In Rangamati, Chittagong, at a picnic spot above the Kaptai hydroelectric dam

Picnicking on a summer day with the A T Islam family: Lisa and Tariq on the bench, Anna, Macil Islam and their daughter – both back to the camera, with me laid up with my hand covering my face

Above: Henrietta and Kiki with Anna and Lisa at our residence in Chittagong

Left: Beryl and little Razia Momen, Anna and Lisa at Cox's Bazar beach, Chittagong

Top: I am seen at the Joint
Steamer Company Pilot
Bungalow, Fenchuganj, Sylhet

Above: Anna and me at the
bungalow compound

Right: Anna on a boat ride
during a tour of my section
of Waterways in the River
Kushiyara, Sylhet

*We are crossing the flood waters on our way to Fenchuganj
railway station from our bungalow*

*Anna with my cousins on an IWTA launch while
on a visit to see us in Fenchuganj*

*Henrietta, sons and my friend Enam after their visit to us,
crossing to the railway station*

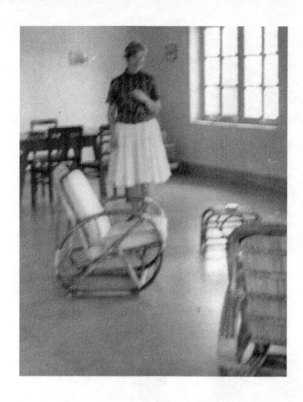

Left: Our flat was furnished with bare essentials

Below: We lived in the downstairs flat, much nicer than in my earlier posting in rural Fenchuganj

Our life together continued when I got transferred to IWTA Chittagong with responsibility of conservancy and pilotage of a larger section of Waterways

*Above: Here Anna and Lisa
seen in the sitting room*

*Right: Anna and Lisa on the
veranda, Lisa ready in her
buggy to go out*

*Below: I am playing with Lisa
in our sitting room – I am just
back from office*

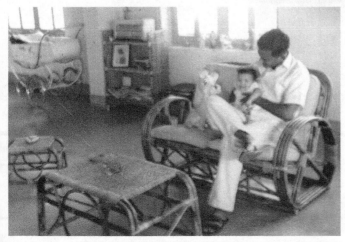

Above: Anna, Lisa and my brother Raja, at Lever Brothers factory gardens. Not long after we decided to come to England. At that time, about 1965, Raja lived with us while working as an executive at an insurance company in Chittagong

At Lever Brothers (Unilever), Chittagong

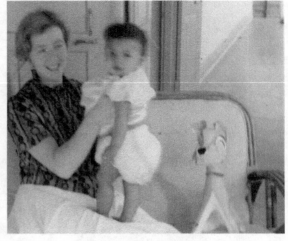

Above: Lisa with a very happy mum
Left: Lisa gaining confidence

Above: I was on a visit to see Detroit, the seat of car manufacturing in the USA. Here I am seen about to enter the Henry Ford Museum to see how it all started

Below: At the end of 100-years of Rotary celebrations in Chicago, Anna and I decided to to visit some of our relatives in Ann Arbor, Michigan. Here we are seen with my uncle Kamal, his wife ('Loni chachi'), and other family members

Above: Anna and I always happy to have students stay with us when they came to learn English language. Here Anna is with students from Japan, Spain and France in our West Norwood house

Below: Our house, 126 St Julian's Farm Road, West Norwood. It had six bed rooms, three reception rooms including an attic flat. We lived in the house for thirty three years

*Above from right: Leah and Jacob
– Lisa and Frank's two children;
Eleanor and Konrad – Rebecca
and Rickard's two children: our
four grandchildren growing up*

*Right: Lisa and I attended the
Britannia Association's summer
2019 Reception at the Royal
Naval College parade ground. I
am a member of the Britannia
Association keeping my link with
the BRNC Dartmouth. We attend
the Dartmouth Royal Regatta in
August every year*

Chapter Ten

Politics

Although when viewing my life and career, politics would seem a far cry and a contradiction, I always felt it was in there somewhere trying to come out but prevented by circumstances.

It must have been my father's influence because I saw a bit of his commitment to high-level politics during the India-Pakistan partition time, from 1945 to 1947, and then until he retired from politics after losing Sylhet to Pakistan (East Pakistan/East Bengal, now Bangladesh) from Assam, India, after a referendum.

From age ten I was taking part in demonstrations against the impending Japanese invasion, taking part in resistance activities, hiding in trenches from imminent bombing, frightened, worrying about the unknown and very alien Japanese rule under a different culture, different from the British rule with which we were familiar for generations past. The threat from the Japanese was real; they were already in Burma, over the border from Assam. That was 1944/45. We felt it was better 'with the devil we knew' (the Brits) than the alien one (the Japanese)!

As the war ended it was time for the independence movement, to get rid of British rule in India – the Quit India Movement. I could see in my father and his close friends that passion ran high. Mahatma Gandhi's call for the British to leave India was reverberating everywhere. My father had already quit his studies in engineering at the call of Mahatma Gandhi. I was joining political demonstrations, joining the chanting and slogans, the street processions responding to calls for marches and meetings demanding the end of British rule in India. The chant was: '*Cholo cholo Dilly* [Delhi] *cholo, Lal Kila dokhol koro*', translated as 'March on to Delhi, capture Lal Kila, the powerbase of the British Raj in India.' I joined my friends, some of us in bare feet, marching on the dusty streets, day and night; sometimes I would leave the house in the morning, not to return till late evening or night, my mother worrying about where I was. She would ask the maidservant to keep the food warm for me in the pans in the kitchen. I would tell the maidservant off if she put cold food in front of me, no matter if I was late for breakfast or lunch or very late supper. Poor servants!

The arrival on the scene of Mr Mohammed Ali Jinnah, demanding recognition of the fact that 'the Muslims are a nation', divided the independence movement into two: the Congress, predominantly Hindus, wanting an undivided India; the Muslims wanting a land of their own wherever there was a Muslim majority. Gandhi and Nehru visited Sylhet, my hometown, in the famous Eidgah Maidan, explaining how an undivided India would be best for all Hindus and Muslims and all other religious groups, living together in an undivided India. Jinnah also visited Sylhet and addressed a very large Muslim gathering at the Eidgah Maidan. He kept pressing on with his demand that Muslims, being a nation, needed their own homeland; the Muslims did not want the dominance of the British to be replaced by the dominance of the Hindus. The political alignment was: the Congress Party under the all-India leadership of Gandhi, Nehru, Patel, Moulana Azad; the Muslim League under the leadership of Jinnah.

I was about twelve when, as it happened, I was torn between the passionate conviction politics of my father, Mohammed Azizur Rahman, supporting the Congress, and its Muslim associate group, the Jamat-e-Ulema Hindh (the Muslim part of the Congress Party).

Most of my political compatriots supported Mr Jinnah and the Muslim League. Outside of my house, out of sight of my father, I would be with my school friends and most family members. I got caught up in the politics of compromise. Outside of my house, I would be following the Muslim League with my peer groups, my two grandfathers, my uncles and aunties, both maternal and paternal – all supporters of Jinnah and the Muslim League. However, inside my house I would be a quiet supporter of my father's Jamat-e-Ulema Hindh. How I divided myself between outside and inside my home was quite clever. I had a cap known as the Gandhi or Nehru cap – essentially a small sack, made of home-spun *khaddar* cloth, stitched on three sides, the open end to fit my head, and folded up twice to put on my head. The improvisation was that in one fold I had the black and white stripes of the Jamat flag stamped, 1 inch by 1.5 inches, a mini-flag showing my allegiance to my father's party and the politics of Congress seeking an undivided India. On another fold was a mini-flag, of similar measurements, showing the crescent and star in red, the logo of the Muslim League, showing to the outside world my allegiance to the Muslim League and Pakistan. Of course I had to be careful that my cap was correctly folded, inside and outside of my home. At all cost I had to avoid a mix-up, or a caning by my father would follow! If I failed to show allegiance with my cap badge to the Muslim League it would bring the severe displeasure of my friends, relatives and many others who would know me as one not following them!

One day I joined a Muslim League student demonstration. Most of my school friends from Sylhet town local secondary boys' schools – the Government High English School, the Aided High, the Raja Girish Chandra High, the Model High and numerous others from adjoining areas – were taking part. The procession arrived at the town centre, near the deputy commissioner (DC)'s bungalow, the bungalow of the superintendent of police (SP) and the district courts. One of us, I understand Obaid Jaigirdar, broke out of the procession and went straight into the DC's court buildings nearby, climbed the walls and reached the top of the main building flying the Union Jack, while the Gurkha soldiers guarding the court buildings, had their rifles trained on him ready to fire. Obaid pulled the flag down and hauled up the Muslim League red crescent and star flag. Fortunately, the DC (probably it was Mr Dumbreck, British?) did not order to shoot. That would have made a bad situation worse. As an aside, this was a skill of the British rulers – they had the judgment how not to provoke to make a bad situation worse except for the Jallianwala Bagh massacre!

Early in my life my politics was thus ambivalent. Was I to become a man of solid views, uncompromising, single-minded, no matter the cost, just in the mould of my father, 'like father like son'? Was this to develop as a character trait in my later life? At that point in life I did not know. Much later in my life that trait – single-mindedness, uncompromising, sticking to my guns – was there no matter the cost! Only time would tell.

The politics of Labour

Why Labour? My natural inclination to politics has always been to the 'left' of centre. I never felt comfortable with the Conservatives who I viewed as the party of the 'haves'. I always sided with the 'have-nots' rather than the 'haves'. This must have had something to do with my poor upbringing, my humble background, as one of nine children, my father, a civil lawyer, not earning a great income. We were not 'well-to-do' as I was growing up. In fact in the environment in which I grew up I saw a lot of poverty and deprivation. All this must have impacted on me during my childhood and youth.

Therefore, my perception of the Tory Party is that it is a party of wealth, the rich, the employers' rather than the employees' party; the party of the 'exploiters', not the working class, the 'exploited'. I was never a rabble-rousing revolutionary of either extreme. I felt at ease with the political middle ground. I always liked to move on, to progress, not to waste time and energy navel-gazing, in following unrealisable dreams. Maybe I was too pragmatic in my political inclination.

But it was also a feeling that I never liked the politics of Labour where policies were decided by a few, perhaps in a smoky corner of the local pub next to the council building, as happened when I worked at Lewisham Council in Catford, South East London. Then those policies determined by the few got imposed on the many of the local party. That gave rise to resentments, disagreements, disenchantment, leading invariably to what became known as the 'tyranny of the majority'. I liked moderation in Labour politics. I joined the Labour Party, my local party being the Knights Hill Constituency Labour Party (CLP), later with boundary changes to become West Norwood and Dulwich Constituency Labour Party. I did not like the politics of the hard left led by Cllr Ted Knight in Knights Hill or Derek Hatton in Liverpool in the late '60s and early '70s. As I saw happen, such politics were unsustainable as they withered away over time or ran out of steam. And leaders of that ilk slowly drifted towards capitalism, setting up in successful businesses. The resentment of the 'left behind' would be intense to the nth degree! Hypocrisy never wins; sooner or later it gets found out by shrewd voters. But I regarded Labour as my natural political home.

It was the late 1970s/early '80s. My ambition was to become an MP. I was in a hurry, wanted to become an MP 'soon', not via the time-consuming councillor route of a local borough council. With my background in the navy and with some experience in the British civil service, I wrote to Mr Neil Kinnock, leader of the Labour Party, expressing my interest in Labour. He passed it on to Mr Alf Dubs MP (later Lord). Alf Dubs showed some interest in me. I was invited to see him in his Constituency Labour Party (CLP) office in Battersea. I recall how our conversation went. He said, 'Thank you, Suhail, for writing to the leader. Mr Kinnock has asked me to see you.' After some small talk, he came to the point. He continued: 'To become an MP there is a route to follow. At first you must become a councillor in your local borough, Lambeth. That, I am afraid, is a must to progress in Labour politics.' He gave me his own and other examples. It was a cordial meeting. I left him thinking I must review my strategy; this was going to take time.

I have mentioned Colin Bryant who was a neighbour and became a friend when I lived in West Norwood, South London. He was Labour. He and I decided to contest councillor seats in Lambeth. As expected, all safe Labour seats were taken a long time ago and there was no chance of any seats falling vacant soon. Usually there would be two councillors in each ward. Colin and I went through the selection process, got selected for two seats, very safe Tory seats in Clapham Park! Undaunted we carried on, just in case. We campaigned from the home of a Labour activist who lived near Clapham Common station. He kindly offered us the front room in his substantial home on Clapham Common to use as our campaign HQ. Once or twice a week we would go to his house to prepare for street-by-street, door-to-door campaigning. Generously, he would leave us a bottle of expensive red wine with snacks. Colin and I campaigned together. While door knocking I would feel the 'cold breeze' of racism – a feeling of 'not one of us', 'strangeness and foreignness'. A look of shock would appear on the faces of people opening their front doors, indicating a feeling of 'Who are you? You are not welcome here,' though a few were warm and welcoming. In those days, in the 1990s, I was naive enough to put it down as a temporary

Politics

phenomenon. I felt that in time, as I became known in the ward, I would overcome it. But I was going to be in for a shock!

Come the voting day, all day I was hopeful of a pleasant surprise. With the swing of votes nationally favouring Labour, I thought both Colin and I had a good chance of winning the Conservative seats of Clapham Park, as most neighbouring seats were Labour. Voting finished. Colin and I went to Lambeth Town Hall in Brixton to see the counting of votes in progress. It was about 2am. Again and again, while looking over the shoulder of counting clerks, I saw the same Labour supporters had ticked in favour of Colin, but abstained from voting for me. I put it down to the voters' deeply held racial prejudices or an unfamiliar name; the sight of a foreign name, Aziz, on the paper had put them off. As the final result came out, the Labour support for Colin was much larger than for me in the same ward. Of course, neither of us won the safe Tory ward. It would have required an unrealistic swing to Labour in a traditionally Tory seat. I obtained an insight into the deeply held prejudices of white voters in Lambeth. Never mind the merits of a person, there was racial bias, bias against a foreign name, a pattern of racial discrimination even amongst white working class Labour voters. I experienced a disheartening switch-off within myself. I never tried local elections again. Alf Dubs' advice to me that I must follow the council route first before trying to become an MP did not work for me; my hope was dashed to the ground. Probably if I had persevered I would have become a councillor in some safe Labour ward in Lambeth, but as I said, I was a man in a hurry in politics!

The revelation came to me that, faced with a choice between a foreign-sounding name, like a Muslim name, Aziz, and an 'English'-sounding name, the voter would choose the latter. That's the instinctive choice they would make and there was not much point arguing about it.

The West Indian Labour Party candidates, however, did not always have to face the same experience, as many of them had 'English'-sounding names – such as some of my friends in that community in Britain: 'Brian Sullivan', 'Maurice Forsyth', 'Lincoln Crawford', 'Sam Springer', 'Delbert Sandiford' and so on.

But times have moved on. Today we are fortunate that we have councillors and MPs, ministers – even a cabinet minister – and mayors in respectable numbers from all of the British ethnic minority communities. Black and Asian men and women are active in the political firmament of this country in abundance. Alex Lyon and other like-minded Labour MPs and peers set up an organisation in the Labour Party called the Labour Party Race Relations Action Group (LPRRAG). Alex Lyon was its chairman; I was elected its national vice-chairman. As alluded above, I was living in Nottingham in those days, working as a personnel officer at Pedigree Petfoods division of Mars Group, in Melton Mowbray (1974–78). At my suggestion Alex Lyon agreed to have a meeting of LPRRAG in Nottingham. It fell to me to organise the meeting. I booked Rushcliffe Town Hall, in West Bridgford. I invited Alex Lyon MP, Clare Short MP and the secretary of LPRRAG (the name escapes me) to have dinner at my place before proceeding to the meeting in Rushcliffe. Anna and I cooked a delicious curry dinner for them – I called it the 'Aziz menu'! My guests met Anna and our two children, Lisa and Rebecca. After the dinner my guests thanked Anna and the children; we proceeded to the meeting. I took Alex Lyon and Clare Short in my car. He got talking about racism in Britain. When I described what I saw on the vote-counting night in Lambeth, Alex Lyon said, 'It is not racism as such. It is what I would describe as "strangeness and foreignness". People find new experience with new people as "strange". After a time they get over the "strangeness" and become familiar with new people. Slowly the "strangeness and foreignness" disappears.' I believe that in the past few decades, this has happened in Britain. The 'strangeness and foreignness' of black and Asian people have largely disappeared; minority ethnic people are seen in politics, media, sports, and the cultural and social life of Britain in large numbers. In twenty-first-century Britain, Alex Lyon's prediction has probably become true. That is not to say that ingrained race prejudice, racism or racial discrimination have disappeared. Minority ethnic people still experience these in subtle forms; the undercurrent is still there – it will take a long while, if ever, for it to completely disappear. Racial prejudice is so deeply ingrained because of Britain's colonial past that it is unlikely to disappear. Tolerance rather than acceptance would become the norm. Things will get better; but prejudice based on and because of colour will not disappear.

After talking to my Labour friends and colleagues, I decided to start taking part in the selection processes of prospective parliamentary candidates (PPCs) up and down the country. Once again, safe seats were all taken. There was no chance that I would be offered a safe Labour seat on a plate! Even if one became vacant due to a sitting MP's death or retirement, being selected as a PPC would be difficult. My Labour friends gave me all sorts of advice. Some would tell me to keep trying for seats in Greater London and the home counties where black and Asian people lived. Others would tell me to try for seats outside the metropolis because the area was crowded and the politics of London were tricky!

I took up a subscription to *Labour Weekly* and *The Tribune*, where upcoming seats and selection timetables were advertised. I was naive in responding to these ads in a straightforward manner, without researching the local politics or talking to CLP members to find out who the strong contenders were, and what was the nature of competition one would face. I just relied on my naive, strong faith in people, believing that all was well and that I would be considered on merit. But this was not to be the case. People were groomed and lined up years before. For example, I expressed my interest in Diane Abbott's seat, Hackney and Stoke Newington. I got invited to one ward Labour Party selection meeting. I was told later that at the final selection meeting, out of some twenty votes, I got only one and that was due to some 'social engineering work' done in the background by a friend of a friend! I never researched that seat, nor Diane's formidable strengths. She was bound to get in as she had been cultivating that seat for a long time. There was a strong presence of black people in that constituency, she was black with an English name, she was highly qualified, Cambridge educated, so she had the favourable wind in her sails. Years later in 2005/06, as chairman of the London Probation Board, I was meeting London MPs to tell them about the work of the board. I met Diane Abbott in her office in Portcullis House. 'By the by,' I said to her, 'I competed for your seat all those years ago.' She gave me a smile; she was kind and generous with her words, saying, 'Look where you have got to.'

Some of the seats I tried were such longshots and totally un-researched that it baffles me fifty years on! I attended ward meetings of several CLPs, incurring some expenses from my own pocket: Stirling, Edinburgh Pentlands, Strathkelvin and Bearsden in Scotland. One Scottish lady, now a baroness, told me: 'Don't try Scotland, Scottish CLPs are very parochial.'

Other seats I tried were Croydon North East, Watford North, Bethnal Green, Nantwich, Henley and Halifax in England; Powys in Wales. Some London feedback would be: 'Don't try London – too much competition and "nasty politics" here.' Lesson: politics is a game; one has to keep trying, but success can be rewarding.

I even tried Mr Michael Heseltine's seat in Henley-on-Thames, a true blue Tory seat! I would have easily got the CLP nomination for that unwinnable seat! I had my ward selection meeting in the front room of the home of some substantially wealthy Labourite lady in Henley. There were about eight or nine members at the meeting. I felt honoured to have been shortlisted. There was a very positive vibe at the meeting. I felt comfortable. One question was from a youngish lady: 'How do you feel about taking on such a big beast of the Tory Party?' She spread her arms wide to emphasise the point. Another said, 'Of course you won't win this seat but if you were to be selected, it would give you such good exposure – "Suhail Aziz takes on Heseltine" could be the banner headline of some national and local newspapers. That publicity and exposure would surely enhance your future chances in another winnable seat.' I agreed with that insightful advice. I got selected at that ward of Henley, only to withdraw for reasons I give below ('A comment on my constraints'). But the bottom line is: I was not a young enough candidate to be wasting time trying for seats which were unwinnable for me.

I experienced some encouragement and some 'knifing' at some of the other selection meetings. I think it was one of the safe Labour seats in Croydon – Croydon North East or Croydon Central. I got selected at one of the ward meetings. I remember a friend was on the selection panel from the Lambeth Co-op Party. I got selected there. But it was most probably at another ward selection meeting in Croydon that I got 'knifed'. I was those days working in Lewisham Council. There were a couple of people, a man and a woman, who I must have crossed regarding filling a particular post in my division. These two people were pushing a particular candidate to get the job. One of my section managers got overridden by those two people. I put my foot down and got someone better suited for the post selected. Anyway the man amongst the two must have lived in the ward within Croydon CLP. The evening I appeared at the ward selection meeting in Croydon, I saw this man again. When the meeting got going, I remember his question, designed to trip me. Something very personal like, 'Did you send your daughter to a private school?' I remember driving home that night feeling that my candidature got spiked, in all probability, by that man settling his score. I did not get that selection.

I believe that I have an inner capacity to see through people. When I was chairman of the London Probation Board, my board secretary, not a well-wisher of me, while sharing a drink at The Speaker, Great Peter Street, said, 'Suhail, you have a reputation, your board colleagues at the London Probation Board think you are very perceptive.' Quite often I have found that if I have some negative thought in my mind about someone, then sooner or later, I find that my instinct proved right, that person got found out, or fell away!

Jennifer and Colin Beever were our close neighbours when we lived in West Norwood for over thirty-two years. Colin was my boss, mentor, colleague, friend, when I worked at the Commission on Industrial Relations (CIR). We were frequent dinner guests at their house in Thornlaw Road, on the next street to ours, St Julian's Farm Road. At those dinner parties we met some very powerful Labourites, quite a few of whom had become 'Baroness' or 'Sir' or 'Lord', though Jennifer had never had such ambitions. Jennifer and I, with other friends such as Lorna Boreland-Kelly (later a Dame, chairman of the board of governors at Lambeth College where I was also a governor – but that was to become another saga, mentioned elsewhere), were members of the Lambeth Co-op Party. Jennifer and I were members of the Fabian Society.

A comment on my 'constraints' – things which I believe held me back

On one occasion, The Rt Hon. Edward Heath, MP for Bexley and former Prime Minister, was being interviewed by Mr David Frost on *Frost on Sunday* after a visit to Japan. In answer to a question about what he found to be the most striking thing in Japan, Mr Heath replied, 'Respect for education.' He contrasted that with the situation in Britain. I think it was in the same interview that he opined that one must have enough 'financial means' to be in politics. He was talking about principles in politics. There are times when one has to stand up for what one believes in. Why I am saying this? Time and again, in seeking Labour Party nominations, I would say, 'Thus far, no farther!' I found that I could have carried on seeking nominations leading, I am sure, to a good CLP selection for a winnable seat. But I could not continue because I did not have the financial means. One must have the financial strength to carry on in politics or to make a stand on a matter of principle, resigning from a position if necessary. I had a family to support. As a relatively newly arrived immigrant, I was still finding my feet, trying to catch up on where I left off. I had a family, with two daughters in school. Anna and I were both working to pay our mortgage and live. I could have carried on but I just kept getting cold feet whenever an opportunity arose. My friends would frequently say that I could have been an MP and a minister had I persevered, because I had made enough headway to be noticed by people in positions of power and influence within the Labour Party hierarchy. I would have got enough support to be recognised within and outside the party and the country. Opportunities came for me and I let go! There was Labour Party organisational support and financing available once one got selected as a Prospective Parliamentary Candidate (PPC). So it would have been possible.

In the late 1980s, I was doing an assignment as a consultant/tutor at the Civil Service College, Sunningdale, the seat of training of Britain's senior civil service. I was selected by Ms Georgina Winkley to undertake training and tutoring with a German consultant/tutor, Mr Cornelius Bughart. The course was designed for assistant secretaries/senior principal-level participants. There were some ten participants in the group. Two consultant/ tutors – Cornelius and I – were attached to the tutoring class to run the course. At the feedback session at the end of one of the programmes, one of the participants, told me, 'Suhail, it's time you moved to the centre of the stage!' I vividly remember that statement, it was quite unprompted. Time and again opportunities have come my way and I let go, with 'excuses' not insurmountable. With hindsight I say to myself: Mr Alf Dubs was right. I should have become a Labour councillor first, then persevered to become an MP. I would have got somewhere in the Labour Party and Labour governments. But I let opportunities go. True, my financial circumstances were a constraint but as I speak now (2020), they could have been overcome. As a Bengali song says: 'It is all mistakes, in this life it's all mistakes – as written in pages of my life's book, it is all mistakes' ('*Bhul Shobi Bhul…*'). Has it all been a mistake? No, I don't think so! Some maybe. But not all. Whenever I have thought about entering politics in the UK, and did not do so for personal reasons and constraints, I have looked back and thought, *I could have been an MP, probably a minister, but didn't do so because I pulled back!*

The Labour Party general secretary shortlist!

'The jewel in the crown' was when I was shortlisted, with five or six others, for the Labour Party general secretary post. I was then working as the head of employment and economic development in Lewisham Council. I think I saw the ad in *The Guardian*. President Obama called his book *The Audacity of Hope* and I must have felt audacious to apply. To my surprise I was shortlisted. Friends and family thought that it must be 'statutory Black (or Asian) on the shortlist' phenomenon – political correctness! The coverage of the shortlist in the national press was extensive. At Lewisham Council my colleagues, especially my economic development division team, were pleasantly surprised. They came up to congratulate me. I told them it was my 'audacity of hope'! The day of the interview came in the party's then HQ in Walworth Road in South London. I met other candidates in a waiting room, all male candidates, no female. Tea and biscuits were offered. The arrangement was that nobody would leave the room until everyone had been interviewed and the result had been announced. So it was an all-day affair. I do not recall the names or background of the other candidates.

When I was called in, I was taken aback by the sight of the entire Labour Party National Executive, some twenty-five or more, sitting round the table in a half moon to face the interviewee. The Labour Party chairman welcomed me, went through the quick drill to introduce the panel, to be followed by my chance to ask any questions. I saw Neil Kinnock, leader, Roy Hattersley, deputy leader, Tony Benn and Gwyneth Dunwoody, who I recognised easily, having seen them many times on television and sometimes in person. The chairman asked routine questions like 'Why have you applied? What would you bring to the table?' Then Roy Hattersley, seated next to Kinnock, asked a question about how I would deal with a particular situation – angling his question to the fact I had very little experience of 'Labour' politics! That was true. I think Gwyneth Dunwoody asked a question. That was that. My interview was at most twenty-five minutes. My ordeal had ended. I glanced at Mr Benn who looked thoughtful. He didn't ask a question; no doubt he knew it would be waste of time as I was a non-runner for the job. I don't recall if he was smoking his pipe or not!

When the result was announced, Larry Whitty (now Lord) got the job. He was invited back in, the rest of us were thanked and we said goodbye. I felt greatly honoured to have been shortlisted and considered for the general secretary post of the Labour Party, the party with such a history and tradition, champion of working class Britain, and which was to form the Government of the United Kingdom soon.

I noticed as I was leaving Walworth Road HQ, there was heavy presence of press reporters at the steps. As I was coming down the steps past them, I felt it strange that not a single reporter took the slightest bit of notice of me, the sole Black or Asian on the shortlist. I had a feeling of being discarded. But that happens in politics. Once gone, you are soon forgotten – history. After the general secretary application I decided to retire from active Labour politics or trying to get selected for Parliament. I retired, and with that my ambition in that direction got extinguished.

When I think of my audacity, it must have been my ambition and drive to achieve. As Lord Young told me once when I was receiving him in my capacity as a council member of the Institute of Management Consultants (IMC) at a reception at the Grosvenor House Hotel in Park Lane, London: 'You keep pushing!' I kept thinking that starting with a job as a ticketing clerk in a tiny British Rail station, Motspur Park, in Surrey, all those years ago in 1966, to be able to apply for the Labour Party general secretary and getting shortlisted couldn't be a mean achievement – I had come a long way with God's blessing, everyone's good wishes and above all Anna's and my children's sacrifice and support for whatever I sought to do in England. Opportunities were there.

One other positive outcome from the Labour Party general secretary application was that my interest in politics of Britain and current affairs was also getting deeper. Over the years my letters got published in *The Guardian*,

The Times, *The Economist*, *The Tribune*, *The Times* daily Comment on Line, U3A publications and professional journals.

University of the Third Age (U3A)

U3A is a nationwide organisation of retired people (www.u3a.org.uk). Some years after I had joined the U3A Croydon branch, attending the group's monthly meetings, I became an enthusiastic participant in one of their numerous activities groups – the Current Affairs Group. The group was led by a very able person, Mr Barry Gifford, he always made sure that all members got their chance to participate in the deliberations. My areas of interest were Brexit, President Donald Trump, other current issues in the news – local, national and international. I was still pursuing the politics of 'left of centre'!

My view of current American politics is that the election of Donald Trump could turn out to be a mistake but only time will tell. My particular concern is that good quality people will be withdrawing from US politics. This might result in a phenomenon known in economics as a 'Market for Lemons'! When a market is full of secondhand cars for sale, it is not easy to sell a new car because it will not be trusted as new. So the new car is withdrawn from the market.

Who suffers? A country's standing in the world suffers. The poor, the deprived, the disadvantaged suffer. The countries concerned do not prosper, development is held back. People become disillusioned with politics. People begin to reminisce about the good days of the past. So the mainstream politics drift towards populism, not necessarily a good thing. We will see how Mr Trump's America – 'Make America Great Again' – pans out.

In discussions at the Current Affairs Group of the U3A Croydon branch, at a very early stage of the Brexit debate, I had strongly expressed my view that it would be wrong for Britain to leave the European Union. Britain's voice in the comity of nations of the world would be diminished. In international trade, in world economics and politics Britain would feel cast away, lonely, a diminished voice. It would be a folly of immeasurable magnitude. As the veteran MP Ian Mikardo used to say, 'If something works, leave it alone!' After forty-three years or more of working the EU was still going strong. At this time, in early 2019, we could see the movement of the tectonic plates of politics; there was no saying which way things would end up. The politics of both the main parties, Labour and Conservative, are fractured; a middle-ground party could be born, who knows. Brexit is proving that this may be so. The sadness would be when people realise that Brexit did not mean something good for Britain; Brexit could turn out to mean disaster for the nation. I hoped that good sense would prevail and Britain would return from the brink and would remain an influential strong partner within the European Union and a voice in the world. In our deliberations at the U3A Current Affairs Group, my views seem to get some acceptance or are not vehemently opposed; I feel I am listened to with respect.

Britain was most unprepared to undo what had been put in place after over forty years' membership of the EU. The complexity of the treaties, rules and regulations were found to be too much to handle. The British negotiators could not cope with the unravelling of what Brexit meant. One item, 'the Irish backstop', became an enormous hurdle for PM Theresa May to the neglect of all other current issues facing the country. The political parties were all divided, cabinet government had all but failed, so there was no chance of 'whipping the MPs' into line. In their heart of hearts the British knew that remaining within the EU was hugely beneficial. The proponents of Brexit began to be seen more as 'rabble-rousers' than responsible politicians working in the interest of their country. As at February/March 2019, seven Labour MPs had left their party; likewise three serious capable Conservative MPs left to join the other seven, plus one more Labour – they formed The Independent Group (TIG), later the Change UK Party. The latest 'breaking news' was that Mr Tom Watson, elected deputy leader of the Labour Party, might be leading a band of fifty or so middle-ground Labourites to bring about some cohesion in the Labour front bench. Most of these MPs did not give support to Jeremy Corbyn when he was elected leader of the Labour Party.

As for the Tories after Brexit, there would be many contenders for the party leadership after Mrs May steps down or is pushed out. But no one is emerging as the leader yet (March 2019). There would be complex negotiations during the transition period to put in place new rules in every aspect of life: food, medicines, environment, employment, trade, security and so on. The new leader of the Conservative Party would be required to navigate through the aftermath of Brexit. There is no saying how things would shape up, or settle down. Judging by the extent of the Tory Brexit fiasco, it would have been better if David Cameron had shown some wisdom and stood up to the hardcore Tory right-wingers, thus saving the country from a waste of time and global humiliation. The Brexit referendum turned out to be an exercise in parading lies and misleading statements from both sides – the Leavers and the Remainers. Sensible people on the Remain side, such as Sir John Major or Lord Michael Heseltine or Tony Blair, spoke out at critical junctures of the debate, but all their advice fell on deaf ears. The country was not in listening mode, though the IMF, the OECD, the World Bank and the UN all counselled Britain not to jump into the unknown with Brexit. Britain would be put into harm's way – politically, economically and socially. But no one was listening to wise counsel.

Finally the characters. Mrs May was too much of a 'tunnel vision leader'; she could not raise her sight to take a 'helicopter view of things'. She was not seen as a statesman, rather a bureaucrat. Her Brexit team? Well, Mr David Davis could not do it. So he was sidelined by the PM who preferred Mr Olly Robbins, a bright, retired civil servant who had a deeper insight into the development of the EU. He was also the architect of the Maastricht Treaty. David Davis was followed by the short-lived Brexit secretary, Dominic Raab, an ex-army man; reportedly he was hardly of the calibre needed for the job, but nourished a premature ambition to become the next leader of the Tory Party. He resigned after Mrs May's Chequers meeting. The third Brexit secretary of state was a junior minister, promoted by Mrs May, who was asked to focus on domestic aspects of Brexit, thus leaving 'Brussels' to Mrs May herself, Olly Robbins and the UK representative in Brussels. She was comfortable with civil servants but, as it turned out, most Brexit ministers were uncomfortable with her. The enormity of Brexit negotiations with such people as the President of the European Council, Donald Tusk, and the President of the European Commission, Jean-Claude Juncker, proved daunting, backed as they were by the *crème de la crème* of the European Commission. Mrs May failed to have politicians of calibre and weight by her side to tackle the politicians on the other side of the negotiating table. Frankly the widely held view was that she lacked the experience or understanding of the job. As her former chief of staff had said: 'May was fighting the negatives, not seeing the opportunity that Brexit presented.'

Sadly the Coronavirus COVD19 from early 2020 has become a major event affecting the lives of people across the world. Faced with this Pandemic Brexit takes a back seat.

India, Pakistan, Bangladesh

First some historical perspective. We need to go back some years. The creation of India and Pakistan was done in some haste. The Second World War ended in 1945. Election in Britain brought in the Labour Attlee Government. The new government had decided to give India independence and quit India quickly, as agitation was growing there. Vast population movements took place, many lives were lost. India and Pakistan were established in August 1947 on the basis of religious divide: Hindu India and Muslim Pakistan.

A degree of haste accompanied the partitioning of India. As a consequence some fourteen million people moved across the newly created borders; many were slaughtered by the opposing sides; tens of thousands died of disease. The human cost of the partitioning of India was enormous and vast. The responsibility for this human tragedy must be shared: by the British; by the Indian leaders at the time unable to restrain those bent on murder (although Mr Gandhi had a restraining influence in Bengal); and after partition, by the administrations in India and Pakistan.

There are two explanations: first, the appointment of Lord Mountbatten of Burma as the new Viceroy of India to implement the Government's decision to partition India as quickly as possible, reportedly in six months. Also Lord Mountbatten had, upon being appointed Viceroy and after sizing up the situation, pressed for an early deadline for independence. Second, the artificially created borders between India and Pakistan, which came to be known as the Radcliffe Line, created problems. Conflict was inevitable. Sectarian violence dimmed hopes for a quick and dignified British withdrawal. Mountbatten was not given adequate resources to do his job. He had created a border force which could not maintain the peace; they could not protect the cities or exercise any control over the hundreds of thousands of refugees who were fleeing their homes as a consequence of the Radcliffe Line.

The haste was further compounded by the Government's decision to appoint Sir Cyril Radcliffe (the architect of the Radcliffe Line in the partitioning of India), as the chairman of two border commissions – one for Bengal and one for the Punjab – charged with equitably distributing 175,000 sq. miles (450,000 sq. km) between the western side of the Indo-Pakistan border and the eastern side of the India-Bengal border.

Radcliffe was essentially a civil servant, sent to do a very complex job. Other accounts describe him as a 'lawyer of great intelligence, probity and intellectual toughness that was to enable him to withstand intolerable pressures' (Philip Ziegler in Mountbatten's biography). After arriving in India on 8 July 1947, Radcliffe was given just five weeks to decide the borders of Bengal and Punjab. All sides had agreed the dividing lines had to be drawn and finished by 15 August, the agreed day of independence. The Radcliffe Commission was instructed to demarcate, giving due regard to natural, geographical, as well as socio-political considerations, and taking account of which areas were majority Muslim and Hindu. Radcliffe had never been to India before, a fact which probably worked in his favour in a difficult situation. But there might have been some truth that Radcliffe showed no understanding of the complex issues or emotional aspects of the job. He knew nobody important in India, nor did he show any inclination to consult even Mountbatten, the Viceroy. But Mountbatten did not want to be consulted; he thought the Viceroy as the King's representative should not get involved. It was said at the time, 'the fact that Radcliffe had not visited India before was probably a good thing, he would do his job without any interference, he was thus seen by the authorities as an asset, unbiased, able to give an appearance of impartiality'. Radcliffe justified the division with the truism that no matter what he did, people would suffer; nor could he please everyone. The Hindu and Muslim leaders could not agree on a unitary India. Demarcation was therefore inevitable. It was likely that whoever did it, and whatever the line, there would have been trouble. To avoid disputes and delays, the demarcating lines were drawn in extreme secrecy. Final awards were ready on 9–12 August 1947, but not published until two days after independence on 17 August 1947. By then Radcliffe had already departed

India; he left before even his boundary award report was distributed. The truth is that border and other disputes from the Radcliffe Line continue even to this day: Kashmir resulted in three Indo-Pakistan wars, and a fourth almost happened over the division of water resources between India and West Pakistan, a dispute that continues.

By his own admission Radcliffe was heavily influenced by his lack of fitness for the Indian climate and his eagerness to depart India. Thus a crucial determiner of the outcome of partition was devoid of commitment and emotions required for the job.

It is recorded that when Radcliffe ended his assignment, he did not even accept his fees. He did, however, collect all his papers, drafts, maps, which he took to England and burnt. He preferred not to say a word even to his family as to what he did or what happened.

History was ignored: the Danish war against the Germans over borders and the Papua (British) and New Guinea (German) conflict are examples.

Creation of Bangladesh

On the partitioning of India in 1947, Muslim Pakistan was established in two parts: West and East, separated by 1,000 miles of Hindu India. It was an 'unnatural' marriage, of Bengalis in the East and mainly Punjabis in the West. The former comprised 130 million people and the latter 80 million (1947).

The first clash of cultures between West and East Pakistan took place in 1952. The Punjab- dominated government ordained Urdu to be the official language of the whole country, thus setting aside the cultural identity of the Bengalis. This generated anger amongst Bengalis, who formed the majority of Pakistan. The main political party in the East, the Awami League, under the leadership of Sheikh Mujibur Rahman, led an uprising. Students of Dhaka University were at the forefront of demonstrations. The Government banned all public meetings. That fuelled more violence. On 21 February, police fired into a crowd, killing five students. This date was subsequently declared as 'Martyrs' Day'.

In 1956, after years of conflict, the Government relented. Bengali became the second state language of Pakistan, alongside Urdu. However, the seed was sown for the separation of the two wings of Pakistan. Other differences arose. Although West Pakistan had the minority population, it exercised political, economic and industrial power, and had the maximum share of revenue and foreign aid. Bengalis saw themselves as economically deprived and exploited. The bulk of the army came from the West and the civil service was under the control of the West. It was becoming clear that the creation of Pakistan, with two distant wings bound together only by the common religion of Islam, was becoming untenable.

In 1958 General Ayub Khan abrogated the constitution and declared martial law. He tried to placate Bengali nationalism by addressing some of the causes. But it didn't work. In December 1969 he handed over power to General Yahya Khan. In 1970 a general election was held in the whole country. Bengalis overwhelmingly supported the Awami League, whilst in the West the Pakistan Peoples Party of Zulfiqar Ali Bhutto won an overwhelming victory. The East, having the majority of voters, demanded that Sheikh Mujib's Awami League should form the government. Bhutto would have none of it. The powerful Pakistan Army supported him. The country headed for a deadlock.

Troop movements took place from the West to the East to quell the uprising. Bengalis were largely unarmed, so the military suppression was effective. But the uprising spread like wildfire in response to Sheikh Mujib's call to fight the enemy. He was arrested and moved to the West. In the UK, *The Sunday Times* reported that the military had committed genocide. Over a million Bengalis were killed, and over ten million became refugees in neighbouring India. A war of liberation had started for an independent East Pakistan.

India was becoming concerned at the presence of 92,000 Pakistani soldiers at its eastern borders and the potentially huge refugee crisis. Mrs Indira Gandhi, Prime Minister of India, supported the Awami League, and allowed it to form a government in exile in Calcutta. The Indian Army moved over the border on 3 December 1971. The Pakistan Army surrendered without a fight. Bangladesh was established with the support of India. Bengali, the mother tongue of Bangladeshis, became the state language. Sheikh Mujibur Rahman was returned from a West Pakistan prison and became the first President of Bangladesh (and later, with the adoption of the constitution, the first Prime Minister). The UN recognised

Bangladesh in 1972.

The creation of Bangladesh illustrates the importance of language and cultural identity. Artificially constructed borders prove to be impotent. Religious considerations cannot hold together a people faced with economic exploitation. The emotional side of life must be respected. It was the language – the Bengali mother tongue – that started it off. Minority groups know the importance of holding on to their mother tongue; it is their cultural heritage. No amount of artificially constructed borders will satisfy various groups, particularly where language and religion are concerned.

On 17 November 1999 UNESCO declared 21 February as International Mother Language Day in tribute to the language movement and the ethno-linguistic rights of people around the world.

Bangladesh movement in Britain

During 1970/71, Bangladeshis in Britain joined the demand for an independent Bangladesh. Action committees were formed in most UK cities and towns where Bangladeshis were present in some numbers. Processions, demonstrations, meetings and rallies took place to tell the world about the case for Bangladesh.

Some of my fellow Bangladeshis and I formed a Bangladesh action committee based in Streatham. Meeting and office space was generously given by the late Mr Talukdar, on the top of his restaurant, Kulaura, on Streatham High Road. From that base we campaigned day and night: leafleting; joining others in demonstrations and processions; writing to the press; making media appearances on TV and radio; marching to Downing Street to ask for British recognition of Bangladesh; holding rallies in Hyde Park. Some British activists joined us in our campaign. Mr Simon Dring of *The Daily Telegraph* reported about the Pakistan Army action in Dhaka city on the night of 25 March 1971; this was further strengthened by the effective reporting of the late Mr Anthony Mascarenhas of *The Sunday Times*, notably his reports on the Bangladesh 'genocide' and 'pogrom'; support also came from MPs and Lords. All this support for Bangladesh helped the process of obtaining early recognition of Bangladesh internationally as an independent country.

Having achieved independence, I feel that Bangladesh politics should be left to our brothers and sisters who are running Bangladesh. We can't do it from the UK or overseas. We can only keep an eye on the country with the hope that the country will be run well. We want our hard-earned independence to be allowed to develop and flourish as an independent nation.

Some of us wanted to provide political support to the Awami League from London to gain international exposure for Bangladesh. There was already an old branch of the Awami League in London. However, following the establishment of Bangladesh, and with a view to supporting Sheikh Mujib's Awami League from an international platform in London, I, with others, formed the Bangladesh Awami League Overseas. Our organisation showed effectiveness and promise. But sadly when we sought recognition from the Awami League HQ in Dhaka, they decided to continue with the old established Awami League in London. This was apparently because Sheikh Mujib had received a great deal of support from them. Therefore, we packed up the Bangladesh Awami League Overseas. As I said, the politics of Bangladesh can't be conducted or managed from the UK. We must leave it to our people there to run the country. We should support their efforts in whatever way we can.

Like all developing countries, changes happen, trials and tribulations have to be endured. Sadly, only a few years after Bangladesh was born, Sheikh Mujib and most of his family were assassinated in a military coup. A martial law government followed, converted into a civilian government under General Zia ur Rahman. He too was assassinated, to be followed by another military government, then converted to a civilian government under General Ershad. Since then, democracy is taking root. Two women feature prominently: Begum Zia (wife of the assassinated General Zia ur Rahman), a former prime minister, leader of the Bangladesh National Party (BNP); and Sheikh Hasina, the daughter of Sheikh Mujib (who, with her sister, had escaped death as they were in London at the time of the bloody coup), the current Prime Minister and leader of the Awami League.

It is to be hoped that the present economic growth will continue. But corruption and nepotism are rampant. Despite these, the country is showing remarkable economic progress, with GDP growth of 6% to 7%. The population shows resilience and motivation in the face of natural disasters caused by global climate change. Education of the rural poor is seen as a priority. Poverty is much reduced. Women are gaining freedom to work and prosper, with the size of families under control. Altogether, the country is a remarkable success.

Chapter Eleven

My diverse family

I have a diverse family. I am from Sylhet, in the north-eastern corner of Bangladesh. I married Anna. She was from the other end of the world, a remote corner of South West England – Dartmouth in Devon – over 5,000 miles (8,000 km) in between! So, that was the first bit of mixed, interracial marriage, the coming together of two diverse people – Suhail and Ann (Anna). Our two children, Lisa and Rebecca, were therefore of mixed parentage. When Lisa grew up into adulthood and was in a fantastic television journalism and broadcasting career starting with TV-am, she was introduced to Frank ter Voorde, a Dutch man, by a Swiss friend of hers, Effi, which eventually led to Lisa marrying Frank. So it became an interracial, multicultural mix of Bangladeshi/English/Dutch. Likewise, Rebecca was working in Europe at the EU Parliament, Toyota Marketing and the British Retail Consortium in Brussels. She met Rickard Granberg in Brussels, which led to their marriage, which meant we had a Bangladeshi/English/Finnish cultural mix. Lisa's children are of Bangladeshi/English/Dutch heritage; Rebecca's children are of Bangladeshi/English/Finnish heritage. My friends often say, 'You can't get a better cultural and interracial mix than that in one family!' They are right.

Lisa Soraya Aziz

My friends and colleagues have always read about Lisa in newspapers and upmarket magazines and said in admiration of our elder daughter, 'Suhail has got a famous daughter.' Not only were they referring to Lisa's elegance and beauty, but also to her enormous achievements. Starting her first broadcasting career job at Radio City Liverpool, she rose steadily to become a media star, a TV personality, a newscaster and presenter of style and weight, breaking new ground in the mainstream media. After Radio City Liverpool, she worked at TV-am, Harlech TV, BBC TV channels, ITV, CNBC and for thirteen years at Sky TV. When TV-am was just starting in the UK Lisa was their anchor as a newscaster/presenter. One of her distinguished colleagues, Jeff Berliner, had once commented, 'Lisa knows how to *read* news.' Her reputation as an effective media person spread fast in industry and commerce, resulting in numerous invitations to host important TV events and numerous communication assignments from multinational corporations, globally. She had become famous.

Lisa was born in June 1962 in Bromborough Hospital, Totnes, South Devon, some twenty miles from Dartmouth, my wife's home and home of the Britannia Royal Naval College, where I got my naval training, and of course the place where I met my wife-to-be, Anna, back in the summer of 1956. I had just left the Pakistan Navy and was in East Pakistan Inland Water Transport Authority (EPIWTA). As described elsewhere, I was sent for training with Trinity House, London, to learn about how the navigational aids were organised around the British Isles, the lighting and buoyage system and their workings and maintenance. This training was of course fortunately 'arranged' so that I would be in England to be near Anna at the final stages of her pregnancy until the birth. So it all worked out fine for us. I express my deepest gratitude to my friendly ex-Pakistan Navy chief executive, Capt. C. S. Ahmed, and my friend and well-wisher Cdr Erfan Ahmed, also ex-PN, for making all that happen working in the background.

Lisa studied arts and comparative religion at Goldsmiths, University of London. Her education was in state schools except in Nottingham where she was at a grammar which had just converted to a comprehensive as Nottingham High. She was diligent in her studies and took part in social activities at school and university. She was very active in sports and drama, and was editor of the college magazine. Her mother and I felt that Lisa was showing promise, was determined and ambitious and that she was going to go places. We encouraged and supported her as much as we could. Personally I was sorry that because of my financial circumstances I could not send

Lisa to private schools and to Oxford or Cambridge. But she achieved a lot nevertheless. We thank Allah for His help and guidance of Lisa. Lisa is a proud, self-made person, extremely talented. She has been regarded as a role model to many black and Asian young people aspiring to enter the British media industry. Today there are many TV and radio broadcasting personalities from the ethnic minority communities in Britain.

Lisa's talent in school was spotted early. In Nottingham, the BBC Asian programme, *Nai Zindagi Naya Jeevan* ('New Life [Urdu], New Life [Hindi]'), led by the distinguished BBC Asian broadcaster Mr Mahendra Kaul, a friend of mine, organised an outside broadcast for a cultural show for the Nottingham Bangladeshi Association, hosted by Lisa, which she conducted brilliantly. Her talent was noted widely in the Asian community through the programme. She was only about sixteen. From that time on Lisa developed an interest in the media. This interest matured in her university life at Goldsmiths, where she also edited the college magazine. Already Lisa had become a star with a strong following in the media world.

After completing her training at the National Broadcasting School in London, and after hundreds of meticulously handwritten job applications, many ending in tears and disappointments, Lisa kept her resolve and kept pushing the media companies, eventually culminating in her first job in her broadcasting career at Radio City Liverpool as a trainee journalist. She was only twenty-one, having just obtained her degree. She was very brave living in a flat across the River Mersey in New Brighton and taking the ferry every day to her office in Liverpool city centre. She has good memories of Radio City Liverpool where people were nice and warm to her. There was an exciting event she told us about. It was in the days when the extreme left of the Labour Party controlled Liverpool City Council – in about 1983. One morning Mr Derek Hatton, then deputy leader of the Labour-controlled city council – a very powerful man in the city – walked straight into Lisa's studio, handed her a piece of paper and said, 'Here, love, broadcast this.' Of course the power of militant tendency was well known. That piece of news bulletin from Hatton had to be read out on air by Lisa; there was no arguing with Derek Hatton by her station seniors in Liverpool of those days!

Lisa began her television career at BBC TV West where she qualified as a BBC graduate trainee and ran their news magazine programme. Soon after that she was headhunted by HTV West at Bristol where, soon after, she was anchoring and co-presenting HTV's award-winning current affairs programme, *The West This Week*. Her career at TV-am saw her flourish in TV broadcasting working as reporter, presenter and main anchor. She won *The Daily Mail*'s prestigious 'Media Personality of the Year'; and got the 2004 EMMA Award 'Best Television News Journalist' for her coverage hosting the first ever continuous live coverage of the Muslim Hajj from Mecca, Saudi Arabia, for Sky News where she worked for thirteen years; and was acclaimed for her coverage of the Bangladesh Cyclone. Lisa was declared 'Asian of the Year' in 1989 by The Rt Hon. Douglas Hurd MP, Home and Foreign Secretary, for her work in broadcasting. In 2005 Lisa moved back to ITV West in Bristol to present their flagship evening news show. In 2009 Lisa and her team at ITV West won the Royal Television Society Award for 'Best Regional News Programme'.

In 2010 Lisa returned to London to work as a freelance journalist at BBC Radio and then at LBC Radio. In her career Lisa had hosted many events for private, public and voluntary sector organisations, including large multinationals, UK and international banks, government departments and charities. She had been ambassador and trustee of numerous charities which she had championed. Lisa has politics in her blood. Of course my father, Lisa's grandfather, was a politician of high standing in pre-partition India. I, too, have been active in politics as narrated above. Like me, she has always supported the Labour Party. When we lived in Nottingham (1974–78), Lisa was always keen to join me in campaigning work, leafletting door-to-door at election time – rain, snow or shine! Her political instincts are strong. Lisa is a very perceptive journalist with a finely tuned skill in 'zooming' in for the truth.

Lisa switched to radio broadcasting, reading news at LBC, occasionally freelancing at BBC regional stations. She continues to be a successful media person, well liked, very much in demand as a newsreader of repute and weight. She has toughened through her career in TV and radio.

Lisa married Frank ter Voorde in 1990. The marriage was a media event in London. *The Sunday Times*, *The Daily Express* and some other newspapers and magazines ran stories with pictures of Lisa marrying Frank at the Kensington and Chelsea Register Office. The ceremony was followed by dinner at the Hurlingham Club in Fulham in the presence of selected relatives and friends and invited guests mostly from Lisa's media colleagues at TV-am and contacts. Frank was in commodities trade. In the early days of trading Frank found it difficult going – as happens in that kind of trade where there are numerous competitors. Middlemen like Frank couldn't be competitive with people who had the resources to buy and sell outright at source without having to go through a middleman. Frank was losing money. Lisa was in a well-paid job as newscaster/presenter at Sky TV. She kept helping Frank. But the losses were causing Lisa some concern. Eventually the pressures became too much. Lisa decided to divorce Frank. One morning Frank was on the phone. Anna took the call. I could see she was worried, so she passed the phone to me: 'Frank, please talk to my husband, I will hand you over to him.' I took the call. Frank said, 'Did you know Lisa wants to divorce me?' I said, 'No, Frank. OK, we will come over as soon as she is back from work.' We four met at their Louisville Road house in Tooting. Lisa's mind was made up. From what we heard, she had had enough. Our extreme sadness was about their two kids. It would fall on Lisa to bring them up in a one-parent family. Lisa and Frank's divorce took place after ten years of marriage, in 2000. Lisa never married again. Frank returned to his childhood love in Holland – a divorcee with grown-up children. They got married.

Frank and Lisa's two children, Leah ter Voorde (now twenty-four) and Jacob ter Voorde (now twenty), had a fascinating childhood. Leah was enormously energetic – 'hyperactive'! Anna became Leah and Jacob's loving nanny, practically bringing them up while Mum Lisa was busy with her TV and corporate work commitments. They lived in Fulham, then in Tooting. The Hurlingham grounds and Tooting Bec parks were the children's regular outings with my wife; they would climb the trees, play in the children's park and venture into daredevil playfulness. Leah studied at Graveney School in Tooting and went to the University of Derby to study teaching. Lisa, Jacob and I went to Derby on the day of Leah's degree award ceremony, a joyous occasion – 'regulation' picture-taking, joy and laughter. Leah got her degree in 2015 and obtained a job very quickly, working in a Nottingham primary, teaching kids. She proved to be very popular with children, very patient – a latent strength in her character which we didn't know anything about. Now she is flourishing.

Jacob is a scholar, privately educated. He was at Dulwich Prep, a feeder school of Dulwich College, South London. He got 97%, 98% in most of his GCSE subjects. Jacob showed promise. At times, if he got lower marks than he was expecting he would query the tutors: 'Why less than 98%?' He got his GCSE A-levels in 2016 and studied bio-chemistry at King's College London. Being very strong in chemistry and biology, physics and mathematics, Jacob wants to go into medicine drugs research. Having completed his studies for his first degree at King's College London, obtaining First Class passes, Jacob planned to take a gap year to spend time doing other things that interested him and spending time with his *papa* in his business; then a Master's, maybe PhD research at Oxbridge or in the USA.

After Lisa's divorce from Frank, happily both Leah and Jacob keep in close touch with their *papa* in Holland and with their grandparents – *uma* and *upa* – in Zwindrecht, Holland. Frank is now well established in commodity trading, with offices in Rotterdam and Switzerland. He is very kind to his children, often having them for holidays or giving them money whenever they ask or need it. Lisa is pleased that Frank is generous with the children. After bringing up the two kids single-handed as a one-parent family, Lisa is a lot happier now, seeing the success of her two children. Happily our grandchildren Leah and Jacob will continue to keep in close touch with Frank and their grandparents in Holland. That side of the family relationship is being nicely maintained.

Rebecca Sophia Aziz-Granberg

Rebecca is the younger of our two daughters. She was born in Streatham, South London, on 30 April 1971. The date is interesting. Anna was pregnant, with Rebecca expected at any time. The Bangladesh independence movement was in full swing in London; we were supporting the political activities in Bangladesh and the interim government in exile in Calcutta (Kolkata). I was very active in the movement with the Bangladeshi community and some British supporters (MPs, Lords, intelligentsia, community leaders and supportive British activists) in London. Those days I was working as an industrial relations officer at the Royal Commission on Industrial Relations (CIR). My office was at GKN House, in Kingsway, Aldwych, near Holborn. After work on some days I was attending two meetings in a day and had full diary engagements at the weekends, such was the tempo of activities during the Bangladesh movement in Britain.

On Friday 30 April 1971, I arrived home pretty late about 10pm after attending two meetings after work in central London. When I arrived home, I went upstairs. A pleasant surprise was to hit me! Our GP, Dr Marszalek (Czech or Polish), a very pleasant lady doctor, and a district midwife were in attendance. Anna had just given birth to our second child, Rebecca (again Anna's choice of name). Dr Marszalek said to me, 'Mr Aziz, congratulations, you have a girl, you are very lucky that we were called by Mrs Aziz just in time.' I was very worried and embarrassed, quite shocked. Anna could not contact me as I was at meetings – no mobile phones then. I felt very sorry that I was being very irresponsible not thinking that Anna was in advanced pregnancy. We had not booked her into a hospital for the childbirth. She being a very strong person, never in a panic in crises, managed. I was thankful, but felt guilty that I was not present in the house when Anna was giving birth. I prayed and asked for Allah's forgiveness and Anna's wellbeing.

Our lifestyle was very simple. When I was leaving the RAF in 1970, Anna was expecting Rebecca. As a flying officer in the RAF, I left without a penny in benefits because I had not even completed three years in the service. I had just bought a terraced house on an endowment mortgage for £5,250 (2019 price = £400,000) in Streatham Vale, South West London, our first step on the property ladder. The night Rebecca was born, we had only a paraffin heater to keep the room warm on a cold April night. By the Grace of God we managed; Anna was very happy that we had two daughters. We did not want any more children.

Rebecca went to the local Julian's Primary School, just at the top of the street we lived in, St Julian's Farm Road, a three-minute walk from the house. Like all mums, Anna would take Rebecca to school and bring her back. Rebecca did well in her primary school, took part in school activities and played tennis at the local tennis club. She started with local state schools in West Norwood. But we were getting a bit concerned about her progress with her GCSEs at the local schools. So we discussed in the family and decided that, despite the help we received with Rebecca's school fees from the Girls' Day School Trust at Streatham and Clapham High School, she had to be moved to another private school to finish her GCSE A-levels with good grades if she was to go to university, which she very much wanted to do. Luckily my income from international management consultancy was good enough for Rebecca's private education for two years at James Alleyne's Girls' School (JAGS) in Dulwich.

She had to take JAGS' admission tests, which she passed; she was accepted. In due course she obtained her A-levels with good grades to enter university. Of the offers of places Rebecca decided to accept, she took up the University of Leicester offer of a place to study history and politics. After obtaining her degree with a 2(i), Rebecca embarked on her career. Some years after, she obtained a Master's in European studies at South Bank University, London.

Rebecca began her career as a *stagiaire* at the European Commission, Directorate General VIII, which was concerned with the developing world in Africa, Asia, Latin America and the Oceanic Islands. She was very interested in development of underdeveloped countries. After successfully finishing the *stagiare* she got a job in the European Parliament working for a British MEP. She continued working in Brussels at the British Retail Consortium and in the marketing division of the European headquarters of Toyota Motors. While working in Brussels, Rebecca met Rickard Granberg, a young lawyer from Finland. Rickard was working at a Brussels law firm. He had studied law at the University of Stockholm.

Rebecca decided to come back to England. Not long after, Rickard also moved to London. They got engaged. I was pleased to arrange their engagement party at the old Army & Navy Club ('The In & Out') on Piccadilly, an associate club of my club, the Royal Air Force Club, also on Piccadilly, W1. It was a memorable occasion when they got a picture taken standing under the life-size portrait of Lord Palmerston at the club. They got married at the Kensington and Chelsea Register Office in London, followed by a family gathering for afternoon tea at the world famous Ritz. They have been working in London since then. Rickard is a legal adviser to a media company. Rebecca worked as a senior civil servant at the Department of Trade and Industry (DTI, now DIT). Later she concentrated on bringing up her young family, at the same time as having a part-time job.

At Rebecca's wedding I had invited relatives from Bangladesh. Due to distance involved, only my youngest brother Koysar, who sent his elder daughter

Farah; and my brother Lama, my youngest but one brother, a former MP in Bangladesh, who had attended Lisa's wedding in 1990, accepted my invitation to join Rebecca's wedding ceremony in London. Lama wanted visas for his entire family of five. I was of course pleased that they would all join Rebecca's wedding ceremony. I knew the then British High Commissioner to Bangladesh, Mr Peter Fowler CMG. I requested him to kindly arrange visitors' visas to Farah and Lama and his family members, which was duly done. I was most obliged to the High Commissioner. Farah attended the event and we enjoyed having her. But Lama and his family did not attend the event. To my utter surprise and disappointment, they went into hiding with no communication with me. Unaware of his designs, I was to learn later that Lama and his family overstayed their visa, became illegal along with his entire family, and remain in England as asylum seekers. To date they remain completely cut off from me. I asked Lama several times to return to Bangladesh rather than remain as illegals causing huge embarrassment all round, but to no avail!

After Rebecca and Rickard's wedding, Anna and I visited Oba, Ăland Islands, in the Finnish archipelago, Rickard's home. We saw his home, and met quite a few of his close relatives at the continuing wedding ceremony there, dining and dancing. We went fishing in Rickard's uncle's boat. We had a tremendous time.

Sadly, not long after our visit to Finland we heard that Rickard's mum, Greta, accidentally died when the ice she was walking her dog on cracked and she fell in. Her dog went running to get help; people arrived but sadly it was too late. A helicopter came from nearby Mariehamn, capital of Ăland, to recover her body. I went again to Oba to attend her funeral service. She was a very nice, sincere, caring person. She died quite young and is sadly missed.

Rebecca and Rickard are blessed with two beautiful children, our lovely grandchildren, Eleanor now fifteen and Konrad eight (in 2019). Their education is progressing at a private school, Surbiton High.

Eleanor is already excelling in school, having received two music scholarships (oboe and recorder). She takes part in music festivals and shows on the South Bank, Barbican Centre and at the Royal Albert Hall. She goes away to places like Liverpool for her concerts. Anna and I went to see her play in groups at John Lewis, Kingston. Eleanor is studying hard for her GCSEs under the strict supervision of her mum. She wants to go to a good university to study music.

Konrad is working hard at school, both in his subjects and at numerous sports – football, cricket, hockey, rugby – in which he shows skill and promise. Whenever I can I go to see him play for his school. He has just told me that he has been selected for his school A-team to play cricket this summer (2019). He's an all-rounder!

Anna was extremely keen to spend as much time as she could with Rebecca's two children, so she used to go over to Surbiton quite often. Anna was very fond of Eleanor and Konrad, frequently looking after them in their home in Thames Ditton in a lovely location by the Thames. Anna was to visit them for the last time on 26 April 2014 while her illness was already advancing. I still have a picture of her bending down playing with Konrad in their garden.

Our 50ᵗʰ Wedding Anniversary on 31 January 2010, at the Royal Air Force Club, Mayfair, London

Our wedding anniversary was a great occasion for us and our family. Obviously I had to give a speech. My family – Anna, Lisa and her children Leah and Jacob, Rebecca and Rickard and their children Eleanor and Konrad – were all there. There were some 110 guests: my relatives and friends, former colleagues and fellow Rotarians. There was a sumptuous dinner and music when Anna and I had a chance for a little dance for the occasion. We were deeply touched by the love and good wishes of all present.

My speech, lasting about ten minutes, covered most of what you would have read in the pages of this book. But there are a few things I would like to highlight:

First: I said my marriage to Anna, held in our Karachi flat on 31 January 1960, took place in extreme secrecy lest the Pakistan Navy agents found out. Only a handful of close friends were present. But it didn't have to be like that. It could have been held with razzmatazz, with drums beating and trumpets blaring! So this fiftieth wedding anniversary, at the Royal Air Force Club in London's Mayfair, was my heartfelt gift to Anna, going some way, I hoped, to make up for things I could have done differently for our wedding. I remain very sad and sorry.

Second: The creative work of my grandchildren, presented to my guests at the anniversary dinner to thunderous applause, is given below:

(ALL)
FIFTY!!!
A POEM BY LEAH AND JACOB
ACCOMPANIED BY MISS ELEANOR...

JACOB
WELL DONE TO YOU TWO...
FROM NEWLYWEDS TO RETIREES,
50 YEARS MARRIED, THOUGH NOT ALWAYS A BREEZE!
WHAT WITH NAN'S POOR HEARING,
AND GRAMP'S DODGY KNEES!

LEAH
THROUGH THE UPS AND DOWNS,
FROM DELIGHTFUL DARTMOUTH TO ALL OVER THE WORLD...
IT'S GOOD YOU BOTH LIKE DANCING,
SO WERE PREPARED TO GIVE IT A WHIRL!
FROM SAILING UP THE SUEZ TO DOWN THE NILE,
FROM LEEDS TO LINCOLNSHIRE,
VIA THE SQUARE MILE,
YOU'VE BEEN THERE AND DONE THAT
AND MUCH MUCH MORE!
BUT WHEREVER GRAMPY'S WORKED...
NAN KNOWS THAT HE'LL KEEP HER AWAKE AT NIGHT WITH A SNORE!

JACOB
THROUGH THICK AND THIN,
THROUGH LEAN TIMES AND FAT...
YOU LOOKED AFTER EACH OTHER,
AND NOW EVEN MARMITE, OUR CAT!

LEAH
SO THANKS NANNY AND GRAMPY FOR BEING THE BEST,
FOR GETTING THIS FAR,
YOU'VE CERTAINLY PASSED THE GOLDEN WEDDING ANNIVERSARY TEST!

At the end of our anniversary dinner a distinguished friend of mine, Mr Benny Dembitzer, came over to me and said, referring to my dismissal from the Pakistan Navy: 'Good, Suhail, you have no rancour!' To be honest, those wise words of the lawyer friend of my captain, Cdr Awan, on PNS *Khaibar*, written in the letter to the Pakistan Navy chief, came back to me: 'Not to grant permission to this young officer would leave him disgruntled for the rest of his life.' I feel that disgruntlement remains. Even though I say 'no rancour' after the President and Governor Tikka Khan's offer to go back to the navy if I wished, even though I regarded that as the Government's 'apology', I don't think my deep feeling of being 'disgruntled for the rest of my life' has ever gone.

It was Lisa who said, 'Mum, you and Dad have been talking about going on a P&O cruise. You go, I will pay for it, and let me find you a ship and cruise schedules.' So we all poured over a P&O brochure, and Lisa identified a two-week Mediterranean cruise on the ship *Ventura*. Lisa drove us over to Southampton and saw to our embarkation. We took a picture at the entrance to the ship; and Lisa met us off the ship when we returned. She was working at Sky TV in those days. She was very pleased we enjoyed what was for us a great cruise.

During the Med cruise we visited two ports each in France, Spain and Italy. We visited great places like Monte Carlo and Monaco, but unfortunately it rained a lot. Our call at Barcelona coincided with heavy rain! Life on board every evening was having cocktails before the second sitting dinner at a table reserved for the two of us, then time for the evening show. At the captain's dinner-dance, we got our picture taken by the side of a huge flower arrangement; that picture adorns our sitting room in our bungalow. A very enjoyable experience on the *Ventura*, thanks to our very thoughtful and generous daughter Lisa.

Chapter Twelve

Anna – our life together

Anna was always a strong, sturdy woman, always fit and well. If she got minor ailments she never made a fuss; she was clear in her mind about her treatment and hardly visited doctors. Whatever the ailment, she always pulled through. It must have been in 1986, when I was working at Lewisham Council, London, that Anna was first diagnosed with a malignant lump under her left arm. Our GP referred her to the Royal Marsden Hospital in Sutton. After numerous tests, she was given radiotherapy for some weeks, following which she was put on tablets. Oncologists kept a monitoring eye on her during this time, seeing her every six months or so. This treatment lasted for five years with tablets. Anna pulled through; she got the all clear. During this period following her radiotherapy, Anna kept well and got on with normal family life.

This ability in Anna to pull through was remarkable. She would always be calm and composed, never in a panic or anxious; if there was something, she kept it to herself. During her treatment at the Royal Marsden, every week I drove her to the hospital, waited until she finished her radiotherapy, then drove her home. She never spoke about any worry in her mind. She took it in her stride. She pulled through her first attack of cancer. We felt no concern in our minds. The consultants at the Royal Marsden were very able people; they looked after her well, giving us all encouragement and support. The NHS service was at its best, as always in these situations. We both felt reassured, even though it was cancer. Anna knew somehow, and I with our two daughters Lisa and Rebecca believed, that she would pull through. It was our strong faith and belief that she would be alright. By her calm demeanour she generated confidence in us.

Anna had developed some varicose veins in her legs which were painful. Doctors decided that there would have to be some surgery. She was admitted to East Dulwich Hospital, which was near us as we lived in nearby West Norwood, in South London. After a few days in hospital, she was discharged to the care of district nurses, got her bandages off and all was well. Anna pulled through, no problem.

When we were living in Nottingham, our GP had found that Anna suffered from excessive bleeding during her monthly cycles. So when we had moved back to London, it was another surgical operation, again at East Dulwich Hospital. This time it was hysterectomy. The surgery went well. Anna recovered and successfully pulled through. Things were bright and happy again.

During these times, Anna attended to her household duties as normal. We used to have students from the Victoria School of English staying with us. Anna would dutifully attend to them. She wouldn't in any way let herself or the school down. There was strict time-keeping for the young kids: breakfast on time and then seeing them off to the bus stop; everything went perfectly.

We went on driving holidays to England, Scotland and Europe. I always enjoyed driving. I would be driving, with Anna in front, young Lisa and Rebecca in the back of my Volkswagen Beetle, with food and drinks all fully stacked up. We travelled through France, Germany and Spain. We stayed in holiday places – large hotels or small B&Bs. On one holiday in a Spanish resort we met a family – an American gentleman and his English wife. We became friends. The gentleman and his wife would drive us through Spain, seeing the vineyards on the hills, occasionally stopping to eat and to taste the local wines. We kept in touch with him for some years. It is strange how a friendship comes about through casual encounters and continues as a close friendship for years.

Once we proceeded on holiday, planning to visit France and Holland. We drove from Nottingham. We completed the crossing but at the Calais passport check we were stopped. I hadn't thought about it, I still had my Pakistani passport! Anna and children were all holding British passports. We didn't want to turn back. The French immigration officer told me to leave my family with the car in Calais and go back myself to Dover, where there was a French immigration office, explain the situation, obtain a visa and return. I had no option but to take the return ferry to Dover. I found the French official, obtained my visa and luckily caught a ferry just in time. Anna had kept the children jolly with food and drinks while they waited for my return. Thankfully it all happened during a long summer day, so it was all over during daylight. Thus the calamity of not checking things before a holiday was plain!

We arrived in Holland pretty late in the evening. There was heavy rain; we could not even see the road signs clearly. We kept driving, with not a soul in sight, no lights of any village or town. With two small kids in the back, Anna and I kept wondering what to do. Where were we? Eventually we arrived in Haarlem. But it was quite late. We didn't have any advance booking for a hotel or B&B. However, we found a reasonable-looking hotel; we went in and got a lovely big room for the whole family. But we needed something to eat. It was too late for a meal at the hotel. The restaurant was closed. So off we went in the car to find a restaurant or a café. After a long drive and search in heavy rain, we were lucky to find a café. We ate a big meal and returned to the hotel. Next morning, after a nice long sleep, we drove to Amsterdam. We had a lovely time there.

During a routine cancer-monitoring visit to King's College Hospital, doctors diagnosed cancer, in Anna's left breast. The dreaded disease had come back after about fifteen years. The doctors decided that she needed to have a mastectomy.

Naturally it was scary. In those days our Lisa lived in Bath, Somerset, working at ITV West. Anna and I discussed how to break this worrying news to the children. Instinctively Anna suggested, 'Instead of talking over the phone, we should go to see Lisa to tell her.' We arrived in Bath. We could see Lisa was apprehensive at our sudden arrival. Gently, both of us told Lisa the bad news. Lisa embraced her mum, tears flowed and not many words were said; she just said, 'Poor Mum.' Lisa had encountered such bad news before because one of her very close friends, Fiona, after a short illness had died of cancer. Lisa knew what her friend had experienced. So she was quite strong in helping her mum and me to prepare ourselves mentally for this upcoming major operation.

Anna's operation took place at Guy's Hospital, Bermondsey, East London, under the care of Macmillan Cancer Support and NHS doctors and oncologists. The operation lasted about eight hours. I was scared. I kept praying to Allah to make Anna well again, to grant her longevity. Anna was in hospital for five days. During this time I would visit her and sit by her bedside, holding her hands, having little talks. There were other patients who had gone through similar surgical procedures. It was amazing to see how people were courageously facing their individual ordeals. My daughters Lisa and Rebecca would visit their mum, sit by her and encourage her. Friends were always kind and visited Anna, but they were short of words because words are always difficult at such times. Anna had her beautiful smile on her face as she greeted her visitors and talked to us, her grandchildren and friends. She showed her determination; her composure remained unperturbed. She coped with the onset of cancer and the major surgery that followed with great fortitude.

After this major operation, there was a long treatment plan of five years with tablets – Tamoxifen. There were visits to Guy's Hospital to see the oncologists for six-monthly monitoring checks. Things progressed well. Anna was declared all clear after five years. Once again, Anna, by the Grace of God with her strong will and undaunted nature had pulled through – (*Alhamdulillah*).

During all her operations, all major ones, and associated treatments, Anna showed a remarkable diligence in adhering to her treatment plan. She would never miss taking her medicine, or an appointment with doctors and hospitals. She never needed to apologise for missing an appointment or being late! This characteristic was evident in all her family; we all attached great value to this discipline, which I think stood us in good stead.

Summer 2012: After living in West Norwood, South East London, in a large house with an attic flat, seven bedrooms, two reception rooms etc. (friends used to say, 'Suhail has bought a mansion'!) for over thirty-two years, with our two daughters having 'flown the nest', Anna and I decided the time had come to downsize. It was too much work for her. Not only was she a housewife, but often we had young students from Japan, Spain, France and so on staying with us while they attended the Victoria School of English. She worked extremely hard, looked after her home perfectly, supported our young families, maintained excellent relations with friends and families. Occasionally she would take part-time jobs, as my income was not all that great, and, being proud, she would rather earn her own pocket money. All in all, Anna had a very busy life but never would she moan or express unhappiness. Her upbringing in a working-class family taught her to be strong, hardworking and at the same time a nice person.

After a long time on the market, we eventually sold the big house and from the proceeds we bought two smaller houses: a modern townhouse in nearby Sydenham in South East London and a very nice Edwardian townhouse in Dartmouth, Anna's birthplace. Anna loved Dartmouth and the house we bought, No. 1 Northford Road, just above on the hill near the market square, was perfect. It had great sentimental value for both of us.

Our two daughters were very fond of Dartmouth, Lisa having spent a lot of time with her Dartmouth grandparents – Nanny and Grampy – during her school holidays, and Rebecca, too, grew very fond of the place, so much so that, to this day, Rebecca and her family go to Dartmouth every Easter break for a week, see family and friends, and do a lot of crabbing. We all knew that Anna's love of Dartmouth was profound.

We moved to Sydenham in March 2011. We bought a townhouse in Lawrie Park Avenue, with five floors counting upwards from garden level – townhouses were built vertically. Ours was the third house in a block of four – 21, 23, 25, 27; we had No. 25. The block of houses was built on a gentle slope. The entrance was at the first floor front garden level. You went down one level to the dining room, with doors opening to the rear garden – the ground-floor level. From there you counted five floors to the top, quite a climb. The kitchen/breakfast room was on the first floor, the living room on the second floor, then the study (or third bedroom) and bathroom were on the third floor. The main bedroom was on the fourth floor and the third bedroom (guest room) was on the fifth floor.

Little did we realise at the time that buying the Sydenham townhouse was to turn out to be a big mistake, a wrong decision for both Anna and myself from our health point of view. I had had both my knees replaced (total knee replacement – TKR – in 2008/09), so climbing the four sets of staircases, six to eight steps each flight of stairs to each floor, was going to prove difficult!

And as it turned out Anna too was becoming unwell. The mistake was of course getting clearer to us as we persevered in the townhouse climbing the steps all day. By the end of the second year we thought that another home move was in the offing. It is always difficult to admit such a colossal mistake to one's own self but it was beginning to play us up. We were embarrassed to admit to friends and our very fine neighbours at Nos. 21, 23 and 27 Lawrie Park Avenue that we were going to move after just under three years – rather too soon after moving in. Our neighbours at No. 27 were a charming couple, David and Joules. As the estate agent's 'For Sale' sign went up, Joules came running into our kitchen/diner, saying, 'What have we done?' I engaged in a little dialogue with her to explain that we were truly very sorry to be leaving, especially leaving our neighbours in the block.

Saturday 28 July 2012: Anna had a routine blood test appointment at our GP surgery on Thursday 26 July. On Saturday 28th, Anna noticed a change in her skin colour. She asked me, 'Can you see if I am going yellow?' I said, 'Yes.' So we quickly made an appointment with an out-of-hours GP at SELDOC (South East London Doctors). The doctor confirmed Anna had jaundice and suggested we go to King's College Hospital A&E immediately, but also said there might be many hours' wait as it was a Saturday. So we decided to leave it for our own GP on Monday.

Monday 30 July: We saw one of our surgery GPs first, Dr Thekkakari, a fine South Indian doctor, who completed the paperwork procedure online, gave me some papers and asked me to take Anna to A&E immediately. As we were leaving his room, he firmly told us to, 'Go to King's.' That moment was to be the start of Anna becoming ill, but given Anna's track record of 'pulling through' all her ailments in the past, we thought nothing of her jaundice as we waited at King's College Hospital A&E. The doctors were very good. They got on to the case after initial assessment very quickly. At first the A&E doctors thought they would follow the 'medical route', but soon after they changed their mind and decided, 'No, it should be the surgical route.' Anna was admitted there and then for tests and examinations, and had to be admitted to hospital. Consultants and senior registrars became involved over the next few days. She stayed in hospital for nine days. At the end of these tests and the assessment period, Anna was seen by a very fine Indian consultant surgeon, Mr Ameet Patel, surrounded by his team and medical students. He said Anna would need a 'big operation'. He took time to explain what was to happen. He drew a diagram of the abdomen, showed where there would be cuts to take out the obstruction which was causing the jaundice and how everything inside would be reconnected. He told us it was called the 'Whipple procedure'. We were told that Anna could go home for a few days and would be readmitted to hospital for the surgical procedure on 14 August. The date of the actual operation was to be 15 August 2012.

We celebrated Lisa's daughter Leah's eighteenth birthday on 2 August 2012, followed by Lisa's second child Jacob's fourteenth birthday on the 13th August. We all had a good time. Anna made sure that presents were given, beautifully wrapped, plus of course some cash pocket money for the two of them. But at the back of our mind there was the worry that Anna was soon to be admitted to hospital for what the doctors at King's called her 'big operation'. On 10 August, Anna had her pre-assessment (to determine if she was fit to undergo the op or not). After a few days at home, I took Anna back to King's College Hospital, Denmark Hill, South London, as appointed, on 14 August. She was given a room of her own where routine checks were carried out. That night I stayed at home and went to the hospital early in the morning to be with her. On the morning of the 15th Anna was prepared for the operation, then trolleyed along the corridor in the direction of the operating theatre. I was walking alongside, holding the side of the trolley, trying to talk to her but found no words; I was traumatised. I told Anna to pray; I prayed for her surgery to go well. There was nothing else to do. Farther along the corridor, I saw Mr Patel, the consultant surgeon, heading for the wards to see the patients he was going to operate on that day. He stopped. I spoke to him. He held my hand and spoke the reassuring words 'Don't worry, she will be alright.' Those words were very providential. As we arrived at the last point before entering the theatre, the porters stopped and said, 'Sir, this is where you stop, you can't go beyond this point.' I let go the side of the trolley, kissed Anna and said, 'Cheerio!' The trolley was pushed along; after a yard or so, Anna shouted, 'Love you.' The trolley was turned into the theatre out of my sight. I had never heard Anna shout out so loud anything personal like this in public! I said goodbye to her, turned and reached for the window near me, put my head out and cried bitterly for some minutes, praying to Allah, 'May Anna's operation go well.' It was an extremely upsetting day for me. She was taken in about 11am and it was an eight-hour-long procedure. She was not out till about 8pm when she was taken to the high dependency unit, then to intensive care and then to the recovery ward. I went to the recovery ward that evening and saw a member of the surgical team whom I recognised; talking to him earlier he told me he too lived in Lawrie Park Avenue, Sydenham! That gave me a rapport with him. I asked him, 'How did the operation go?' He said, 'It was all fine, everything went well.' I was keeping Lisa and Rebecca informed all day. They visited their mum when she had been transferred to her ward. For three days after the Whipple procedure, Anna was not allowed anything to eat or drink, only her lips could be moistened with wet wool. She lay lifeless.

Anna made a slow but steady recovery from the 'big op'. She remained in hospital for a fortnight, during which Mr Patel regularly visited her in the ward to see her progress. After fourteen days, on 28 August, Anna was discharged from hospital and allowed home for rest, recuperation and recovery. There then followed various clinic, doctor and hospital visits. After about three months Anna was quite mobile and feeling well. I happily wrote to friends and relatives that Anna had pulled through, she was well again. Excited, we booked a second P&O cruise, a Baltic cruise to visit St Petersburg. Anna was keen on St Petersburg.

In August 2013, we went to Devon for a week's holiday. Anna's sister, Linda, lived in Newton Abbott with her husband, Gary, in a lovely house. We stayed with them. Gary's sister and brother-in-law came to meet us. Linda was familiar with Teignmouth as she had worked there as a nanny so we all decided to go there. It was a lovely hot day. We walked along the front, bought ice cream and took pictures. (I have a copy of the photo on Anna's favourite dresser; in the picture Anna is holding a cornet ice cream. Who could tell that that was the last time Anna would have a cornet ice cream? I titled the photo our 'last cornet in Teignmouth'.)

While in Devon, we saw our friend Hilary Farouk in Torquay. As mentioned before, Hilary and Anna grew to be close friends during their voyage together from Liverpool to Karachi, with our little Lisa and Hilary's little Kim, aboard the *Circassia*. Hilary lived in Torquay on her own, near her parents' home. Her husband, Farouk, had died of cancer some years before. Their two children, Kim and Elona, live away and visit her regularly or she spends time with them on holiday. It was lovely to see Hilary; we had afternoon tea and cake at a lovely leisure centre in Torquay. Hilary and Anna took pictures together; all now adorn our albums. Hilary was not keeping very well, so she needed to be home in Torquay for visits to doctors, consultants and hospital. I have tried to keep in touch with Hilary. I try to take her to lunch at the Grand Hotel, Torquay every August when I am down at Dartmouth for the Regatta, provided she is home and not away staying with one or the other of her children. Lisa accompanies me, with Leah and Jacob if they are with us, for the Regatta. She likes to meet our grandchildren. I do this in memory of Anna. I hope that Hilary's ailments will be cured soon.

After that 'last cornet in Teignmouth' in August 2013, we drove back to London.

A few months after the Whipple procedure, Anna had a follow-up appointment with Mr Patel, her consultant surgeon at King's College Hospital. He told Anna that following the procedure, they had done a biopsy and although there was no sign of the dreaded disease, cancer, as a precaution she should undergo a programme of chemotherapy and he would arrange this with Dr Paul Ross at Guy's Hospital. This plan of chemo was to take place for six months from November 2012 to April 2013. A very fine oncologist, I think a Tunisian lady doctor, looked after Anna during this programme of chemotherapy. All went well. To our delight Anna got the all clear in April. The oncologist discharged her on 24 April 2013. But she told us that even though it was all clear, nevertheless she would keep Anna on her books at Guy's so that Anna's case 'did not fall through the net', as she would like to keep an eye on her. I recall saying to the doctor, 'Thank you, Doctor, this has been an anxious time.' She asked me, 'Why an anxious time?' as if to tell me that Anna was cured. Sadly, this decision to keep Anna on her books to keep an eye on her got changed rather thoughtlessly by another oncologist on a regular monitoring visit at Guy's Hospital. We saw an Indian oncologist for the first time; it is really a concern that you rarely see one doctor twice on such visits, especially on routine visits. He said, 'As Mrs Aziz is well, she will be discharged to the referring doctor.' He took the view there was nothing else to do, so he would send her back to Mr Patel at King's. As it was to turn out, this was a big mistake. I wish Anna and I had realised it. We didn't think at the time that that was exactly what her Tunisian oncologist did not want to happen. A fatal gap was to develop when no one was monitoring Anna's condition till about October 2013.

Happily from April to October 2013, Anna was fit and well. After our trip to Dartmouth over the summer, we booked again to go on a P&O Balkan cruise (to visit St Petersburg). We were looking forward to it. So I told relatives and friends Anna's good news. We booked a fortnight's cruise; Anna had become particularly keen on P&O cruises after our first wonderful experience on the *Ventura*.

Anna was fine for some months from April 2013. We were feeling wonderful. The cruise had been booked; children and grandchildren's birthday celebrations were taking place. I wrote to friends giving them our good news that she was fully recovered. I did not know anything about cancer or that it might return. All the knowledge and experience was to dawn on me slowly over the following months. One friend, Veronica Smith, wife of my management consultant colleague, the late Brian Smith (he died of cancer a few years ago), wrote to me expressing happiness at Anna's news. But there was a slight query in my mind reading her letter, a tinge of suggestion that the disease might return. As it happened, that haunting query soon turned into reality; sadly it had to happen: Anna's illness returned.

One of Mr Patel's team, Dr Chakraborty, a very bright Indian doctor (a fellow Bengali from West Bengal), saw Anna a few days previously and said that there were quite a number of lymph nodes showing on the screen. He arranged an appointment with Mr Patel.

On 13 January 2014 Anna and I saw consultant surgeon Mr Patel again. He also said there were signs of lymph nodes but he wanted to make doubly sure, so he was arranging an urgent PET (Positron Emission Tomography) scan and would see her again immediately after that was done. At 9am on 27 January Anna had her PET scan at King's as an urgent case. This was followed by an urgent appointment with Mr Patel on the same day at 2pm.

There was bad news to hit us both. Mr Patel confirmed the return of cancer and he said he would refer her to see Dr Paul Ross, the oncologist at Guy's, again. Ominously Mr Patel fixed his eyes on mine for some long seconds and quietly uttered the words, 'I am very sorry.' I felt devastated. I tried not to show my nervousness to Anna. I was shocked at what was happening.

As we left Mr Patel's room, Anna asked quietly, 'What about the move?' We had decided on the move to a bungalow to avoid the stairs of the townhouse. Our sale of the Sydenham house was well advanced, coming on to exchange of contracts. I don't recall what I said to Anna in reply, I was traumatised. I couldn't think what to do.

As we were driving back, Anna asked me quietly, 'Why did Mr Patel say he was very sorry?' I could not reply, so I made light of it. I said, 'Probably he thought you had to undergo another round of chemo.' Anna went very quiet. We headed for home with very little conversation. I was feeling quite scared. Knowing Anna, I could feel that she was frightened but showed no sign of it; that's my Anna in crisis: calm as a rock, a very sturdy woman, keeping her thoughts to herself. Her home, her children and grandchildren – what was to happen to all this?

11 February 2014: At an appointment at Guy's Hospital cancer unit Dr Paul Ross, the consultant oncologist, saw Anna, me by her side listening. He had a chat with us. He said he would arrange some more chemotherapy but he also said that he would refer Anna to St Christopher's Hospice in Sydenham, South London. He said they were very good in palliative care and in helping to maintain a good 'quality of life'. The mention of the word 'hospice' was scary. We knew that very ill, terminally ill, patients go to hospice. But Dr Ross didn't explain more; the fact that people go there with terminal illness was never mentioned. Anna or I didn't think it necessary to ask for more information. We left things unsaid. We were as though on an escalator – keeping going, one way, not able to turn round. In our heart of hearts we both felt that it wouldn't apply to us. As I said before, I had the profound unshakeable belief that, as on previous occasions, Anna would pull through again, *Inshallah*.

Ten courses of chemo were to be administered once a week over ten consecutive weeks, along with a programme of visits to St Christopher's

Hospice for various activities aimed at improving quality of life, to help keep Anna cheerful.

The first dose of chemo was on 19 February 2014. Each half-hour chemo session was preceded by a blood test to ensure that the blood cells were up to a certain level of strength for a chemo dose to be administered. The first two or three blood tests were alright, so chemo doses were administered. Then after four or five weeks, the blood measure was not found to be at the level needed for the chemo dose. So we were sent home on two or three occasions, which meant that Anna would miss a week to allow blood cells to come up to the right level. We didn't quite understand it; in fact I was quite annoyed being sent home when Anna was mentally prepared for the chemo sessions.

15 April 2014: This problem of going to Guy's for chemo, the blood results not being up to strength, having to be sent back home became a regular pattern and a cause for concern. So we got an appointment to see Dr Paul Ross, the oncologist, again. He said to Anna that the chemo was not working and that he wanted to discuss options. These were: do nothing; or a 'combination drug' which might show results but he explained that there were risks that the benefits would be far outweighed by side effects – severe tiredness, loss of hair, negative impact on quality of life – and still there could be no guaranteed success with the treatment. During this discussion I also asked Anna if she would like to go to America. I cited the case of my Uncle Kamal's wife in Detroit who had undergone chemo for her cancer. Her experience was that she would take a couple of hefty doses and be laid up for a week or more every time, with no food and pretty miserable side effects. But the good news was that she recovered and lived for some years afterwards. Anna gave an emphatic 'No' to both Dr Ross's suggestion of a combination drug and my suggestion of treatment in America. Dr Ross said the services of the hospice would be good at this stage and that he would arrange for the hospice to make contact with us.

We were not sure we understood what was happening. We were traumatised. I felt very confused. The vagueness of Dr Ross's advice and decisions, the unexplained whys and wherefores hit me. We said goodbye to Dr Ross, but I was feeling worried. I asked Anna to go and sit in the patients' waiting area, then I went back to Dr Ross's room, knocked, entered, shut the door behind me and asked, 'Dr Ross, please tell me, what are you saying?' He said, 'Mr Aziz, please sit down. Mrs Aziz's prognosis is not good.' I asked what did that mean. How long had she got? Dr Ross asked me, 'What do you think?' I said, 'I don't know, you are the doctor!' He said, 'Short months.' Then he added, 'Mr Aziz, I could be wrong.' By that time my eyes were welling up with tears. I said to him, 'Dr Ross, she is a good woman.' He came out of his room to say goodbye to me. I wiped my eyes, walked to the reception area where Anna was waiting for me. Without engaging eyes I said to her, 'OK, Anna, let's go.'

While driving back, I could feel Anna was extra quiet; I was trying to make small talk. After a while, Anna asked, 'You went back to see Dr Ross, what did he say?' I could not say it, so I spoke a half-truth. I said, 'Something about the hospice routine.' Once again at a critical juncture I did not have the strength or courage to reply to her honestly. Again I made light of my reply. I could see in her face that she was not happy with my reply and small talk, but didn't press me. Anna knew I was upset. In both our hearts we knew things were not right. Even at that stage we both believed in our innermost minds that, as before, 'Anna would pull through'. I now realise how naive or ignorant I was. As an explanation for this naivety I can only think of my faith in Allah and my profound belief in the professionalism of British NHS doctors – that they knew best. Anna always said about NHS doctors: 'They know what to do.' My mind was closed to the thought that anything untoward would happen to Anna; as I said, she had always 'pulled through'. Really we never thought anything like death would happen to her! There followed a couple more trips to Guy's Hospital for blood tests but they were negative, so Anna could not be given any more chemo doses. That chemotherapy plan ended.

I began to take Anna to St Christopher's Hospice, once a week. The routine there was that she would spend a couple of hours at art classes or such like upstairs while I waited at the hospice's very nice Anniversary Centre, an extremely friendly place where terminally ill patients, their relatives and nursing staff would mix and mingle – with amazing laughter and cheerfulness on the surface but with a deep undercurrent of extreme worry and sadness. It offered a waiting area, a café with facilities for meals, tea, regular piano players playing music. It was a very nice visitors' centre, with beautiful gardens where people could sit, have tea and chat. Anna would join me after her art classes. We might have tea or head for home. While driving back I would ask her, 'What did you do today?' Anna: 'Not much.' I could see she didn't want to talk much about it but seemed to be happy spending a bit of time at the art classes – because she was a pottery artist in Dartmouth and it was still within her to do painting and drawing. A painting done by Anna on 11 April 2014 was handed to me by her art class supervisor on the afternoon of 25 June, the day Anna passed away. I got it framed and it hangs on my study wall, along with Anna's portrait and pictures of my Rotary clubs – for my constant viewing and speaking to Anna!

Sadly Anna's jaundice reappeared. Towards the end of May it became quite serious. She became quite ill and restless, her face and hands went yellow – reminding us of her jaundice attack back in July 2012 and that attack starting the serious prospect of a major operation, the Whipple procedure. She was getting agitated, unable to eat or drink, throwing up what she tried to eat. We called the ambulance and went to Croydon University Hospital A&E. It was getting late, about 5pm, and Anna was there till about 11pm while various tests were done and medication given. An Indian A&E consultant looked after her extremely well. He stabilised her restlessness and brought her back to normal. The consultant very kindly asked Anna if she wanted to stay the night in hospital, she would be very welcome, or she could go home. It was up to her. We both thought for a moment and decided that as her condition was much better she would be happy to go back home. I took Anna home at about 11pm that night. She slept well.

Meanwhile, following Dr Ross's referral, things were progressing with the hospice. On 3rd June we had the district nurse's visit, followed by visits by other nurses from St Christopher's covering the Croydon area. The 'Black Box' for cancer patients for treatment at home was duly placed at the foot of our bed – an ominous sign but there it was! Seeing that Anna needed a period of rest after her jaundice attack and the visit to A&E in Croydon, a very kind and highly professional senior nurse at St Christopher's, Ms Tracey, began to look after Anna. She said that she would try to get a bed for Anna at the hospice for a short time. Tracey rang me that weekend to say a bed had been found and that I should take Anna along on Monday 9 June 2014 – which sadly was to be Anna's last day at her home. Tracey made clear however: 'Suhail, we have found a bed only for a week. You must understand that she has to return home after a week of rest and comfort at the hospice.' Of course we both agreed. Anna was given a very nice single room on the second floor facing the front of the building, a sunny and warm room overlooking the grounds and the Sydenham tennis courts and the views beyond. The nursing, the care by the doctors and nurses at St Christopher's Hospice were all excellent. The facilities were tip top. The attitudes of all staff we came into contact with were consistently positive and remarkable. So Anna was settling in at the hospice at least for a week.

Anna's condition was stabilising a lot; she was quite comfortable, talking, joking, seeing her family members who kept visiting her during the week. Despite the jaundice, we all felt Anna was feeling better.

Meanwhile, unbeknown to me or Anna or our daughters, the hospice doctors were exploring with the Guy's oncologists familiar with Anna's case the possibility of fitting a stent to drain out the pancreatic and liver fluids so as to ease the jaundice effects. After discussion with us, on Friday 13 June, an urgent CT scan at Guy's was arranged. I drove Anna to the hospital and back. At 5pm that Friday, I was told by the hospice doctor that the CT scan confirmed that Anna was fit to undergo the procedure for fitting a stent. I was asked by the hospice doctor if I would be able to drive Anna over to Guy's on the previous evening, Sunday the 15th, for the procedure the next morning, 16 June. Accordingly, after our lunch at the hospice, we proceeded to Guy's Hospital. After the admission procedure at the Borough Wing of Guy's Hospital, Anna was allocated a room on her own. The surroundings at this wing of the hospital seemed a bit strange and unfamiliar, in fact quite poor. Anna said to me, 'I want you to stay the night with me.' I was given a put-up bed to sleep on in the same room, which we felt was good of the hospital staff.

On Monday 16 June, we were told by a Borough Wing ward nurse that the operation was cancelled. After being directed by the hospice to take Anna to Guy's on a Sunday evening for her procedure on Monday morning, I wanted to learn a bit more about why it had been cancelled. So I asked to see the senior registrar. He was apologetic and told us that the consultant had another urgent case, so Anna's operation would now be on the following day, Tuesday 17 June, in the morning. However, that was not to be so! On the Tuesday morning, we were told that the stent fitting would be performed at St Thomas' Hospital. We were at Guy's near London Bridge; St Thomas' was quite far, by Westminster Bridge. An ambulance was arranged. Anna, accompanied by me in the ambulance, left Guy's for St Thomas' at 12.15pm, arriving there at 1.30pm. At 2.20pm a Chinese consultant came to have a preliminary chat with Anna before performing the operation. But as he was talking I began to feel that he didn't seem to be fully briefed on Anna's case. I wondered if he had read her medical notes. So I offered to fill him in a bit about Anna's history. As I began to tell him that in July 2012, following her jaundice, she had had the Whipple procedure, he stopped me speaking and said, 'Oh, I didn't know she had had the Whipple procedure. In that case I can't do the stent fitting because the camera can't follow the endoscopy route to fit the stent to drain out the fluid, as her inside has been cut and reconnected. But not to worry, let me go and speak to my colleagues and come back.' After about an hour he returned to say that he had spoken to his radiologist colleagues and that they would do the 'skin procedure' to fit the stent, that is, the operation would be done from the side. At about 3.30pm, the consultant's senior registrar came down to see Anna. He apologised for not reading the notes and briefing the consultant about the case. He also said that the skin procedure was to take place at Guy's, so we were to return there by ambulance! Regrettably her frail condition was not taken into consideration in taking her back and forth by ambulance.

We were at St Thomas' all afternoon that day but Anna was not offered a cup of tea all the time we were there, even though one could see staff flitting about the place doing nothing. The radiologist couldn't tell us when the stent fitting would take place, it would depend on the radiologists' schedule. We returned to Guy's as the rush hour was starting and the traffic heavy with a lot of stop-go during the journey by ambulance.

Upon return to Guy's, Anna had a sandwich, which she asked me to share. There was still no news as to when her stent fitting would take place. I rang the hospice, spoke to Anna's doctor there and explained the fiasco arising from the consultant or senior registrar not reading her notes about her history as to whether a stent could be fitted or what procedure would have to be performed. The hospice doctor was very sympathetic, felt sorry for what had happened and promised to talk to the oncologist again in the morning – it was already 4.45pm. He was trying to get it organised for the following day, Wednesday 18 June. We hoped that it would be done on Wednesday without any other hold-up. The hospice doctor apologised, felt sorry and said things could have been done better.

Wednesday 18 June: Anna was scheduled for her operation at 2.30pm. By the time she was taken down to the anteroom of the operation theatre it was already 4.30pm. Then she was to wait till about 6.30pm when she was taken into the theatre for the surgery. I was waiting in her room, walking up and down, talking to the nurses on duty with very little information as to what was happening. What was the reason for the delay? My anxiety was mounting. She was in the theatre from 6.30 to 10.30pm. When Anna was trolleyed back to her room, she looked like death, absolutely flattened, lifeless after the four-hour ordeal. Then more bad news followed. As a temporary measure the radiologist consultant had fitted two tubes on her two sides to drain out the liver and pancreatic fluids. I gathered it was getting too late for him. So he put off the actual stent fitting to Friday 20 June; failing that it would be done after his weekend, on the following Monday, 23 June! There was absolutely no regard to the fact that Anna had become extremely frail and weak after her ordeal in getting the two draining tubes fitted. There was no consideration at all that her pancreatic cancer was at an advanced stage and the draining of the fluids to ease her jaundice was imperative. She was dying. I stayed the night in hospital with Anna.

Thursday 19 June: The senior registrar of the wing came to see me. He said that he had spoken to the hospice doctor and he in turn had been in close contact with the senior registrar at the oncology unit (Dr Ross's unit) at Guy's. He said to me (I summarise), 'Mr Aziz, Mrs Aziz's condition has become very weak. In her condition it is not wise to subject her to more pain to fit the stent. And the underlying cancer is in an advanced stage. The doctors feel that she should go back to the hospice and spend her time there recovering from the surgery and spend time with family in the care of the hospice.' Seeing Anna's condition, I and our two daughters agreed that Anna should not be subjected to more suffering. She was taken back to the hospice by ambulance in an extremely frail condition. We arrived back at St Christopher's at about 12.15pm. She was taken to the same room and given something to drink. We were glad she was back with the caring doctors and nursing staff at the hospice. The fiasco over the period Sunday 15 June to Thursday 19 June was worth generating a formal complaint to the NHS. But I thought that the underlying pancreatic cancer was advancing and there was nothing much to be gained by complaining, so I decided we should remain focused on Anna.

By Friday 20 June Anna was gaining some consciousness but still remained very weak, not eating or drinking. The hospice doctor spoke to me on that Friday afternoon. He said they would keep an eye on her over the weekend and speak to me again on Monday 23 June, and review her condition with me. I spoke to Lisa and Rebecca. Over the weekend, Saturday and Sunday, Anna began to speak a little; she was getting back her consciousness. But she was still very weak and in pain from the surgery. On Sunday 21 June, I was sitting by her bedside, crying. I said to her, 'Anna, don't leave me.' In a very faint choking voice Anna replied, 'I don't want to leave you but I can't go on like this.'

I felt terrible. I could not speak to her as I would have liked to share our private moments. In the privacy of my home I had so much to say to Anna and to hear from her if only she came back home, as it was planned by senior nurse Tracey, after a week in the hospice. I wanted to say so much to Anna and I know she wanted to talk to me too; a lot of things remained unsaid; they will remain heavy in my heart for the rest of my life. On the afternoon of Saturday 21 June Anna said to me, 'I forgive you.' I cried. In my emotional state I could not say to her, 'Thank you, Anna. I am sorry I could not give you a better life with me. I am very sorry to have put you through so much, so many ups and downs in our life, but you took it all in your stride, without a moan, you have been so strong and resilient, you never complained. For all this, Anna, I thank you. You never gave up on me. Please forgive me.' All this remained unsaid.

Monday 23 June: The hospice doctor, Dr Gough, saw me about eleven o'clock. He said that my wife's condition had not improved over the past weekend, in fact her condition had worsened. He said that it would be wise that my family members be asked to be with her that evening and that I should let relatives know that her condition had deteriorated. The nurses had taken out her two draining tubes as they had almost dried up. The chaplain of the hospice, the Reverend Andrew Goodhead, visited Anna. She was fully conscious. Rev. Goodhead told her that he would visit her again on the following day, Tuesday 24 June. Lisa, Rebecca, Rickard, our grandchildren were all by her bedside that Monday evening. Anna was in full possession of her senses. She said to me that there was some money left in her account. She asked me to give £500 each to our four grandchildren, which I said I would do (since done). She also asked that the few decorations in her hospice room be taken home. She even remembered to tell me to draw the sitting room curtains at home during the day, as it got very hot! During Tuesday some friends and relatives visited her for the last time.

Lisa and I kept vigil all Monday and Tuesday night. Anna's breathing was getting heavy and she was in discomfort. The nurses told me to sit by her and hold her hands and gently rub them as she, although not fully conscious, would still know that someone was with her. The presence of someone is felt by the patient. I stayed with her over the weekend. I tried to talk to her but she was not conscious. I set holding her hand. Praying.

Tuesday 24 June: Rev. Goodhead visited Anna. He stood by her bed; Anna was half sat up, I was standing next to her facing them. The chaplain asked, 'Ann, what do you want to do?' I saw Anna engaged, looking into his eyes; I had never seen Anna look so penetratingly into anyone's eyes or at anything like this in my life, then she very firmly uttered the words, 'I want to go.' Then the chaplain read out the last rites, read out prayers from the Bible and the last rites were performed.

Lisa and I stayed up all of Tuesday night with Anna. From about 6.10pm, as the hospice booklet says, I could see Anna's breathing definitely began to change; she was breathing less frequently with a chesty rattling noise; it was scary. I was reciting from 'Surahs' from the Quran and praying to Allah to grant her comfort for I could see my Anna was in extreme discomfort.

Wednesday 25 June: Anna's breathing changed and became less regular, emitting a painful noise. The hospice doctor said one by one her organs were failing. Later that morning the doctor and nurse disconnected the oxygen. Anna, with her head on my arms, heaved a long breath followed by a second long heave trying to recover her breath. Alas, that was not to be. At 1.10pm, my Anna breathed her last; she passed away peacefully in my arms. *Innalillahi Wainna Ilaihi Razeun*. May Allah take Anna to Heaven.

Lisa had gone to City Airport to collect Jacob coming back from visiting his *papa* and *uma* and *upa* in Holland. I called her to hurry back. Rebecca, Rickard and children arrived and stayed in the room. They had just gone downstairs with the children for a drink. I asked the nurse to go and find Rebecca to come quickly. Sadly Lisa and Rebecca could not see their mum and children's loving Nanny in her last moments. I had never seen Jacob and Leah cry so bitterly; I recalled that Anna had literally brought them up while Lisa, their mother, was working at Sky TV. We lost a fantastic person. I lost someone very dear; Anna was very precious to me. Now she was gone. May God take her to Heaven. I felt alone.

We remained in vigil by Anna in her room. Senior nurse Tracey came down later that afternoon to express her condolences. Her attitude was so positive and helpful. The hospice doctor was most apologetic, saying that things could have been done better in Anna's last days. I contemplated whether to make a formal complaint against the NHS for the atrocious behaviour of the consultant radiologist at Guy's who subjected Anna to so much pain and yet left an incomplete job, attending to his personal matters like weekends whilst ignoring a patient in a dangerous condition. He should never have accepted the case upon request from his Chinese colleague at St Thomas' Hospital; the mess-up over the period 16 to 19 June, forcing her to go to and fro between two hospitals – Guy's and St Thomas'. But I decided not to complain. What was the point? Anna's pancreatic cancer was at an advanced stage, its growth was overwhelming; it was only for a time that we would have Anna with us. Nothing could be done. A hospital apology was not going to help us in our tragic loss or bring my Anna back.

Looking back, Anna's last days at the hospice were so sad and tragic. Had she returned home after a week, as was originally planned by St Christopher's Hospice staff, we would have had Anna for a bit longer with us. I feel so sad that in the hospice room there was no privacy for me to talk to Anna; so much remained unsaid and she could also have spoken to me and told me what she would have liked me to do. My regrets I could not talk to her about so many things I would have liked to about our life together, the hardships, the trials and tribulations, the experience and impressions, and above all I could not say to her privately, about my deep love for her, nor could she – because both she and I were constrained in the hospice room. It gave some privacy but not when Anna was in full consciousness. So I just sat holding her hands, as she was asleep or unconscious, during the last two nights of vigil at the hospice. With hindsight so many things could have been done better. We did not have to take her through the ordeal of trying to fit a stent to drain out the fluids; we could have left her with her jaundice because her restlessness had been overcome at A&E at Croydon Hospital.

I feel angry. I know Anna, even though she lay asleep or unconscious, was thinking because suddenly she said to me, 'I forgive you.' I wanted to talk to her about our life together for the past fifty-seven years, through the frustrations and irritations, problems and challenges we faced together; as I say, it all remained unsaid, caught up in the trauma. She lay in the quietness of the room, as if we had nothing more to say to one another. Anna occasionally stared quietly. I kept saying, 'I love you, darling, don't leave me.' She said, 'I don't want to but I can't go on like this.' Anna spoke little, but when she said something, the few words she spoke were always so thoughtful and meaningful, they summed up so much of our life's span. I have lost someone very precious in my life. I am angry with myself that I could not talk to Anna in quieter private moments in her last few days. I wanted to ask Anna for her forgiveness again and again and to say, 'I love you, darling.'

Why am I angry about her last days in the hands of the NHS hospital? I have guilt, I feel angry with myself because I could have done things better for Anna in her last days. I think that anger is festering inside me. With hindsight, I think I was traumatised. I just couldn't think what was best for her. I was just drifting along, both of us taking things as they came. I don't think I had the experience or judgment to see what was good and not good for Anna. I just went along, in consultation with Anna and obtaining her agreement, to whatever the doctors were telling us. We took it all in extreme good faith, not arguing or challenging the doctors' decisions. We believed in our fate, whatever God had wished upon us.

Lisa and I had visited Beckenham Cemetery and Crematorium to see the manager. He, with considerable thought and empathy, described arrangements and costs. We felt content. Lisa and I visited the Co-op Funeral Service at Sydenham. Once again a very kind and sympathetic manager took us through all the arrangements. Luckily the manager lady knew the manager at the cemetery, so it was all put in place with very little running around from us. On 17 July 2014, Anna finally parted company with us. She was buried at Beckenham Cemetery, Grace's Gate enclosure. *Innalillahi Wainna Ilaihi Razeun.*

A repeat encounter with HRH Princess Alexandra

Earlier in this book (Chapter II), I described my encounter with HRH Princess Alexandra when I was an inpatient with a duodenal ulcer at the Royal Naval Hospital Devonport. HRH was visiting the hospital as the head of Queen Alexandra's Royal Naval Nursing Service (QARNNS). Princess Alexandra paid a visit to my cabin, accompanied by the surgeon captain and the matron looking after my care. I was presented to the Princess by the captain – a memorable occasion for me. Now, fifty-eight years later, 1956 to 2014, at St Christopher's Hospice, where Anna, my beloved wife, passed her last days, I was pleasantly surprised to see a portrait of HRH Princess Alexandra proudly displayed by the hospice entrance, commemorating a royal visit to the hospice when HRH saw for herself the good work the hospice was doing providing palliative care to patients in their dying days.

Some pictures in my life

Of course there are hundreds of snaps and photos taken to remember Anna and my life together. I have my second project which still remains as my 'unfinished job', which is to go through the boxes of photos and prints accumulated over a lifetime, deciding which to discard and which to put into albums. I hope to complete that project after sending off this manuscript of my memoir to the publishers.

Meanwhile, I have got hanging on my study walls some important pictures. They are, going anti-clockwise as I face the east wall: a beautiful large picture of Lisa when she was at Sky TV; underneath, she with Tony Blair and her co-presenter at ITV West when Mr Blair was on a visit to Bristol; then a picture of me, as president of the Rotary Club of Streatham; me shaking hands with my counterpart president of the Rotary Club of Manila Bay, while I was visiting officials at the Asian Development Bank on Brettonwood, my company, business, in Mandaluyong City, Manila, Philippines; a photograph at the Royal Air Force Club at the ceremonial function when I was taking over as president of the Rotary Club of Streatham, succeeding past-president Leon Quomina. Alas, five from that group photo of eighteen are no longer with us, including Anna – may God bless their departed souls. Underneath that photo is one taken on board the *Spirit of Chicago*, on Lake Michigan, during the centenary celebrations of Rotary International – the Rotary movement formed by Rotarian Paul Harris and a handful of his colleagues in Chicago in 1905; next is a beautiful large portrait of Anna, enlarged from some of the pictures on Rebecca's mobile phone and printed by a famous professional photographer in Surbiton, Surrey, England, as arranged by Rebecca; next is a painting by Anna as she was receiving palliative care at St Christopher's Hospice.

The tutor in charge of the therapy class at the hospice came down on the afternoon of Anna's passing away to hand me the painting, which read, '*Made at St Christopher's by Ann Aziz, on 11.4.2015*'. It showed two potted plants, one pink and one blue – no prize for guessing the meaning! I used to take Anna to the hospice for her routine care. I would ask, 'What did you do today then?' She would not give a full answer. 'Oh, something!' I knew how sad she was feeling those days having to leave it all behind. In my study underneath the clock is a recent addition of a group photograph with five of my school friends taken during my visit to Obaid Jaigirdar's Cuban Consulate in Dhaka, Bangladesh, in April 2018.

On the three shelves are my family pictures: children, grandchildren, travels, including one with Prince Charles at the Commonwealth Institute when I was a director at the Commission for Racial Equality; one with Lisa when she was declared 'Asian of the Year' by the Foreign Secretary, Douglas Hurd (now Lord Hurd); Rebecca and Rickard's wedding; Lisa receiving her degree from HRH The Princess Royal Princess Anne, at the Royal Albert Hall; Anna, Lisa (age three) and my brother, the late Raja, in 1965 at Lever Brothers Pakistan, Chittagong; and Anna's thanksgiving service at Beckenham Cemetery chapel on 17 July 2014.

Then on the wall behind me are: me when I was a director at the CRE; BRNC Dartmouth; a group picture of me at the passing-out, Dartmouth, July 1958; an older picture of the naval college buildings; HMS *Vigilant*; my four grandchildren, Leah and Jacob, Eleanor and Konrad; and Anna and Lisa with enormous smiles as they appeared in an M&S magazine during a food festival.

In the sitting room there are more pictures on the shelves. One important one is a famous painting by a local artist from Dartmouth of the Royal Naval College Dartmouth. During a visit to Dartmouth after Anna's passing away Lisa and I found this painting. I bought it. It hangs on the south-west wall of my sitting room. I explain to my visitors the meaning of that painting and particularly the extreme western cabin on the first floor. The significance is that it was the painting showing my cabin in the St Vincent division of the college close to the western fire escape which I frequently used while dating Anna especially on occasions when I was running late returning to the college after pipe down!

A holiday in India

It must have been winter 1990. Our elder daughter, Lisa, then a TV newscaster/presenter at Sky TV, said to us, 'Mum and Dad, you have been talking about a holiday in India. You go this winter, I will pay.' Anna said, 'It's very generous of you, Lisa.' I added, 'OK, Lisa, we will take you up on that.' So we did some research, found just the thing: an all-inclusive two-week package holiday to Rajasthan, India, a west-central state, rich in culture and heritage and kingdoms of many Hindu maharajas with their palaces, pomp and grandeur, partly also a desert region. All rich in history. Our package included food and accommodation in 4-star hotels and a chauffeur-driven Ambassador car. The trip was to cover the circuit New Delhi, Mandawar, Udaipur, Jodhpur, Jaipur, Fatehpur Sikri, Agra and the Taj Mahal, and back to Delhi. Although a subcontinental myself, as I said I have been through some changes in my nationalities: I was born an Indian, Pakistani for a while, then Pakistan broke up, and I became

Bangladeshi, dual British. Anna was English, from Dartmouth in Devon; we had met while I was training at the Britannia Royal Naval College Dartmouth. After our marriage we lived in Pakistan and Bangladesh for some years; she took to the culture and the people with fascination and great understanding. She really liked the people. We discussed our flight for the holiday. We decided that this time we would travel to India taking the great circle route over central Asia, the former Soviet Union. For cost and for novelty reasons, we decided to fly Aeroflot, Uzbekistan Airways. The plane was a brand new Airbus for the first London–Tashkent sector. It was an evening flight. Upon arrival in Tashkent airport, the waiting began. The hall where passengers were to wait for connection to New Delhi was cold; a cold breeze was blowing through the halls. We almost felt the cold blast of a different culture. It was getting late. The grim-looking airport staff were most uncommunicative; asking for a cup of tea felt like hard work. It gave us a feeling of being unwelcome, burdensome guests. Sitting around in the airport lounge not knowing what was going on, with nothing to read, it was quite a strange place for foreign travellers. One felt that nothing had changed from Soviet times, even though countries of Central Asia had become independent republics some years ago with the break-up of the old Soviet Union. We boarded the plane (it was an old Russian plane), for the Tashkent–New Delhi part of our journey. The seats were most uncomfortable, not cushioned well; these planes were frequently used as cargo carriers. Taking off was scary; as it gained height and got to cruising, the engines made a screeching noise as if something was wrong, vibrating and shaking! Anna looked at me as if to say, 'What have you done? What a start to our holiday in India!' I began to feel guilty and embarrassed. I recalled these planes were very much in use in this region when India was closer to the Soviet Union than to the West. The three-hour flight to New Delhi was soon over. We were met at the airport by the holiday staff. The driver (named 'Rana', my name sake!) was an Indian from Uttar Pradesh. He spoke good English, was polite, courteous, cultured and fairly well educated. The Ambassador car looked clean and smart. After a good dinner we settled in for the night. Our travels round Rajasthan were to begin in the morning. Hotels in Mandawar, Udaipur, Jodhpur, Jaipur, Agra were good, welcoming, hygienic, with excellent service; it made all the difference. We began to feel good. I was relieved, as I'd been fearful that I was incurring Anna's displeasure by wrongly selecting this holiday with Russian planes!

The return journey home via Tashkent again was to prove problematic. Waiting at the Tashkent airport at the dead of night was a nightmare. Once again the atmosphere at the airport was quite awful.

Anna said to me, 'It's beginning to feel like a grim situation. The handful of staff on night duty are most unwelcoming, they seem quite unhappy.' As we came off the plane to the transit lounge for our connecting flight to London, the first thing that happened was a couple of immigration staff in military uniform met us and started a process of separating the passengers in a very suspicious and worrying way. For no apparent reason they began separating white passengers from non-white passengers, mostly from India. So I and fellow Indians were grouped on one side, while the white passengers stood some feet away across from our group. Then one by one they began checking our passports. I had heard that British Home Office rules impose hefty fines on airlines if they are caught bringing illegal immigrants. There was no problem with the Home Office rules but it was the way the Uzbek military-style immigration staff were doing their checks in the most offensive, rude and discourteous way at the dead of the night. I did not see one staff member with a smile on their face! The process of separating white from coloured people reminded me of scenes from films of the way treatment was meted out to Jewish people in Nazi Germany. I was standing there with a few other Asians separated from my wife at about three in the morning; I was asking myself what was up. After the passport checks we were still standing separated from the white passengers. I thought this was getting ridiculous. It was getting to about 4am; the building very cold; the military staff did not seem to be in a hurry at all; we were left standing, couldn't even sit anywhere. As time was getting on, I took a look at the staff carefully; they seemed quite tired and sleepy anyway. So I decided that I would just drift across toward my wife's group. Anna looked concerned; I could see her mouthing at me, 'Be careful now!' Thankfully, I was successful, not caught out! I embarked on the plane with the 'white' group who were allowed on the plane first. After a while I saw the Indian 'coloured' group slowly boarding the plane. It was a relief that they were OK. What I was experiencing was the sheer strangeness and foreignness of what was going on, no communication, no talking, no welcoming gestures and no smiles. It was quite fearsome and frightening. I felt we'd got caught between two cultures.

Thus the worry of having to experience something like this, which had never happened to me or Anna before, was thankfully over. It showed how different cultures clash. My wife was able to take it much more calmly and quietly, with her quiet disposition from her upbringing; whereas I and my fellow Indians were showing our emotions and reactions quite differently, verging on panic and anger! On the part of the Uzbeks it was different again; serious, grim, the people were so un-understanding and bullying in their style. Happily, I was able to drift across from one group to another without being seen. They were at the end of their night shift, half asleep. I felt the British Home Office was just as much at fault, making UK-bound passengers go through a humiliating experience like this, at the dead of a very cold night. Surely a more civilised and practical method of checking people in transit could be put in place rather than subjecting passengers of many nationalities to such an ordeal. But 'all's well that ends well'! The flight back to Heathrow was once again on a new Airbus, with smart cabin staff, good food and wine, courteous, a welcoming feeling. The cold unfriendly suspicious culture soon gave way to a very pleasant experience. Things have moved on for the airline. Aeroflot has modernised beyond belief, its planes are mostly Airbus and Boeings in western hemisphere flights; old Soviet planes have been scrapped; the airline today enjoys a good safety record. Flight attendants are smart, well spoken, welcoming. It shows things can be done, change can happen.

Soon Anna and I were back at Heathrow, a feeling of being back to 'England's green and pleasant land'. It truly was a great experience seeing Rajasthan. I said to Anna, 'Sorry, never again a flight over the Great Circle route over the old Soviet Union.' Clearly I was caught up between two, if not three, cultures. It is the phenomenon often of 'strangeness and foreignness'; it is overcome with openness, dialogue and understanding. One has to adapt to new situations. There are great places to visit in the former Soviet Republics: Samarkand, Bukhara, Tashkent, the Silk Route, the Balkans, St Petersburg etc. If tourism to those famous historical places is to become safe and attractive, attitudes and behaviours must change and become welcoming, not grim or harassing. Indeed they have begun to change since the break-up of the former Soviet Union. But there is some way to go yet.

Chapter Thirteen

The aftermath

Tributes

Tributes from relatives, friends, colleagues and acquaintances started to arrive with deeply touching words of condolence, sympathy and offers of help:

> '... *looking at her portrait in your living room I could see the lady had serenity about her*'

> '*We are stunned by the news and will truly miss the beautiful person your wife was...*'

> '*Ann was gentle, kind and most loving... you have wonderful memories of her so hang on to those during the dark days ahead.*'

> '... *Ann has been a rock of support to you through your travels around the world.*'

> '*Ann was truly a lovely and charming lady*'

> '*We are devastated for your loss*'

> '*I have fond memories of her as she was a real lady*'

'*In loving memory of our friend who we knew many years ago at Dartmouth Pottery*'

'*Members stood in silent tribute at the start of their meeting of the Rotary Club of Tooting*'

'*She was always so kind to us – she was family*'

'*We are feeling so very sad at Anna's passing*'

'*Ann was such a lovely, sweet brave sister – always in our hearts forever*'

'*We are part of something that goes on ad infinitum. You will see the lovely Ann of your life again forever and be re-united*'

'*She was always our most elegant and gracious chachi* [auntie]'

'*… the wonderful memories that Anna has given you all as her GIFT*'

'*We always found Ann to be a friendly and pleasant person, and we looked forward to meeting up with her at the Rotary Conference*'

'*The portrait of Ann's life that you sent us gave us a glimpse of a remarkable woman… we wish that we had had the time to get to know you both better*'

'*… we will cherish her memories of her love and care and her beautiful smile*'

'*… very moving Service… the readings and the music very apt… you have really "done Ann proud' as they say… that beautiful portrait on the front just catches Ann's whimsical expression perfectly and having your photo on the reverse is such a lovely touch…*'

'She was a great lady and we know she suffered greatly with you in your early days in England'

'We are blessed to have known such a remarkable and lovely person'

'Aunty was a warm, gentle and fantastically kind person who can be compared to no other'

'... there was something special about that woman'

'Thank you for sharing your story with me. It was very interesting and moving. Your wife was extremely clever and beautiful... very moving and emotional but adventurous and also exciting. You and Ann had many trials and disappointments but you weathered the storm and persevered. These are the qualities of a good marriage and love that lasts forever... keep writing because real stories are ones people want to read'.

'I speak as an old friend of the family. I have known Ann and Suhail for over 40 years – since Suhail worked with my late husband and lived not far from us. I remember visiting them when Rebecca was a baby and Lisa still quite small and Ann still managed to be calm and unflustered and to welcome friends warmly. The family then moved to the Midlands but when we heard they were returning to London I was very keen to have them as neighbours so went round to the local estate agents collecting details of houses to send to them. We were really delighted when they bought one of those houses and moved to the next road.

'Ann was an extraordinary woman. Brave, determined and adaptable – imagine moving to another culture and continent far from home in Devon, at 21, to get married. Her sensitivity to others and their needs of course made her the ideal wife, mother and grandmother, but I also thought that those qualities, combined with her determination and adherence to high standards, would have made her a first class teacher or social worker. Her qualities of endurance were sadly tested as she had much to bear with her own health problems which she faced bravely and stoically.

'Ann was also a beautiful and elegant woman who created charming and harmonious homes. She was the warmest and most generous hostess who provided feasts for her guests, carefully taking into account all possible needs. Her family is a living example of multiculturalism at its best – how the world ought to be – taking the best from a variety of cultures and creating a harmonious whole. This requires special talents of diplomacy and awareness of others, continually being alert to them – listening rather than judging and smoothing out any possible problems or misunderstandings.

'We are all much poorer without Ann's serene, self-effacing competence and warm support for others, and everyone who knew her will miss her sadly.

The strong family she created will support each other in their loss and grief and know how grateful they are for Ann's life and for her loving care of them through the years.' – Jennifer Beever at Anna's funeral service, Beckenham, 17 July 2014.

Anna's burial took place on 17 July 2014 at Beckenham Cemetery and Crematorium, a very old and long-established cemetery, located in Bromley, Kent. Anna is laid to rest in a double grave; she is buried at seven feet and I will join her at five feet. The headstone will be shared: Anna's inscription is on the left, mine on the right.

Anna is not coming back. Nothing could be done. What now? How was I going to live a life after Anna, without my life's partner beside me? How to live life with its loneliness and sadness? From the time I first met Anna all those years ago in the summer of 1956, it has been a fifty-eight-year partnership, three years courting while at Dartmouth, and fifty-five years of married life, with all its ups and downs, trials and tribulations, joys, happiness and fun. So, what now? And my guilt that I could have done more to make Anna's life with me better and more comfortable.

I live on my own in the bungalow which Anna and I made our new home in Selsdon, South Croydon, Surrey. Sometime the loneliness gets overwhelming. So I go to my desktop computer in my study and listen to some very old songs on YouTube, listen and often cry:

'*Amaro Porano Jaha Chay*' by Rabindranath Tagore (written 1888): *That which my heart desires /'Tis you. 'Tis but you / That which my heart desires/Bereft of you in this world/ Bears no one, nothing for me/ That which my heart desires.*

Another song:
(We had) So much to say to each other/ So many songs to sing/ Will the pains of our parting/ Will they ever end…

'A letter' by Jaganmoy Mitra – (about 1944): *Today you are so far away/ You are so far away/ As we were parting, you held my two hands/ And said/ Please write to me/ Today you are so far away.*

A Bengali film song by Geeta Dutta from Bengali film '*Harano Shur*' *(about 1950):* *You are mine, oh yes you are mine/ Whisper into my ears at least once/ That you are mine…/ In our life and death/ You will come dressed as a bride/ That is all I pray for/ There is nothing more I wish for.*

Another song from an old Bengali film *Chandrashekhar* (about 1950): *Do you know my friend/ How much you are making me cry/ My friend, oh my friend/ I am crying for you…/ Why have you left me my friend? You have given such hurt/ What did I do wrong?*

Counselling: I went through the processes of counselling, first one-to-one sessions followed by group counselling held as part of St Christopher's Hospice's support programme for bereaved relatives after the loss of dear ones. I found my one-to-ones very helpful. Those were the early days of my loss; I was in a high state of emotions; I cried a lot in those sessions. The counsellor (an English lady lecturer in Arabic from City University, London) said, 'Cry, it's good to get it out of your chest as much as you can.' It certainly lightened me a lot, but grieving never goes away.

A couple of years after Anna's death I got depressed again. I didn't feel like doing anything, just sitting, gazing at nothing with my eyes fixed on nothing or looking blurred at something. I saw my GP and immediately she gave a prescription for antidepressants. I took the tablets for a few days, then I didn't like their side effects: zombie-like, always feeling sleepy. So I told the GP I was stopping taking them and tried to carry on, managing myself a bit more cautiously. And I sought the help of another counsellor identified by my GP from Cruise Counselling, Croydon branch. She was called Fiona. She was very clear in what she thought I needed. She gave me some practical, valuable advice at a time of my feeling so confused:

- 'You cannot ignore your grief'
- 'Allow yourself space in time'
- 'Understand the change that has happened in your life'
- 'Time will allow perspective'
- 'We are ruled by emotions'
- 'You are not the same person now, change has made you vulnerable'
- 'Who are you now? You are in a new situation'
- 'Dual process: You have lost your wife; your children have lost their mother. Dual process of emotions – intensity is different'
- 'Confusion – adding to that not helpful'
- 'Shed the baggage'
- 'Does it work for you?'
- 'Give time to yourself; give yourself space.'

Anna has entrusted to me our children Lisa and Rebecca, and our four lovely grandchildren: Lisa's two, Leah and Jacob, and their sweet cat Marmite that Anna was very friendly with – no biting, no scratching, just good friends; and Rebecca's two – Eleanor and Konrad. All are on trust with me. I am to try to keep them happy.

Our beautiful bungalow in Selsdon, South Croydon, London, Anna had got done up to her taste and choice ('I want everything painted white'!) by Romanian builders and decorators as her cancer was advancing. As she would say to the decorators: 'I want everything white.' The bungalow was decorated to her absolute and elegant choice; everything was painted white, all sitting room furniture white, everything in sight in fact white! IKEA furniture all white.

Anna's cancer was already advancing menacingly as we moved from the five-storey townhouse in Sydenham to Selsdon in January 2014. Despite her discomfort she wanted to see that everything was done to her taste. We had gone to buy the curtains in the curtain shop in Streatham. Anna walked round the shop and made the selection. The young man, the curtain fitter serving us, saw Anna was in discomfort. He kindly said, 'Madam, would you like to sit down?' He offered her a chair. I could see in Anna's painful state she appreciated it. I felt guilty that I was causing all this extra pain to her having to go shopping in her condition. She knew I couldn't do it on my own, I didn't have a clue, so she insisted she came to the shop with me.

I decided that the house was on trust to me to keep alive Anna's memory as her parting gift to me. I recall the day at the breakfast table she began to cry loudly, with tears running down her face as she looked out of the kitchen window at the garden. I went over and embraced her and asked, 'What's wrong, Anna?' With tears running down her face she said, 'I am angry with myself. I got it all done and I won't be here!' Heartbreaking. I felt very hurt. I could not speak, just sadly looked at her. Words failed me. That is why I feel that I must look after this bungalow and maintain it to Anna's high standards.

Many people have visited this house since Anna's passing away. They have always commented in admiration: 'what a beautiful house!'

My pain clinic consultant at King's College Hospital and some friends have suggested that rather than living on my own at the bungalow, with the risk of falls at my age, feeling lonely and sad, I should move to a 'sheltered home' or to a flat nearer my daughters and friends and where I would see more people. I have considered that proposition carefully. But I can't leave this place, Anna's memories are attached all around me. I regard it as entrusted to me by Anna. So I will live here until I die. I am not going to be around much longer anyway. 'It is only for a time!' After that it will be for Lisa and Rebecca to decide what they want to do with the bungalow.

It's over five years since Anna's departure. Not a day has passed without thinking of my beloved Anna. I have her large portraits hanging in every room – bedroom, sitting room, my study, guest room. Rebecca got them done for me from recent mobile phone images at a Surbiton studio. I am most grateful to Rebecca for this. The portrait prints are good companions for me. They are lovely. I talk to Anna often as I miss her so. People have said I should not have Anna's pictures so prominent as they trigger my emotions and set me off crying. But I couldn't do that. With her pictures in the house plus a whole host of other things, family pictures in various rooms, I feel I am in Anna's company. I can talk to her at moments at my will. It helps me to think of her and 'speak' to her about all sorts of things – in my happy or sad moments – and report to her. A life partner for over fifty-eight years, how could I forget her love, absolute commitment and dedication to our life together?

All marriages go through ups and downs. Looking back I remember when Lisa and Frank were breaking up in 2000, Anna and I felt the pressure. We had some arguments around Lisa and Frank's breaking up. Once Anna just quietly left the house, went to stay with our children Lisa and Rebecca for a few days to allow for a cooling-off period. When she was back I would ask her jokingly, 'Please let me know when you are going off again!' She would say, 'But I came back, didn't I?' Such conversations would be in bed, in quiet comfort, with a kiss and embrace, some quality time, and we would fall asleep. Our partnership lasted a magnificent total of fifty-eight years, for over half a century.

As I said I have my two daughters Lisa and Rebecca and my four grandchildren. Lisa and Rebecca live not too far from me: Lisa in Dulwich about twenty-five minutes' drive to my place; Rebecca in Ditton Reach, Thames Ditton, Surrey, about an hour's drive. I see both our daughters often, Lisa, being nearer, more than Rebecca. With two small children at school and because of distance I see less of Rebecca and children. Lisa is taking good care of me and is very attentive to my general wellbeing ever since Anna's passing away. She accompanies me Dartmouth every August when we raise a glass at Anna's memorial bench with relatives and friends; Lisa accompanied me on a cruise to the Norwegian Fjords. I am thankful to Allah for all He has given me as my family in this world.

Since Anna's passing away almost five years ago now, I have tried to visit her grave at Beckenham Cemetery almost once a week or every other week.

I put flowers on her grave, say 'Hello, Anna,' speak to her. Anna is resting at the very pretty and well-looked-after Grace's Gate enclosure. First thing I do is to kiss her picture on the headstone, fixed at the top of her half side of the stone; as I said the other half of the headstone is blank for my daughters to fill in after I am laid in the same grave. After kissing her smiling face, I stand at the grave thinking of her lying peacefully there, smiling, looking as smart and elegant as she left us. I report to her all that I feel she would like to hear about the proceedings of the previous days and weeks. I believe, 'It's only for a time' – to quote from the book my friend Dawn (my fellow Rotarian, Colin Dawe's wife) had lent me.

When I visit Anna's grave, I tidy up the flowers, water them if needed, then I say my payers ('Ziarath') humbly urging Allah Taala: 'Oh, Allah, please take Anna to Heaven, she has been a very good woman, sacrificed a lot, very brave, gave us a lot, I miss her terribly, please let me join her as soon as You wish me to join her, hoping it will be soon.' I know it is only for a time that I have lost my Anna. Lisa also visits her mum's grave regularly, tidies up the grave, brings fresh flowers every time she visits. Between the two of us we have kept Anna's grave looking nice and smart. Rebecca and Rickard visit the grave whenever they can with the children, bringing flowers.

I usually get the flowers from the friendly florist called Michael at the cemetery gate. He is a very knowledgeable, political person with firm views. Frequently he will advise me how to cope with life after my wife, how lucky I am having two daughters and four lovely grandchildren, I should be thankful to God and move on, learn not to forget, keep her in my heart, but do what she would have expected me to do, finish the unfinished work, not be miserable, smile as she would expect me to, try to lessen the frequency of my visits to her grave, make it from one a week to every two weeks, then once a month, see how I get on. I must say I like chatting to Michael; he is genuinely interested in hearing how I am coping. Our chats can be wide-ranging, from politics to world affairs and his life with his own wife and so on. I find these chit-chats with Michael at the cemetery gate quite an elixir in my predicament when frequently I feel purposeless, biding time, lost without Anna.

There is another fine gentleman who visits his mother's grave every day. Lisa and I have got to know him a bit, always saying, 'Hello, how are you?'

He is moving a bit farther away to Bexhill, so he said he might be at the graveyard less frequently.

We discovered a real coincidence at the graveyard: we saw that next to Anna's grave is the double grave of Gerry and Alice, our late neighbours from across the road when we lived at St Julian's Farm Road, West Norwood. Both they and we lived on that street for many years, they longer than us, and we lived there for over thirty-two years. Gerry was a very nice, happy person, always greeting us with a big smile and asking, 'How are you?' His wife was equally sweet and charming. Her sister lived upstairs in the same house as Gerry and Alice. The sister had lost her husband, who died of a severe heart attack. Once, Lisa and I were putting flowers on Anna's grave. A young lady arranging the flowers at the next grave said, 'Hello, you must be Mr Aziz.' She was the late Gerry and Alice's daughter. A great coincidence how, after years, old acquaintances show up!

After Anna left me some other activities followed. I started saying Juma prayers at the Croydon Mosque some twenty minutes' drive into Croydon; I also started my early morning ('Fajr') prayers. In these prayers I deeply seek God's forgiveness and help, pray for Anna's soul salvation. May God take her to Heaven.

My home help

During Anna's illness, one day I was very upset and crying, asking Anna, 'Please don't leave me.' She said, 'I don't want to.' I recall Anna saying, 'You have got Daniella!' Daniella was a Romanian, she was our extremely efficient cleaning lady; she would do house cleaning, washing, ironing, always helpful and cheerful. We were very fond of her for her friendliness and warmth. She was extremely hard working. Daniella was the one who got the Romanian workers ('the Romanian gang') who refurbished our new house, the bungalow in Selsdon. They did the whole house, did the associated building work, painted and decorated the bungalow, from stripping everything down to a beautiful white finish. It was very professionally done. Then Daniella fell in love with one of the workers in the gang, got engaged and took him to Romania to meet her family. Eventually Daniella got married. She gave up working at my place. I was disappointed but fully understood. What

Anna meant was that even after she was gone, there would be someone like efficient Daniella to look after our home, keeping it nice and tidy to Anna's own high standards. Anna knew I was useless at our household chores and I needed looking after well!

As Daniella's replacement I was fortunate to have got, through my friend and colleague, Mrs Turhan Donegan (secretary at my professional association, the International Consulting Economists Association – ICEA), Sam and his wife, Nadee, a Sri Lankan couple who had just arrived in England and were trying to get on their feet. They proved a great help. It was first Nadee. Then when she got pregnant, Sam stepped in. They looked after me 100% – all aspects of my household chores, plus Sam did the gardening. Nadee had come to England on a five-year student visa to study accountancy. She said she had a Master's degree in business from a Sri Lanka university. Her further study in accountancy at Croydon College was to build on what she had studied back home. Also, because she was married, with a long-term study visa, she was allowed by the Home Office to bring her family with her: husband Sam and a little boy. They are happily settled in Bromley. Sam is not as highly educated as his wife, but he is a practical man, highly experienced as a first-class handyman, having picked up a lot of experience when he spent some years in Korea. In England, having first decided to enter the care industry, he got his training as a care worker from Bromley Council, South London. So with my medical and physical problems Sam knew what to do without having to be constantly supervised or chasing. Although Nadee worked for me to start with, one morning after some months of working for me, she joyfully said, 'Uncle, I am pregnant.' I said, 'Congratulations, Nadee, that's great.' Then after a few seconds' reflection I asked, 'But what is to happen to me?' She had her reply ready: 'Don't worry, Uncle [they called me Uncle rather affectionately rather than 'Mr Aziz' or 'Sir'!], my husband Sam is a trained care worker, trained at Bromley, and he will look after you. I will show him everything and especially I will tell him that you expect things to be done to high standards.' So I felt reassured. Sam started to work here. But in his heart he wanted to become a professional gardener, also because there was more money in gardening.

During her visits to see me, Lisa would randomly check Sam's work standards. She felt satisfied with his work and his diligence. Sam did a diverse range of work for me including home help, housekeeping, gardening, electrical work, help with the computer, some cooking; he looked after my gardens to a professional gardener's standards. He bought a lot of new gardening tools to equip himself to become a professional gardener. He was a fast learner and very versatile. He and his wife Nadee were very committed and very helpful to me – they knew that I lived on my own, recently bereaved, still mourning the loss of my wife, so they showed empathy. Nadee was a real help to me during my recuperation after spinal neurosurgery in 2017. I am most grateful to them.

Christmas after Anna passed away began to be different. It had always been Anna's practice to have everyone at our place for Christmas. We tried to keep it up. Christmas 2014 was here in the bungalow. Lisa cooked the turkey at her place in Dulwich, Rebecca prepared the vegetables at her place in Thames Ditton, both then brought the food to Selsdon and we enjoyed the meal together. We kept up this practice until 2016. From 2017 it changed so that we went to Lisa's place; Rebecca and I took our contributions to Lisa's and enjoyed the meal together there. I hope that this practice of taking turns will continue.

Total strangers!

Another development I have found to be a great help is the programme to support families of bereaved people who have lost their loved ones at St Christopher's Hospice, where Anna had her palliative care in her last days. Anna passed away in June 2014. My one-to-one one-hour counselling sessions ran for twelve consecutive weeks starting January 2015. My counsellor was an extremely qualified person. She had a Master's degree, taught Arabic at City University and did counselling as well as being a volunteer at the hospice. My sessions with her over a three-month period were very supportive at a time when my emotions were raw. This was followed by group counselling sessions for about twenty people, who had gone through the one-to-one sessions first, for seven weeks of two-hour sessions, running from April 2015.

When this process ended, some members felt some cohesion in the group, and close acquaintances and friendships developed. So some of us from different groups thought it would be a good idea to keep in touch for mutual support, to try to do things together, and to keep ourselves occupied and busy to ease the sadness and loneliness from which we were all suffering. We were all 'in the same boat'. So, the idea had wide support amongst some of the recently bereaved. Two people, Linden (who lost her husband) and Shah (who lost his young wife), took the lead. This initiative developed into a group; Shah thought of the name 'New Horizons'. The idea behind the name was that we wanted to look forward and try to get on with our lives and to be happy, as our loved ones would have wanted us to be, rather than sad and miserable for ever. New Horizons had over twenty recently bereaved people. We began to have monthly meetings, going out for meals together, visiting places of interest, going on river trips, to the theatre, etc. While keeping our loved ones in our heart we were trying to move on, learn to live with what had happened to our lives. Not easy but we must try.

None of us had previously known one another. We were strangers coming together with a single thing in common: we were all recently bereaved. St Christopher's Hospice supported the idea. They gave us their best meeting room – Dame Cecilia Saunders Room – named after the founder of St Christopher's Hospice and champion of the hospice movement nationwide. The room is very comfortable, well furnished, air conditioned, with facilities for making tea; we use it for our monthly meetings, from 7 to 9pm. Slowly the group members began to mix at meetings, discovering our mutual interests in various activities. Some would prefer to go out separately in smaller or in larger groups – boat trips on the Thames, visits to Kew Gardens and places of interest, e.g. the Monument in the City, the National Portrait Gallery.

I was sure that, like me, others in New Horizons were making friends, doing new things, going new places, and thereby mutually supportive friendships were evolving. The group was decidedly proving to be of value in all our different grieving situations. To start with we had two co-ordinators: Linden and Shah. Then, as in all human organisations, problems of relationships arise. Linden and Peter left us. Shah remained our lead, our chairman, but sadly due to his ill health he could not attend the group meetings. In early 2019 Shah passed away. We all know that it's easy to form an organisation but difficult to sustain it. We hoped we could continue with New Horizons. It was really by chance that New Horizons came together.

St Christopher's Hospice now regularly refers recently bereaved people to New Horizons, which they find supportive. This natural evolution had practical value in replication. The hospice was letting its nationwide network know about our New Horizons group. Our group received mentions in St Christopher's newspaper and publicity materials.

Each and every member of New Horizons found the group useful. They were unanimous in their view that it was good to keep in touch. A shared feeling of 'We are all in the same boat!' We shared each other's sadness and loneliness when one was grief-stricken. It is much better to come and join in group activities than to sit at home on one's own, with no motivation to do anything. Our monthly meetings of two hours or going out for dinner or visiting places were all proving to be of value in bringing together people, developing friendships, allowing confidence-building, sharing our feelings of loss. If someone in the group was not well, others were keen to find out what was wrong, what could be done to help. For example, when I had back pain, became immobile and could not attend our group meetings for a long while, the concerns of group members became strikingly obvious; I received 'get well' cards, three of them over the few weeks of being unwell, all signed by members. Every card had a sweet message written by members wishing me well and to 'get well soon'. I could see I was being missed! I felt so reassured that I would be well again.

When people can talk to one another in complete confidence, trust and harmony, bonds develop. Those bonds are sustained through mutual effort. Over time, 'the strangeness and foreignness' disappear. New Horizons proved to be invaluable in bringing strangers into friendship. Our loved ones are on a journey to Heaven. When they look back at us, they must feel happy because we are happy, trying to find new meanings in life without them, trying to move on.

My life after Anna continues.

There have been a couple of big gaps in my writing this book from 2017 to 2018. This was due to what Prime Minister Harold Macmillan, in answering a question by a journalist once, said: 'Events, dear boy, events!' Some little 'events' in my life during that period created the gaps!

Event 1: *I was shortly to undergo spinal neurosurgery for my chronic back pain. Sam and Nadee had assured me that they would be able to look after me, if needed. Lisa and Rebecca felt quite happy as, in addition to them, Sam and Nadee would be available to give me home help and support. My consultant neurosurgeon had warned me that 'there are serious risks for a man of your age and in your condition, including death'! I had told him, 'I want to be free of back pain; I don't want to end up in a wheelchair for the rest of my life! I would rather die than have a life totally dependent on others.'*

After suffering back pain (lumbar canal stenosis) for over a decade, I had my spinal neurosurgery in October 2017. It took place at King's College Hospital, one of the world-renowned hospitals in South East London. A fellow Rotarian friend, a retired general practitioner (GP), Muhammed Haroon, had given me a word of introduction to Mr Irfan Malik, a consultant neurosurgeon at King's. I suppose it got me a few extra minutes of Malik's attention at his extremely busy clinic at the hospital; at least we could discuss a bit of cricket, a common subject of interest between the three of us. I was hospitalised for a fortnight, with the trials and tribulations of present-day stays in NHS hospitals. But overall it was a success under Mr Malik. I knew he had his engagements at King's College Hospital and he had his own clinic in Harley Street. I referred one of my Rotarian friends for treatment for her excruciating back pain to Mr Malik. I recall Lord Mountbatten's advice at my passing-out at Dartmouth: 'Keep in contact with your civilian friends.' You never know who will be useful and when!

A little incident while I was in hospital: After my operation, I was moved from ward to ward, room to room, because of a crisis in finding beds. I was moved into a two-bed room with a young white man, about thirty, looking rough, punched all over, with dried-up blood all over his face. He told me he had been repeatedly punched by a big white man near a tube station, with whom he was engaged in conversation. Apparently the man started to punch him shouting, 'Why don't you get a proper 'f....g' job then and earn a living instead of being a scrounger!' I felt some sympathy for him. I think I was in that room with him for twenty-four hours. Then, panic! In the middle of the night suddenly I woke up feeling the toes of my left foot being twisted. It was this chap in the room! I realised he was a proper mental case. I called the nurses. They couldn't move me at that time of the night, when it must have been about 2am. So they had to put a big black sentry guard outside the room to prevent that problem guy moving across from his side of the room to mine or walking into neighbouring rooms to disturb other patients. He was most unruly, in fact quite dangerous – pacing about the room continuously, and smoking, which was prohibited. He was seen walking out at will to the streets outside. All in all he kept me awake and in a frightened state. I felt it was quite thoughtless of the ward to put me in a room with a mentally disturbed patient, especially within days of my spinal surgery. I was chairman of two NHS trusts in South London – but I never pulled rank! Fortunately, late afternoon the following day, I was moved to a single room. My family and friends visiting me commented, 'This is a lovely room, you are very lucky having a single room and being comfortable now.' But that single room was located in the midst of female brain neurosurgery patients – nicknamed 'loonies' – who were not without problems. Once in the middle of the night I was awakened by a woman, not very old, standing by my side, only in her loose hospital frock, saying to me, 'I have come to visit you'! I quickly pressed the call-up buzzer and a big black male nurse escorted her out of my room.

And there was another episode! One late evening, two extra-zealous physio nurses almost killed me. They stretched me so much at the physio session that I almost passed away. While being exercised for walking the day after my surgery, I found myself collapsing. I recall I was sitting in a chair, with a few people surrounding me – reportedly the cardiac nurse, the duty registrar, senior nurses etc. I remember a nurse gently slapping my face, shouting into my face, 'Suhail, look into my eyes, look into my eyes...'! I didn't know what was happening. I am happy to be alive!

My discharge from hospital was not without problems. I was visited by two nurses (as I thought), later discovering that one was an occupational therapist (OT) who was assessing my equipment needs after I returned home. I was supposed to have a hospital bed immediately after my discharge for ease of turning and sitting up in bed. Somehow the OT concluded that as I was able to get out of bed unaided, I didn't need a hospital bed. At home, I was in real pain turning, sitting up and getting out of bed. I reported that to my GP who wrote to the district nurse not once but twice, but nothing happened. I was offered a wooden triangular thing to raise my head. The district nurse and the council all tried, but could not get me a hospital bed, though my carers told me that in all the cases like mine they had come across, the patients had hospital beds. The decision of that one OT who visited, cunningly undercover, without disclosing that she was an OT, prevailed! No one could overturn that decision – the GPs, the district nurse, Croydon Council Adult Social Services – while I was struggling in pain in our jumbo king-size bed without proper grab handles.

Long after that, in April 2018, my neurosurgeon, Mr Irfan Malik, saw me in clinic, post-op. All was well with the surgery. I mentioned to him my experience with the hospital OT. He was quite horrified. He asked, 'Have you complained?' I said, 'No.' He then said, 'Write to the senior matron in charge at the neurosciences department,' which I am still to do but knowing how things are in the NHS, I might not. An 'apology' would be run-of-the-mill stuff!

This is not where the saga started by the hospital OT ended! Recently, in May 2018, I was contacted by Croydon Council, as word had reached them about my experience following the 'bed-blocking' (blocking of supplying a hospital bed) by the over-zealous OT nurse at King's. After a couple of visits by Adult Social Services, OT-led, I was supplied with an electrical bed-raiser which enabled me to lie in a head-raised position. After giving it a try for a few days I found the contraption too cumbersome. Besides, I was almost a fit person by then, not needing assistance to sit up and turn in bed, so I returned the device. This was a needless incurring of expenses by the council only to 'clear their yard-arm', rather than be faulted following my GP's and district nurse's interventions.

Event 2: In October 2018, I was to undergo a procedure called a transcatheter aortic valve implantation (TAVI). I was suffering from shortness of breath, dizziness, tiredness, sleepiness, lethargy. Doctors found that the aortic valve in my heart had significantly narrowed and needed urgent replacement. It took place in October 2018. The procedure did not involve surgery and was relatively free of any problems.

This TAVI procedure is part of a research programme to see if this new valve could be introduced into Europe by the valve's manufacturers in California. It has already been successfully tried in California and Canada. I am, with my new valve, included in the research study and I shall be under observation for five years. So far the valve seems to be working alright, although my symptoms have not gone away. But I am hopeful that over time the new valve will bring some improvement in my quality of life, as I still get out of breath on exertion, *feel dizzy and want to rest a lot. I lack confidence but remain hopeful that 'tomorrow will be better!' – if that 'tomorrow' would ever come!*

Things I have done in Anna's memory

This bungalow

The Romanian 'gang' did a good job of refurbishing the bungalow. At first I wasn't sure at all if Anna would like this bungalow because it was in such a terrible state. I would say, 'You don't really like this place.' But after it was done up to her taste, Anna had said several times, 'I like it, I like it.'

I feel that in her memory I couldn't leave this place. In late 2018/early 2019, I discussed with Lisa and Rebecca moving to a McCarthy & Stone retirement living apartment in nearby Sanderstead. My plan to move was pretty advanced and then at the suggestion from a lady at Bairstow Eves estate agents, I went to see some more retirement apartments in Caterham and Caterham on the Hill. I didn't like what I saw; the old-style apartments arranged in long corridors looked pretty grim, almost like prison buildings. After that and upon further consideration, I decided to stay put in my Selsdon bungalow. I didn't want another move, I wanted my body to be taken from here. I consulted my GP and some close friends. I told my children my care would have to be arranged around my own home.

I do not go out much, most of the time I am in my bungalow. I try to keep myself busy with a limited number of activities: seeing my daughters and grandchildren, Rotary club, U3A meetings and activities, New Horizons outings, children's birthdays etc. I try to read. I have a collection of books – business, consulting, political economy, politics, biographies. Anna knew my interest in politics, political biographies and economics. One of several books she bought as a birthday present was Tony Blair's *A Journey*. Inside the cover was a little card from her; it read, '*To dear Suhail, Happy Birthday, Love and best wishes, Anna xxxx*'.

Our house has three bedrooms. Anna and I agreed that the smaller of the three rooms could be my study. I had many books. How to store them? We got one of the Romanians from the gang who was good at carpentry to create space for all my books. He made up shelves on the wall by the door, from floor to ceiling. My books, including the many given to me as presents by Anna over the years, are now stored safely and nicely covering the entire wall. I have read some, but not all. It will take me more than the few years I have left before I depart to join Anna. I had thought of filling up boxes with my books and giving them to charities like Oxfam or the British Heart Foundation, but then I felt I had better leave them as they are on the shelves, and let Lisa and Rebecca decide what they would want to do after I am gone; maybe they would keep some and give the rest to charity.

A memorial bench on the Dart

A memorial bench took a bit of thinking, planning, influencing and 'string pulling'! This is how my plan worked: Anna was a Dartmothian, born and brought up in the Pyne family of the little town. She was a brave girl; she went 'across the seven seas' and two continents to marry a Pakistani who she had met and who courted her for three years while he was training at the Britannia Royal Naval College in the mid-1950s. Anna married someone with the name Aziz – a Muslim, a coloured foreigner in a place like Dartmouth in deepest Devon, 100% white. Circulation of my name must be a first, something to talk about! So I thought I must do something innovative.

Dartmothians have been famous; from the pilgrim fathers departure on the Mayflower from Bayards Cove, Dartmouth, to new world America, historically Dartmothians have gone far afield all over the world – exploration of the high seas, global trading, discovery, inventions. It would not be the first time one of their girls married someone from a foreign country. The people of Dartmouth, and more widely of Devon, were extremely tolerant, courteous, tactful, diplomatic and resourceful. So I felt Anna was a brave girl from Dartmouth, I was a foreigner married to her, I gave up my naval career for the love of her, so what could be done to remember these characteristics of our partnership of fifty-eight years – a very long partnership spanning more than half a century? Goodness!

Anna was a member of the Old Dartmothians' Association, Ladies Section. She fondly kept up her membership of the association. I still have a copy of the invitation to the AGM that Anna received a while ago. We attended a gathering of the association at the Stoke Lodge Hotel, Stoke Fleming, Dartmouth. I also belong to the Britannia Association, which is a membership association of officers who have trained at the Britannia Royal Naval College and keep up their connections with Dartmouth. The association is very active in organising year-round events, arranging visits, etc. College balls are regularly held on the quarterdeck of the college, which are open to Britannia Association members. The association's office is located at the college, with a BA shop for college and navy souvenirs.

In recognition of Anna's profound love of Dartmouth, and my and my children's and grandchildren's continuing affection for the place, I decided I must try to get a memorial bench located at a busy place along the Embankment where local Dartmothians and visitors to Dartmouth would see a plaque placed on the bench, reading, '*In loving memory of Elizabeth Ann Aziz (née Pyne)*'. So, her family name, Pyne, would be placed next to my family name, Aziz – a connection spanning 5,000 miles between her birthplace, Dartmouth, in the south-west of England and my birthplace, Sylhet, at other end of the world, in the north-east corner of Bangladesh.

Finding a suitable spot for the bench proved difficult. The South Hams Borough Council, with offices located in Totnes, twenty miles out of Dartmouth, did not have a local presence since the merger of Dartmouth Council with other little councils in the areas around to form South Hams District Council. Only a couple of councillors represent the interests of Dartmouth in South Hams BC. I discussed my wish about the installation of a bench on the embankment of the River Dart with Kevin Pyne, one of Anna's favourite, respected cousins, a very influential man, with strong views in politics, very much involved with organising the Dartmouth Regatta every year, always writing in the *Dartmouth Chronicle* – a man of Dartmouth. He in turn spoke to a Dartmouth councillor friend and contact at South Hams District Council, Cllr Hilary Bastone. Hopefully between the two of them they would be able to obtain the council's permission to squeeze my bench in an already crowded North or South Embankment (the latter was preferred as more people walk about there). Simultaneously I contacted the council official concerned, Mr Tim Pollard, to start my application process for a bench. While he understood my reasons for wanting to install a memorial bench, like many others, he told me to fill in an application form and he would progress my application at the council. But, like a good bureaucrat, he warned of the potential disappointment because the embankments were already full. I had done the 'needful', the 'string pulling' and an official approach to South Hams District Council.

What else could I do to make it happen, to get a memorial bench installed at Dartmouth on the riverside, in the Mayor's Park, or another prominent place? All these came under the council.

I knew from my short-time membership of the National Trust, and Rebecca's family membership of the NT, that the trust owned a lot of places in and around Dartmouth, frequented by visitors every year. So I made an approach to the National Trust. The local official was most understanding. She asked me to give her a bit of time to explore the availability of sites where a memorial bench could be placed. After a couple of weeks she came back and suggested a spot by the 'Compass'. Now that is a lovely spot; a lot of visitors go to Dartmouth Compass for the view of the surrounding hills and the sea and ships beyond.

I have good memories of the Compass! I knew the spot because Anna used to make me walk miles to it on our weekend dates, as if to search for a suitable spot for us to do a bit of kissing and hugging; we never seemed to find a spot because people were always popping up! So Anna would make me walk back to the town centre; soon it would be near 10pm and my time to return to the college before 'pipe down'. So I remember my frustration of not always getting our kissing and hugging, coupled with Anna's ever-present shyness about doing anything like that in front of people – 'Whatever would they think?' or 'Whatever next?', or, 'Not a done thing!' I used to tease her by calling her 'Queenie' for her queen-like behaviour! So things had to be left for more privacy!

The National Trust's offer was a good one, but I felt it was not what I was looking for. The Compass area did not get visited by all that many people every year. And cost-wise, it was probably going to be as expensive as a council site. So I put it on hold to await the council's decision through my efforts via Mr Tim Pollard, the council official and my supporters Kevin Pyne and Cllr Hilary Bastone.

Not long after, the council approval came through. With great efforts of Cllr Bastone we got a most desirable spot bang in the middle of the South

Embankment, most popular with visitors and locals, right opposite the old post office across the street. The spot was next to a high, permanent plinth with a desert plant in the middle, very nice. I signed acceptance of the council's offer, with drawings of the spot. After a month or so, the memorial bench in loving memory of my wife, Elizabeth Ann Aziz (née Pyne), was installed. So this was my number two memorial for Anna.

Since its installation, I have invited relatives and friends at Dartmouth Regatta time in August to assemble by the bench to raise a glass in memory of Anna. This has happened every year since 2015. Following this prayer I had invited the guests to dinner at the Royal Castle Hotel.

At our gathering in August 2016 a reporter from the local paper, the *Dartmouth Chronicle*, was present. She wrote a piece with glowing words of tribute about Anna and some aspects of her life with me in the Pakistan Navy, East Pakistan, now Bangladesh, and our life afterwards back in England. Whenever I had visited Dartmouth since my days at the naval college, I had always noted and read with interest the inscriptions on plates on memorial benches along the banks of the River Dart. I thought that it would be very fitting, and in loving memory and recognition of Anna's life with me and all my family, for a Dartmothian Anna to have a memorial bench on the embankment of the River Dart. This would also reflect her profound love for Dartmouth. It would also be a 'novelty' for visitors and residents to see the name Aziz combined with the English names Elizabeth Ann, inscribed on a brass plate on the bench.

Anna left us in June 2014. In August 2015, Regatta weekend in Dartmouth, I had arranged a get-together of Anna's relatives and friends in Dartmouth; occasionally a reporter from the *Dartmouth Chronicle* would be present. First, at about 6pm, we gathered around Anna's memorial bench to raise a glass in her memory (usually serviced by a staff member from the nearby Royal Castle Hotel, Dartmouth). Then at about 6.30pm, we all proceeded to the Royal Castle Hotel for a memorial dinner. Usually there would be about twenty, seated at a special table, overlooking the harbour, the busy river during the Regatta, with views of Kingswear beyond. Guests would include my family members – usually Lisa and her children Leah and Jacob – Anna's best friends and their husbands (those available), Anna's close relatives, a representative of the *Dartmouth Chronicle*. At the dinner of 2015 we had about twenty guests. It ended about 10.30pm after raising a glass to Anna's memory.

I repeated the same reception and dinner in 2016. At this dinner one of Anna's closest friends, June (née White), could not attend because she was very upset as one of her two dear dogs had had to be put down on that day because of its age. Also, Anna's friend Anne Piggott (née Cudd) was unable to attend from Weston-super-Mare because of the distance and the fact that Gordon, her husband, was suffering asthma attacks. So my number of guests was quite depleted. Sadly, not long after, Gordon died in 2017 from acute asthma.

My main purpose for this occasion by the memorial bench and the dinner at the Royal Castle was to remember Anna with her best friends before time caught up on all of us and memories inevitably faded away. As mentioned elsewhere, there were six in Anna's group of friends from their school days: four Ann(e)s, and two others, June and Julie. I used to refer to them sometimes as 'the Ann mafia'! For some years Anna and I were wondering whatever happened to Julie, such a charming, lively person, full of energy and fun. The last time we saw her was at a very nice house near Exeter. That was with her second husband (first was Colin when they lived in New Cross Gate, London – referred to earlier). So sadly Julie was not on my list.

Then of course more sad news: Anna's friend, Anne Whitmore (née Chase), lost her husband Keith in 2017 after a short illness – probably lung cancer. A lovely cheerful friend for many years, whenever we were in Dartmouth we would see Anne and Keith in the town somewhere. He always invited us to his flat and to his club, the local Conservative club. (Keith was a member there 'for convenience', but he was a devout Labour man! There was no Labour or workingmen's club in Dartmouth.) He was the volunteer leader of the local fire service, always on stand-by for calls, very mindful of his duties. So Anne could not come to dinner. Another of Anna's group, Ann King, had passed away soon after my Anna's death in 2014. She suffered from the same dreaded disease.

So, after consulting Lisa and Rebecca I decided not to hold our memorial dinner any more. What I did instead was to have our private memorial and prayers (*dua*) at the bench followed by a private family dinner at the Royal Castle Hotel.

Anna's four friends had gone: Ann King (I don't know what happened to her husband, John, a fine likeable person), Anne's Keith, Anne's Gordon, all passed away, five including my Anna. Now apart from Anna's brother, David, and his wife, Lynda, Anna's sister, Lynda, and her husband, Gary, my pull-factor for Dartmouth must be waning! But then, at Regatta time in August 2017, I was able to organise a visit to the Britannia Royal Naval College for Lisa, Leah, Sam (Leah's boyfriend, a charming young man) and Jacob; this meant a lot to them and to me, jolting my memories. A helpful lady called Nicola from the Britannia Association, of which I am a member, was kindly able to organise our visit to the college. I was very proud to show my family round. It meant a lot to me. Nicola was able to locate the group photo of my passing-out batch – now located near the library. I pin-pointed images of myself and Mansur ul Huq (my term-mate in July 1958, the deposed scandal-ridden ex-admiral, commander-in-chief of the Pakistan Navy, who has since died of a heart attack in 2018 in Dubai) and showed the photo to the children. So Dartmouth, the place for which Anna's love was profound, the college, the Regatta, some relatives and friends still remain as my 'pull-factors' for Dartmouth. I would like to continue my visits to Dartmouth at the Regatta time as long as I am able to.

Anna's headstone

I had got Anna's headstone made by the Beckenham Cemetery people, half of the stone written up beautifully with words chosen and formulated by Lisa (Lisa being a professional journalist and TV/radio broadcaster has great skill with choosing the few words and arranging their flow), with Anna's smiling picture engraved on the headstone – half left blank for my daughters to get filled in when I am buried in the same grave. That's the arrangement; I hope Lisa will again choose the words to go onto the other side of the headstone; currently vacant, 'It is only for a time!'

Anna's memorial tea party in my gardens

The other thing I instinctively decided to do *'In memory of my darling wife Anna, Mum to Lisa and Rebecca, and Nanny to Leah, Jacob, Eleanor and*

Konrad – missed by us all' was to hold a memorial tea party on 25 June, the anniversary of Anna's passing away – or on the nearest Sunday.

Every year for the past four years, we have held the tea party at my place in Selsdon, South Croydon, Surrey, inviting relatives and friends. Sam, my gardener, made sure that all my gardens at the front and rear of my bungalow were made absolutely neat and tidy, and his wife, Nadee, almost a part of my family, assisted to make the tea a success. The actual catering for the tea – sandwiches, cakes, scones, strawberries and cream, tea and coffee and cold drinks (with an additional item from me – the samosas from Lahore Karahi, Tooting) – was done by local caterers from Selsdon. The tea seemed to go down well every year. On each occasion we have had some fifty guests honouring me and my family with their kind attendance. Prayers in Islamic and Christian faiths have been said in memory of Anna and her departed soul. In the planning and execution of the memorial tea party, Lisa has been a terrific help to me; her mum would be very proud.

But guest attendance has gone down because of Ramadan, Eid and people's other priorities. During Ramadan for those fasting I had of course made arrangements for 'Iftar' and 'Maghrib' prayers. I am not sure, as I am getting older by the year, how much longer I can organise the memorial tea party, which demands much energy and effort. I have agreed with Lisa that we will review whether we will hold it in the future. I would be sad to discontinue it but, as a recruitment consultant from Odgers, St James's, London, once reminded me: 'Age is something you can't do anything about!' Well, I am ageing, I am five years older than when Anna 'left' me in June 2014. I am sure Anna, if she was around, would be the first to agree with me that maybe I should discontinue it in acknowledgement of my age!

'The Tribute Tree' at St Christopher's Hospice

St Christopher's Hospice has organised many things for the nearest and dearest of those who have passed away at the hospice. These include their famous palliative care, fundraising events, meetings, concerts, tributes and other socials, throughout the year.

One of these is the 'Tribute Tree' – a tree with leaves sketched on the walls outside the prayer hall of the main hospice building. A message in memory of the deceased is engraved on a copper leaf, which is then placed on the Tribute Tree. The contribution for a copper leaf is £1,000. The leaf remains on the tree for up to two years or so, after which it gets passed on to the family. The leaves of the tree are almost all taken; the sight is a tree full of copper leaves! After the costs of making the leaves, the balance of the moneys goes to the hospice fund.

When Anna passed away, we invited friends and relatives to her funeral service at Beckenham Cemetery chapel. We mentioned in the invite that we did not want flowers, but if anyone so wished, they could make a donation to St Christopher's Hospice (a place like a hospital in all but name, except patients are all terminally ill). The hospice told me that donations in Anna's name had reached 'an amazing £600' (their words)! I decided to put in £400 to bring up the total to £1,000, for a copper leaf to be engraved with the words, '*In Loving Memory of Ann Aziz, Wife, Mother, Nanny to Leah, Jacob, Eleanor and Konrad, Always in our thoughts*' (words arranged by Lisa). The leaf was duly placed on the Tribute Tree; it remained there for two years after which it was given to me. I got it framed, the copper leaf mounted on a velvet cloth background by a famous framing shop in Crystal Palace, London. The memorial copper leaf is placed in the hallway of my bungalow.

Monthly lottery at St Christopher's Hospice

The hospice runs a lottery with prizes. Most of the funds thus raised go to the hospice to continue its good work of caring for the terminally ill. With a regular monthly payment of £5 by direct debit from donors' accounts, one gets a chance to win something (£25 to £100 prizes), at the same time helping the hospice fund. I decided to enter this lottery a few years ago in aid of the hospice, which continues.

Apart from the above there are of course many other ways to donate to the hospice.

Our deep gratitude to St Christopher's Hospice

I and my family feel a deep affection for St Christopher's Hospice because that's where Anna died. Circumstances and fate had to be such that Anna passed away at the hospice rather than at her own home, where all the arrangements were made ready by the hospice's Croydon outreach team to look after in her last days at her own home. But sadly this was not to be. The second attack of jaundice meant that Anna left home on 9 June 2014, only for a week to calm her down after the second attack. As narrated before, sadly Anna never returned home.

The care Anna received at the hospice was excellent; the staff were most dedicated and professional. Anna's palliative care couldn't have been more thorough, kind and sensitive. Anna passed away in my arms at the hospice sixteen days after leaving her home, on 25 June 2014. Our admiration for St Christopher's Hospice service remains very high. I and my family remain eternally grateful.

My most recent travels – return to Bangladesh

Even though I have lived and worked in England all these years, I have to admit that I still feel an emotional pull to my birthplace, Sylhet. So I try to travel to my homeland every two or three years. However, for the past six years, since the summer of 2012, because of my late wife's illness, I have not taken a proper holiday – except a few days in August every year to see Dartmouth Regatta and spend a few days with friends and family there. Those are good short breaks but not a proper holiday.

So in April 2018 I decided to go on a three-week holiday to Bangladesh. The non-stop nine-and-a-half-hour flight in a new Boeing 777 of Biman Bangladesh Airlines, from Heathrow to Dhaka, the capital, via a short stopover at Sylhet, was quite pleasant. The plane landed at Osmani International Airport, Sylhet; the airport takes its name from General Osmani, another Sylheti, who led the Bangladesh independence movement from 1970 to 1971. Most of the passengers on the flight were Sylheti men, women and children of the prosperous British-Bangladeshi community, mostly from the successful catering trade – the so-called 'Indian tandoori' restaurants seen in the high streets of Britain, not unlike the presence of Chinese takeaways.

I was travelling business class but I have to admit I was a trifle disappointed to see that even business class passengers were treated to pre-packed meals in contrast to the days gone by when beautiful, smart, sari-wearing, elegant Bengali air hostesses served DC10 business class passengers with care, style and finesse! This time it must have been a sign of global austerity coupled with reportedly inefficiencies and widespread corruption of the Biman airline. They offered not a glass of wine or a beer! Yet, as I understood, the flights are full to capacity mostly with Sylheti passengers. The British-Bangladeshi community has undoubtedly prospered over the years; new generations of young families have replaced the old first-generation immigrants. It was lovely to hear Sylheti language being spoken in the plane; the language has its own unique attraction and cultural heritage; it's certainly different from spoken Bengali. It is said that 'Sylheti and Bengali languages are so different that one needs an interpreter in the middle'! The education system in Bangladesh is generally run in Bengali.

Upon arrival in Dhaka I was met by my nephew Shameem (my sister Mina's son). He is a top civil servant of the Bangladesh Government. I could get a taste of his power as he arranged my smooth, hassle-free clearance while we sat and chatted in the VIP lounge. Shameem had kindly invited me to make his place 'my base' whence I would make my forays to other friends and relatives in Dhaka and Sylhet. The love and affection shown to me by Shameem, his wife, Runa, a very pretty and sweet lady, their son, Naieed, and daughter, Hridi – who had just got married (to a Sylheti husband!) – are memorable. Equally memorable was my brief stay with my youngest brother, Kaiser, and his family, also living in Dhaka. Kaiser's wife, Zereen, was always doing her best to see that my stay with them was comfortable in all respects.

While in Dhaka I made contact with some of my childhood friends who live in Dhaka. Like me, they too are retired having been in substantial positions in government, business and community life. One of us, Obaid Jaigirdar (he prefers to call himself 'OJ' and calls his large charity the OJ Trust), invited a group of us to his place located in a very posh area of Dhaka for a lavish lunch. I was so happy. It was a great pleasure to see my friends all in one place after many years. We had a very enjoyable time at Obaid's. Obaid is a very interesting if somewhat intriguing chap. He is wealthy but no one has really figured out where his wealth comes from! He is so charming, and has a unique style of relating with people. He is also ageing but is still very energetic; he's well read, an author and has travelled extensively. He is honorary consul of the People's Republic of Cuba in Bangladesh; also he has a similar role for Sierra Leone. Obaid knows people everywhere! His Dhaka house lounge is adorned with interesting photos: him with Fidel Castro and Castro's brother, with Che Guevara, Nelson Mandela and others. Obaid is known for his generosity, and has done a lot for his family and friends. In his high school days, he was a courageous boy; we called him a 'revolutionary', as alluded to before when, during agitation for Indian independence, Obaid climbed to the top of the Sylhet deputy commissioner (DC – a British officer)'s office building, pulled down the Union Jack and replaced it with an Indian national flag while the Gurkha soldiers on the ground had their guns trained on him waiting for the DC's order to fire! Happily the situation didn't turn nasty.

By the by, at this lunch meeting, I began to talk to Junaid Choudhury in our group. Junaid was a Shell executive and now acts as a travel guide to Bengali people wanting to visit Shillong, in India, a beautiful hilly place near Darjeeling in Assam, famous for tea. I decided that I would like to visit Shillong, one-time capital city of Assam during the British Raj. Like Darjeeling, and Shimla nearby, the British used Shillong for their cooler summer capital and retreats. Shillong is only eighty miles from Sylhet, over the land border via Tamabil (Bangladesh) and Dauki (India). I have special affection for Shillong: my two grandfathers both served as personal assistants (PAs) to the British Land Revenue commissioners. My childhood memories are still fresh of when my parents, with me and my eldest sister, had stayed with their respective parents in the Laban and Lumparing areas of the city.

But I needed an Indian visa to visit Shillong. Through Junaid and Obaid's very capable secretary, Monisha Chakraborty, a renowned Indian swimmer, and with Obaid's connections in the Indian High Commission in Dhaka, my visa for travel to Shillong was soon obtained. So I was ready to go to Shillong with Junaid as my guide.

In the company of Junaid I took the short flight to Sylhet. Obaid had a bungalow in a nice part of Sylhet town. He insisted we stayed there. That bungalow was massive, neat and clean, with lovely gardens. It was just like a tea garden bungalow except much larger. There were servants to feed and look after us; his car with a driver was put at our disposal. From there, I was able to visit my ancestral home in Thoigaon, Sylhet. I offered prayers at my parents' and grandparents' graves in our family cemetery. Unfortunately I could not on this occasion visit Hazrat Shahjalal's Shrine for which Sylhet is famous. Apart from regular visitors all through the year, every year hundreds of thousands of people of all religions congregate at the shrine for prayers and celebrations. I visited the Muslim Shahityo Shongshod (a literary institution of Sylhet) where I met some of the committee members. Knowing my deep interest in Sylhet and my pride in the Sylheti language, the committee presented me with some of their publications. The institution had received a huge philanthropic donation from my friend of school days Mahboob (one of our luncheon group at Obaid's) who gave it in memory of his father, the late Moulvi Fazlur Rahman, – another most philanthropic person of Sylhet. With Mahboob's help, the committee built a three-storey building to house the Shongshod, to provide a centre for research into the origin of the Sylheti language ('Nagri') by students and others who want to know about Sylhet, its language and culture. Students hold regular cultural functions at the Shongshod. One very interesting little book, presented to me by the editor, was an extract (translated into Bengali) from Robert Lindsay's memoir published in 1821, entitled *My Twelve Years in Sylhet*; Lindsay served in many capacities in British India and he spent twelve years in Sylhet as resident collector and DC around 1778, the subject matter of his epic memoir. Our stay in Sylhet ended with a grand reception arranged by my fellow Rotarian and friend Dr Monzurul Huq Choudhury and other fellow Rotarians of the Rotary Club of Jalalabad. It was their Charter Night. I had to deliver a hastily prepared speech to my fellow Rotarians and others who attended the dinner function.

From Sylhet we travelled to Shillong by taxi. Junaid knew most of the taxiwalas in Tamabil (Bangladesh) and Dauki (India), the land border crossings, so it was interesting to have running commentaries from the drivers about the hill tribes and life at the border crossing. The beauty of the drive was to look down at the gorges while the car passed close to the edge of the roads. The Bangladesh part of the road journey to Tamabil was tough to say the least. For the last ten to fifteen miles to the border the road was atrocious, covered with large potholes filled with mud and water. The constant shaking of the car trying to manoeuvre to avoid them tired me out. The roads were damaged by the heavy-duty trucks bringing down coal and boulders from the Khasi and Jointya hills. Heavy rains and no road repairs! In contrast, the roads to Shillong, after crossing the Dauki Bridge, were well surfaced and well maintained. The Dauki Bridge was built by the British during the 1939–45 war to assist the fight against the Japanese after Burma had fallen. The bridge is an epic piece of engineering: it spans the very deep gorge of the Dauki River, supported by two very thick steel wires tied round two enormous stones sitting high on two sides of the gorge. The bridge is still going strong. The Japanese didn't advance up to Dauki to bomb it.

Shillong is a fascinating place, a place of real beauty with unmatched scenery, streams, hills, parks, forests and gorges. It is home to the Eastern Command of the Indian Air Force and Army garrisons, positioned since the 1960s' skirmish between India and China along India's north-eastern borders with China and Tibet. Native Khasi girls in their beautiful colourful outfits were seen loitering in one of the parks, full of smiles ready for a camera shoot. However, the inner parts of the city are overpopulated, the Police Bazaar market bustling with people. One is unable to move during the evenings when shoppers are out. But Shillong outside its city boundaries remains extremely beautiful. I was able to visit Laban and Lumparing where, as I said, my two grandparents lived with our extended families. But it is all changed now. The areas are transformed with property developments and crowds of settlers. I looked for the house in Laban in which my maternal grandfather, with his very large family, lived, sadly without success. The place is populated by the native (Khasi) hill tribes and Bengali immigrants from Sylhet who came to Shillong during the population movement of 1947. While in Shillong, I visited 'Chera punji', the place with the world's highest rainfall. Standing at 5,000 feet above sea level, I saw cloud at 1,000 to 2,000 feet below me. It was a memorable sight, as was the view of the plains of Sylhet with winding rivers. Definitely, our stay of two nights and three days in Shillong was too short.

No travel is completely without mishap! Junaid, being a travel guide, forgot to get our passports stamped at the Tamabil check-post on re-entry to Bangladesh, for which I had to undertake another journey from Obaid's place to Tamabil, late at night suffering the agony of the atrocious roads.

It was important to get the re-entry stamped on my British passport, otherwise in no time the word would have gone round from the police that there was an illegal in Bangladesh from India. I could not risk being stopped for questioning at the exit on my return journey from Dhaka to London!

Returning to Dhaka to my base at Shameem's, I then spent three days with Babul, husband of one of my most favourite cousin sisters, Nasreen. She sadly is no more in this world. Babul lives well in a plush apartment, close to most western embassies in Dhaka; their youngest son lives with him and keeps an eye on his dad's health needs. Babul has three maidservants looking after him and his son, plus a driver with a BMW and a Land Rover. Coming from a big landed gentry family of Bangladesh, Babul's ancestral home in Korotia, of which he is the sole inheritor now, has an abundance of land and a beautiful ancestral house. His grandfather and great-grandfather and great-great-grandfather were all politicians and very much honoured during the British rule of Bengal. I have a standing invitation from Babul to go and stay with him in Korotia in winter. I also got a chance invitation to a wedding of a niece of mine! It was so lucky for me. I attended the wedding and met most of my cousins without having to try to visit them separately in the appalling traffic conditions of Dhaka city; it could take three hours to travel five miles in the Dhaka traffic! Several flyovers have been built to ease congestion but not enough roads have yet been built able to cope with the traffic flow off them!

All good things come to an end. On my last night in Dhaka, I took Shameem and his family to a thank you dinner at a nice restaurant in Dhaka. Next morning, on 27 April 2018, with a heavy heart and sadness, I said goodbye to them and to Bangladesh.

Epilogue

Years are passing by. Soon it will be over six years since Anna, my beloved darling wife, left me and this world. Coping with the loneliness and sadness has not been easy for me. I have felt to my core what it means to be without Anna, my life's precious companion of fifty-eight years. I miss her terribly. Grieving never goes away, never is it gone. I have been trying to 'move on' with my life. In trying to do this I have been fortunate to have my family of two daughters and four grandchildren around me. The kindness and support of my family and friends have kept me going; I am eternally grateful to them. I have tried keeping busy, filling in time, sometimes with a feeling of being busy without a sense of purpose, experiencing a vacuum and emptiness, asking myself, 'What am I doing here?' and realising 'It is only for a time!'

I have travelled a long distance. Starting with a childhood in a respectable family of Sylhet, Bangladesh, to training and education, and the award of a Queen's Commission at the Britannia Royal Naval College Dartmouth, followed by service in the Pakistan Navy, unfortunately cut short rather early. But I have come a long way. The unique opportunity of entering and training for almost three years at the world famous Britannia Royal Naval College Dartmouth and the ships of Dartmouth Training Squadron was tremendously lucky for me. Then coming back to England, from a ticketing clerk at a tiny British Rail station, Motspur Park, in 1966, to successfully holding two public appointments in succession – chairman of two NHS trusts in inner-city London and chairman of the London Probation Board for two consecutive terms covering Greater London, all secretary of state appointments – is proof of my journey. The opportunities have been many, the sky was the limit. I have always worked in the mainstream of British society.

Looking back I could have done more. If I was able to take a bit more time at the start of my life in England, I could have cut short what I call a period of 'immigrant disadvantage' – the period of up to ten years that it took an immigrant like me to get into a job or career befitting one's position prior to immigration, which in my case was a Dartmouth-trained naval officer and a Unilever personnel manager. With a bit more patience and strategic career planning, things could have been better both for myself, my family here and back home.

Likewise in British politics, I could have achieved a lot more. I might well have been an MP and a minister had I been able to turn my circumstances towards opportunities and positive outcomes. Had I been smarter 'to move towards the centre of the stage' a little earlier! In today's Britain it's so gratifying to see that, unlike the 1960s, 1970s and 1980s, today we have a number of MPs and ministers from Britain's minority ethnic communities – proof that British society too has moved on towards a fairer Britain, opening the doors of equal opportunities to Britain's minority communities. But we are not there yet, there is still some way to go.

Friends had said to me, 'Suhail, write, you have a story to tell.' My memoir is interwoven with my love story: from meeting Anna, her brave decision to fly to Pakistan 5,000 miles away when just twenty-one, getting married to me, a young lieutenant in the Pakistan Navy in the humblest of circumstances and in extreme secrecy, hiding from the Pakistan naval intelligence! Anna and my life together in Pakistan and Bangladesh; happiness and support from some of my family, encountering intense jealousy and resentment from a few others. Then my life's pathway in Britain, starting with a young family, with all its trials and tribulations, my experience, impressions and insights – mostly positives but some negatives – met along the way. Eventually completing my journey, some of it acknowledged as a distinguished record of public service.

My crossroads? After arriving in Britain in 1966 I could have accepted attractive job offers from British Petroleum (BP), or the Trades Union Congress (TUC), or the Constructors John Brown (CJB) instead of the Royal Air Force! I could have gone back to the CRE when invited back. Likewise, I was invited back to the Pakistan Navy, by no less than the Martial Law President of Pakistan and Governor of East Pakistan via my chairman of

EPIWTA, but I declined. I had broken no law. 'The Government of Pakistan is averse to marriages with foreign nationals'; it was a whimsical rule, it did not have the force of law. So I bore no rancour as the invitation to go back to the navy was in effect an apology from the then martial law government of Pakistan. However, my decision was providential anyway as Pakistan broke up, with the creation of Bangladesh, and I became a Bangladeshi. As friends had jokingly said: 'Suhail, you would have been a dead admiral by now!' Looking back, did I take the wrong decisions at those crossroads? I don't think so, for finally it all worked out for me, it was God's will.

But it has not all been a bed of roses! Being a realist and pragmatist, I accept that, as in most societies, there are deeply held prejudices in British society, from top to bottom, in various degrees of ignorance and malice. Dare I quote again what a distinguished columnist in *The Guardian* once wrote: 'British society is dripping in racism.' In particular, I experienced racial problems at the highest echelons of the NHS and London Probation Board. I met jealousy, spite, discrimination from white people; sadly from a few Asians or Blacks as well who could not bear the thought of a Bangladeshi Muslim like me at the top of these bodies! They did everything possible to dislodge, destabilise or discredit me or even oust me. If I was successful in getting a job by beating the competition, they blamed 'political correctness'; if I didn't, they would say 'he was not up the job'. I experienced a feeling of 'one can never win'.

For the future, such prejudiced and racist people, however well they cover up their deeply held racist prejudices, must face forensic 'psychological testing' so that their racist tendencies are discovered in advance of being appointed to senior positions in public service. They must not be allowed the luxury of mischievous, manipulative manoeuvrings. If these ill-intentioned people were allowed to succeed, the downside would be that it would discourage good quality people from Britain's third-generation immigrant population ethnic minorities from seeking private and public sector appointments. The supply of good quality candidates would simply dry up; 'the Market for Lemons' phenomenon will prevail! This is important because society has changed, Britain has changed. Today highly qualified boys and girls from all communities aspire to well-deserved positions in every sector of the economy. Equal opportunities must flourish, not be denied. I believe profoundly that Britain's future depends largely on achieving good race relations. Legislation has an important role to play in securing general acceptance of equality of opportunity in British society.

I consider myself very fortunate to be living in this country. Having travelled and seen some parts of the world, I consider myself extremely lucky to be a member of British society with its general sense of tolerance, fairness, kindness and philanthropy. I believe I have made a contribution to British public life. No society in today's world is perfect, Britain is not, but in relative terms this country is probably the best. Britain has its share of extremism, both from the right and the left. But the law is mostly fairly upheld; lawlessness, deviance into unacceptable behaviour is tackled lawfully and effectively. In case of miscarriage of justice, machinery is in place to correct any injustice. These forces maintain society's balance.

I am glad I came to England all those years ago in October 1966 for the second time (the first was Dartmouth, 1956–58), accompanying my wife and child from East Pakistan – now Bangladesh. I have lived a contented life. I had a lovely and beautiful wife, Anna, a Dartmothian, the mother to our two beautiful, successful daughters, Lisa and Rebecca, and a grandmother ('Nanny') to my four grandchildren, Leah and Jacob, Eleanor and Konrad.

Eventually Brexit will be behind us. Britain will again be united in taking its place in the comity of nations. The traditional middle ground in politics will be found, discarding the extremes. The young people want nothing less than peace, sky-is-the-limit opportunities, a safe environment and having their say and being listened to, for their education, health, employment and everything else that impacts on their lives. We have a 'duty of care' towards our youth. In the Brexit debate I have been a Remainer. I believe strongly that Britain's place has been and remains in the wider world.

But there is something else. With the coming of Coronavirus engulfing the globe, we recall what Mr Harold Macmillan said: "Events dear boy events!" Nothing can be predicted. We have to live this pandemic through. Life surely will return to normal again.

Annexe A

LEVER BROTHERS PAKISTAN LIMITED
P.O. BOX NO. 125
CHITTAGONG,
EAST PAKISTAN.

TO WHOM IT MAY CONCERN.

Mr. S. I. Aziz has been known to me since 1963 when he first joined Lever Brothers Pakistan Limited for training prior to taking up an appointment as a manager in the factory which we were then building in Chittagong, East Pakistan.

After training in West Pakistan Mr. Aziz was made responsible for the setting up of Personnel, Traffic and Transport Departments at our Chittagong factory and for the selecting and recruitment of staff for these departments.

His own pleasant personality and his past training and experience in the Pakistan Navy equipped him well for his duties with us and it is largely due to his qualities and standards that we now have such an excellent operating unit here with a peaceful labour force and an outstanding standard of good housekeeping.

Mr. Aziz is leaving our service with effect from tomorrow for purely personal reasons. I am sorry to lose him and can recommend him with confidence to any employer as a reliable, active and forceful Manager.

LEVER BROTHERS PAKISTAN LIMITED,

(A. S. JONES)
FACTORY MANAGER.

ASJ:PNM.
29.9.66.

Annexe B

From: GROUP CAPTAIN I. THOMAS, OBE, DFC, RAF.

TELEPHONE
SWINDERBY 241 EXT 201

ROYAL AIR FORCE,
SWINDERBY,
LINCOLN.

28 October 1970

To whom it may concern

    Flying Officer Suhail Itne Aziz served in the Secretarial Branch of the Royal Air Force from 24 June 1968 to 30 October 1970 and I knew him for half of this period.

    He proved himself to be a competent executive with a sound knowledge of modern management techniques. He retired from the Royal Air Force to join the Commission for Industrial Relations in a post which offers greater scope for the use of his specialized knowledge and experience.

    Aziz is a good mixer and his conduct and appearance at social occasions were always a credit to the Royal Air Force.

I THOMAS
Group Captain
Officer Commanding

Annexe C

DOCKLANDS Recorder
Tower Hamlets

No. 176 THURSDAY, FEB 7, 1991 22p

The Brettonwood Partnership Limited

TV NEWS STAR LISA IN FAMILY AFFAIR!

TV-AM presenter Lisa Aziz made news herself when she officially opened her father's plush new Docklands office.

Suhail Aziz has launched a branch of the Brettonwood Partnership management consultants at Admirals Way, South Quay, Isle of Dogs.

The company offers a range of services for clients in the areas of urban renewal, inner city regeneration, enterprise and initiatives, equal opportunities and access.

Brettonwood have recently completed a major survey into Docklands' ethnic minorities and their employment prospects.

Now the group aim to help implement some of their findings to improve the employment and training situation for minorities by setting up individual schemes and projects.

The London Docklands Development Corporation are employing Brettonwood to complete the equal opportunities and access programmes.